"A lifetime of preaching and teaching the art of preaching crackles and pops in this bonfire of a book. In sentences of heat and light—blazing passion, luminous intelligence—Calvin Miller, one of our best preachers and writers, tells us what he does best—and why and how."

Eugene Peterson, professor emeritus of spiritual theology, Regent College

"Calvin Miller understands preaching. He understands that it is about the heart as well as the mind, about the imaginative as well as the rational, about reaching people as well as teaching the Word, about exegeting a culture as well as expounding a text, and about painting an image as well as stating a proposition. Most of all he understands that preaching is a work of the Spirit who will not be harnessed by our conventions, but who will bless those compelled to tell his story with a pastor's care for souls, an apologist's zeal for truth, and a poet's ear for his culture's heartbeat. Calvin Miller has long been the poet of preachers; now he comes as a master storyteller to teach us how to tell the gospel to a generation thirsting for narratives to explain our world."

Bryan Chapell, president, Covenant Theological Seminary

"If you are a preacher, read this book! Calvin Miller has a lot to say about preaching, and he says it well. *Preaching: The Art of Narrative Exposition* may take a few hours to read, but it can change your preaching for a lifetime."

Haddon Robinson, Harold John Ockenga Professor of Preaching,
Gordon-Conwell Theological Seminary

"Calvin Miller is a talented preacher and teacher of preachers, and his own gifts are on display in this outstanding volume. Miller's book is filled with practical insights that reflect his own rich experience in the pulpit, and his work on narrative exposition is an important contribution that will help both novice and veteran preachers explore new approaches to proclaiming biblical truth. Any preacher's work will be strengthened by a careful reading of Miller's excellent new book."

Michael Duduit, editor, *Preaching Magazine*

"In this book, Calvin Miller offers an insightful and thought-provoking perspective on one of the central issues facing twenty-first-century preachers: the critical right-brain/left-brain balance in sermon preparation and delivery. Equally important, he shows preachers how to incorporate his perspective in their sermons. For that reason, *Preaching: The Art of Narrative Exposition* promises to be an often-consulted preaching resource for a long time to come."

Argile Smith, professor of preaching, occupying the J. D. Gray Chair of Preaching; chair of the division of pastoral ministries, New Orleans Baptist Theological Seminary

"Some books on preaching follow a dry academic trail, well-worn by generations of homileticians. In reading such books you are left with the distinct impression that you have covered this territory before. Calvin Miller offers us a fresh approach in *Preaching: The Art of Narrative Exposition*. If you are looking for a practical, step-by-step guide to sermon preparation, this is it. But hang on—Calvin will take you places you haven't been. He will encourage you to take risks, to explore new ways of crafting a sermon that will be memorable as well as biblically substantive. This is a journey every preacher should take."

Reg Grant, professor of pastoral ministries, Dallas Theological Seminary

"It's a homiletical autobiography! It communicates the heart and passion of a great preacher as he reveals how he preaches."

David Osborn, director, Denver Seminary Doctor of Ministry Program

"*Preaching: The Art of Narrative Exposition* firmly establishes Calvin Miller as one of the preeminent homileticians of the past half century. Based on decades of solid work in the study and personal experience in the pulpit, this book is simply marvelous. Informative, inspirational, and utterly engaging, it's a must-read for all who are involved in the ongoing challenge of biblical preaching in a postmodern culture!"

Scott Wenig, professor of applied theology, Denver Seminary

"For students and preachers of the Word who desire to turn the ink of the Bible into the blood of living experience through the art of narrative exposition, this book is a necessity and not simply a luxury."

Robert Smith Jr., professor of preaching, Beeson Divinity School

Preaching

Preaching

The Art of Narrative Exposition

Calvin Miller

BakerBooks
Grand Rapids, Michigan

© 2006 by Calvin Miller

Published by Baker Books
a division of Baker Publishing Group
P.O. Box 6287, Grand Rapids, MI 49516-6287
www.bakerbooks.com

Published in association with the literary agency of WordServe Literary Group, Ltd., 10152 S. Knoll Circle, Highlands Ranch, CO 80130.

Third printing, April 2009

Printed in the United States of America

Library of Congress Cataloging-in-Publication Data
Miller, Calvin.
    Preaching : the art of narrative exposition / Calvin Miller.
        p.   cm.
        Includes bibliographical references (p.   ) and index.
        ISBN 10: 0-8010-1290-2 (cloth)
        ISBN 978-0-8010-1290-7 (cloth)
        1. Preaching. I. Title.
    BV4211.3.M55 2006
    251—dc22   2005035546

Contents

Introduction

Sermonizing is an ought-to sport. In fact preachers enjoy one of the few occupations that allow the freedom of telling people what they ought or ought not to do. This can only be done legitimately as long as they read the Bible before they do it and work at keeping their sermons biblical. The truth is most people go to church expecting to be challenged with the ought-tos of life. Most of us know generally what we ought to do, and want to get on with doing it as long as there is something of God in this oughtness. The Ten Commandments are studies in oughtness; so is the Sermon on the Mount. So are the warnings to the seven churches of Asia. The great ought passages of Scripture have been around for millennia, but their age has never diminished our constant need to be reminded of them. The oughts of life leave us unsettled. To serve them is often wrought with feelings of failure. Preachers certainly haven't been able to wrap their own oughts and ought-nots in peace. They ought to do better, live better, and preach better than they do. Preachers ought to quit sinning. Still nobody knows better than those who preach that preaching is an art in which a studied, professional sinner tells the less studied sinners how they ought to believe, behave, and serve. Fortunately the office of "preacher" carries with it a common understanding that as long as the preacher speaks for God, he should be heard even if he is a sinner. Most people not only believe in God but have some notion that if all the world served God, the world would be a better address. But most people also feel that preachers should shoot straight, and when they say, "Thus saith the Lord," they ought to let God do the talking.

This oughtness is what differentiates Christ-centered preaching from public speaking.

Homiletics is an intelligent, high-sounding word, and in moments of ego I like calling myself a homiletician. But I am addicted to simplicity, and most of the time I like calling myself by my simpler title: preacher. After reading hundreds of books on the subject and writing a few, I have taken it upon myself to set forth what I have learned, both as a practitioner and a scholar, and cast it in a simple mode. My desire to do this has come from the realization that none of the books on preaching—even the great books—have done it exactly right. Some get closer to being right than others but none is exactly there. I realize it is just this sort of thinking that keeps creating new books on every subject. New books come from the honest neuroses of scholars who are only trying to make the world better by letting their particular drive to write a perfect book furnish the libraries of the world.

How Will This Book Be Different from Other Homiletic Texts?

How will this book be different? Rather than write out of a compendium of other textbooks, I want to lean heavily on my thirty-five years of pulpit experience as well as my fourteen years of teaching preaching. I want to do something like Fred Craddock did in *Preaching* and write this book a little freer of intrusive footnotes than I usually do.[1] By this I mean that I don't want my argument interrupted by a lot of indentations and block quotes. I don't pretend to imitate Craddock's excellence, only his style of argument regarding external academic authority. I do want to allow other teachers and educators the right to comment on the argument, so I will allow them the space on some pages at the back to make sure the book isn't dependent entirely on my own limited understanding of preaching. Of course, no excellent book was ever written except that the author had done a great deal of reading and while writers may not lay out their sources in ibids and op. cits, their sources are an automatic part of who they are, having been gained in the sweat of personal study. But all good scholarship moves forward on a trail of footnotes. Without mentioning these sources the information gained from all my study may not always be visible but will always remain foundational to my insight.

The style of this book will be what I like to call conversational scholarship. So forgive me if I veer off a "third person stilt" from time to time and borrow from a lifetime of homiletic involvement and say what I personally think and feel about my subject. Quoting others says this is important, but writing in first person says, "this is important to me."

Still, I don't want this book to come off only as heavy *personal* opinion. I want this work to be a dialogue with you, my reader, believing that we both have an eager interest in the same subject. In a way, this is the definition that lies at the bottom of all great preaching. After all, a really riveting sermon is just that: a conversation about a subject in which the "preacher" and the "preachee" have an equal and avid interest.[2] We'll speak more about this idea in an area of the book to which the subject belongs.

Preaching lies at the core of worship and worship is composed of three parts. The first is music and/or praise. The second part is liturgy. Liturgy is the formal teacher—a poetic sort of *didache*—that keeps the church focused on her founder and his teachings. Liturgy is *didache*, the ancient church word for teaching. Liturgy of some sort becomes the focal point of worship. Congregations gather and recite their *paternosters*, Nicene creeds, psalms, doctrines, benedictions, invocations, commandments, covenants, Gospels, Epistles, and pledges. These elements of liturgy have rolled on weekly across the centuries. They poetically nudge the church to remember who she is, what she must teach, how to sanctify baptisms, wedding rites, birthrights, and final rites. Liturgy comes in Latin, Greek, Elizabethan English, and to some degree in Baptist plain talk.

Preaching, the third element of worship, grows from Scripture and conscience, devotion and conviction. It rises from many sources—from Episcopal lectionaries and Pentecostal rambunction. It is there to call sinners to redemption, instruct the church, rebuke the wayward, and—as the cliché runs—to "comfort the afflicted and afflict the comfortable." In this book, however, I will be talking about preaching not as so many homiletic texts do. I want this book to reveal preaching as a dialogue of hope—a verbal rendezvous between the Spirit and the listener.[3]

In writing this book I have taken aim at the oft held supposition that preaching textbooks are written so that boring preachers can read, heed, and become fascinating. Preaching has a calling far greater than just making sermons interesting. Preaching exists to create the kingdom. Merely getting and keeping attention is too small a job description for this critical, redeeming art. Preaching has work to do—a lot of work to do—and honest sermons are in league with God's ultimate plan of conforming souls to the image of his Son.

Is Persuasion a Legitimate Form of Preaching?

Audience interest, then, has never been preaching's main purpose. The sermon is the workhorse of the ecclesia. Preaching was established by Jesus because God has a job to do.

To get the job done preaching must be committed to two goals: first it should be passionate and second, fascinating. Passion makes preaching seem imperative and urgent. Narrative is a force that postmodern preachers must use and listeners must reckon with. Narrative handcuffs intrigue to the ancient text. So, the homily gains relational force when the sermon is passionate enough to be visceral and story-driven enough to be visual.

Neither of these two qualities is enough considered alone. Speaking only to get people to listen is an art that ends generally in egotism. If fascination alone is the goal of keeping attention, a Dale Carnegie course would be as good as the Gospels in preparing the preacher to preach. Still the new homiletic has too often yielded to this shallow goal. In recent years this low road for preaching has become a major highway that runs between seminaries and lifeless parishes. As America has moved further away from the revivalistic zeal that endued the sermon with passion, sermons seemed to grow more congenial but also more sluggish. Thanks to advancements in psychology there is no longer any real sin lurking about and, therefore, no real sinners to reform. Since sin and eternity have been discarded in the ash can of postmodernity there seems to be little serious work for the sermon to do.

So preachers have often jettisoned incarnational preaching and opted for merely trying to be interesting.

This book therefore presumes that there are still many students of Christ-centered preaching who are committed to a biblical worldview and want their sermons to become a reply to secular decadence. Those readers will hopefully side with me that preaching remains a redemptive art, calling the world to align itself on the side of Christ and the creeds.

The manual for this art is Scripture. The fuel for this art is the devotional life of those preachers who have never seen their primary credentials for preaching as coming from diplomas and degrees. Worthy preachers never serve any academy, only their calling.

The serious, scholar pastor wants to be both a sound expositor and strong communicator. Such preachers have a clear understanding that a call to preach is a lifelong call to preach the kingdom and call the church to remember all that was lost in Genesis 3. Preaching is rescue work. It arrives on the human scene with splints and bandages to save and heal—and restore the world to all that was lost when the gates of Eden clanged shut.

I know of no one who has written more clearly about this agenda for the sermon than Bryan Chapell, who speaks of every sermon dealing with what he calls the FCF, the Fallen Condition Focus.[4] Each time a preacher stands to proclaim the gospel, that preacher is out to change the world *back*. *Back?* Yes, back to what it was when Adam was in Eden—back to the pristine business of holiness and relationship. When so much was lost in Eden . . . when so much of the current world is captive to secular values and philosophies, preaching cannot afford to opt for being cute when it ought to be visceral.

From Genesis 4 onward in Scripture, humankind stands at the brink of irrelevance, banging on the gates of Eden, arguing with the flaming angels about all that was lost when the gates clanged shut. The Bible is a book about change: from Noah to John, from Ararat to Patmos, the millennia roll and preachers dominate the Judeo-Christian story. Each of these heralds focused on getting the world back to what it owned before it sampled the forbidden. We all still long to restore that pure rapport with the Almighty that ended at the apple.

I believe that properly nourished this hunger lives in the heart of every parishioner who comes to church. But most of these have not the spiritual vocabulary to articulate how they feel. Therefore they cannot arrive at what's missing in their lives unless someone who knows what's missing helps them understand.

But transformation has become an ugly cultural concept. The idea that sects or denominations have the right to change others drives secularists to the wall. Secular thinkers feel that people should be free to be what they are or want to be without anyone trying to "convert" or "transform" them. This postmodern, post-denominational world we have inherited (perhaps even caused) glories in discussion. Talk is the mode of the day, not argument. Talk—as the cliché runs—is cheap. It's not only cheap, it's a group sport, warm and harmless and so conversational that everybody can participate. But persuasion and conversion, which have always lived at the heart of the Christian mission, are the preacher's mission. Yet persuasion is suddenly taboo. "Just As I Am, Leave ME Alone" is not just the hymn of the penitent, it has become the creed of individual liberty espoused by the media and championed by the libertine spirit of the age.

Still, the current crop of secularists are not very informed. Naïveté is a wonderful quality: it allows even the least informed to enter every conversation with instant esteem. It fashions an equality of all views, without the inconvenience of actually having to study any view. Christians, like the secularists they distrust, also talk a lot. Increasingly they too are unstudied and yet the force of their convictions flies at the world full tilt. But naïveté is a warm cocoon that allows the naïve to be fully authoritative and respected without facing anything dangerous or requiring.

The Apologetic Imperative of Preaching in a Secular Culture

So "thus saith the Lord" seems a weak way to argue, when everyone believes themselves to be "lords" of their own affairs. The authority for all argument is not born in study. It is *sui generis*. It arises from every person's right to run their own show and be who they are without really studying. Most of these super-sovereigns feel that God can comment if he wants to, but God must avoid getting loud. While God is welcome to his opinions, he is only one voice, and he doesn't get extra points just for being God. The unstudied opinionated are prone to say, even to God, "Yes, but here's what I think." In such a world, classic apologetics has lost much of its force.

A popular evangelical wrote a book on apologetics only decades ago that he entitled *Evidence that Demands a Verdict*.[5] The book held its popularity for only fifteen minutes, before the world it was meant to convince began to challenge it. "Excuse me, was that your verdict or my verdict?" There is almost no evidence now that demands a verdict—at least a clear verdict which is evident to all. To put anything in black and white is to be called upon to defend the various shades of either hue.

So preaching has to find an apologetic that is incontrovertible if it hopes to go on making a difference. But the world is tired of hearing what preachers think and so it is increasingly turning a deaf ear to the pulpit. In spite of megachurch success, George Barna argues that church attendance in America has declined significantly since the early 1990s.[6] This means, if such trends continue, that it will decline still further. While in recent years the rate of decline in church attendance has remained flat,[7] the overall prognosis is not good. Philip Jenkins, in his astounding *The Next Christendom*, says that the marked decline of evangelical religion in Europe, England, and now New England will continue until even the Bible Belt of the U.S. has been secularized.[8]

So preachers have passed beyond the easy times. They have lost the wonderful feel of the fifties when the wholesome culture looked at the church and the sermon as traditional and valuable. Still, if this is a brave new world, preaching too must be brave. I once heard a daring prophet say of the new millennium, "There's good news and bad news. The good news is preaching has become all-important in the plan of God. The bad news is, it's not 1950 anymore." Preaching, as always, has a wonderful future, but it will require a fierce kind of bravery to go on practicing its art—a courage that renames pastors as prophets, and anoints the authority of the Word with the oil of truth.

How Listening Patterns Have Changed

In some ways it seems to me that preaching remains too captive to 1950 to transform the third millennium. I travel widely and hear a lot of sermons. Many of them sound to me like some I heard (and some I may have preached) during the 1950s. Could it be that during the past five decades the world was learning to listen in a new way, while preachers continued talking in the old way? Anthropologists and historians have come together on the point that world cultures made some almighty changes in the fifties. It was then that the age of information—often called the age of communication—was born. During those years we moved from the age of print to the age of video. What this really means is that during those decades the world moved from being a huge ear to a huge eye. But instead of becoming more visual, preaching remained too captive to older ideas. That's why in the pages to follow you will read much of the "image-driven sermon" and less of older sermon styles.

But the sermon's twentieth-century captivity was not the only problem. Sermonic passion too seems to have died. There are places where it seems alive—such as in Dixie where I live and work. But in Dixie it seems alive because passion is not so much an intensity of belief but a style of preaching. Many preachers below the Mason-Dixon Line still yell a lot, which often accomplishes little more than to clothe weak sermons with volume. Passion is intense feeling, and merely stepping up the projection does not necessarily mean the preacher is feeling the God-sized burden of the words being preached. A huge discrepancy is born. The hype-as-passion movement settled at the center of evangelicalism in the volume, however. This bogus volume-hype often came not from the gut but from the need to sound urgent.[9]

Passion can never be genuine unless the preacher owns a burning need for a God-relationship. Zeal must own the herald before the herald can preach it into others. I believe that preachers who have no God-hunger may have some good things to say but they lack the passion that is essential to create the kingdom of God and transform the world.[10]

This value no textbook can teach.

It arises from a longing beyond homiletics.

It is sustained by a visceral hunger mere scholarship cannot engender.

Preaching Love and Absorbing Secular Belligerence

Biblical preaching now lies gasping before the onslaught of secularism.

As proselytism became a cultural "no-no," preaching quit saying "no-no." Because the secular culture didn't want a Lord, preaching quit saying, "Thus saith the Lord." Now there are far too few pulpits informing the world that God has something to say to it. In the absence of God's Word, "how-to" has replaced "repent and be baptized."

This trend in some cases makes preachers more interesting but less vital. Preaching is getting more creative, but it is often fluffy and vaporous. Real textual exposition often finds itself coming in a distant second to film clips and drama clubs. Biblical ignorance owns the day. A political contender for president said recently that Job was his favorite book of the New Testament. The odd thing was that nobody in the crowd who heard him spotted the faux pas.

But even in the face of a culture belligerent toward God, the mood of the sermon must remain warm and loving. I offer this book on biblical exposition to remind us that we must never join the secular world nor adopt its bogus values. Honest biblical exposition sets orange cones around the unsafe lanes of the human journey. The book is not written to massage those who want to serve in the Bible-lite megaghettoes of casseroles and softball. Sermons are called to rip the doors from closeted communities of user-friendly "Christians" who would like to see their church get bigger without any real reference to knowing God. This is a book dedicated to that courageous art form known as "encounter!" The kind of preaching set forth in these pages will call for sermons that esteem the pleasure of God more than human compliment.

How Postmoderns Listen

How do postmodern listeners listen? Well, for one thing, they listen with a group ear in order to arrive at a group mind. At the midpoint of the twentieth century, the world changed in two ways. First, the age of communication began. It was an age of dialogue. Lecture died, conversational style was born. "I told you" and "Let me tell you" were replaced by "Whadda ya think?" The culture bowed down and finally agreed to view the church as a vast dialogue. In studying the evening news over fifty years now, I have noticed a progression in the format of national news. It has moved from a single anchor person to a committee of anchorpersons and field correspondents. Even the local news settled down to become a roundtable of lesser luminaries reasoning together.

Great preaching has always been dialogical, but to the indiscriminate layperson, it has been seen as monologue.[11] This view originated out of two qualities of the sermon. First of all, preaching has a style. It is often an upbeat and authoritative style. It is sometimes too loud and struts about very sure of itself. It is often delivered from a pulpit whose elevated visual placement makes it seem high and lifted up. Pulpits are heavy furniture and the persons tough enough to ride them can round up the doggies any way they like, I suppose. But today's mavericks don't respond well to the lasso and prod.

But there is another reason why the sermon seems like a monologue. The preacher reads from the ancient book where God has so many things to say. God often speaks in lightning and thunder and seems—at least in sermons—not to care much what people think of his ideas. "Thus saith the Lord" carries with it a huge foreboding that ends with the congregation saying, "Well okay then."

So as the current age of dialogue proceeds, biblical preaching seems more out of sync with a culture captive to chit-chat. In a culture that goes about asking "Whadda ya think?" the phrase "thus saith the Lord" has become an introduction to Sunday monologues that more and more people are choosing to avoid.

Since the sermon is so out of vogue in the secular dialogue, it may be seen that preaching as a "perceived" monologue is hastening the decline. I say "perceived" because Christ-centered preaching has never been a mere monologue. It has always been a reasoning together and it has always been a tête-a-tête between speaker and listener.

But the world also changed in a second way that has come to bear in how contemporary listeners listen. The age of communication brought with it the technological overhaul of how people listen. The eye joined with the ear to say, "Feed me or I'll take my ears with me and abandon you, Dear Preacher." To some slight degree, the church heard the ultimatum of the eye, but only to a slight degree. While drama clubs and PowerPoint choruses began to punctuate suburban evangelical worship, changing things a bit, sermons remained dull of image and void of light. The church has sometimes castigated television, because it seemed to pipe too much R-rated secularism directly into the living rooms of the faithful. Outside of cable religion, the church seemed rarely to comment on the good aspects of watching television—if there were any.

In his essay *Fourth Temptation of Christ*, the late Malcolm Muggeridge alleged that Jesus's fourth temptation was thirty minutes of prime-time television. Muggeridge said that Jesus rejected the offer because faith had always been an *otic* (a hearing) rather than an *optic* (a visual) experience. He agreed with Paul the apostle who said, "Faith comes from hearing the message" (Rom. 10:17 NIV), and not from seeing it. The church at the end of the twentieth century seemed to agree: the gospel was an "ear" event and not an "eye" event.[12]

But the truth is the gospel was never just an "ear" event. The best preachers throughout the centuries always preached highly visual, image-driven sermons. But if today's listeners have developed great eyes as their ears have atrophied, then the church must do all it can to preach in the same manner that people best hear the sermon. This means that within the framework of all things auditory, sermons must remember the visual age to which they are preached, and create a rhetoric that is image-centered.

By the 1990s, Neal Postman had made the point that the age of print was over and the age of video had arrived in force. Barbara Tuchman said the changes in the twentieth century were equally cataclysmic to those of the turbulent fourteenth century. One of the most striking of those changes had to do with communication. The printing press of the fifteenth century was the magnificent leap ahead that is symbolized in the computer revolution of today.

All in all, we may be sure that the sermon attendee of today listens with the eyes rather than the ears. It would be great to be sure that we are preaching in pictures, for pictures are the language of the age.

Narrative as Exposition

Expository preaching has been the watchword of four hundred years of American evangelicalism. When the term was used in previous decades, it was generally understood to be the basis of sermons that employed linear reasoning, building arguments with highly propositional styles. Because these styles often lacked illustrations and stories there grew up the idea that if a sermon was interesting it was probably not expository. Exposition was hard work for both the preacher and the audience. Preparing it was arduous for the preacher, and listening to it was toil for the laity. But that was the price you paid to have the true Bible preached to you. If preaching didn't defy your ability to care about it, it was clearly not the Word of God. To really be good for you, sermons had to be dull. Exciting sermons were generally seen as heretical, or at least non-biblical.

Many people secretly felt that this "expository" style of preaching was boring, but nobody would say so out loud for fear of being branded as a liberal. Many felt that liberals were more interesting than conservative expositors, but people generally opted to be bored, rather than heretical.

It was after all the theological left that began talking first of narrative theology. But time and interest were on their side. The last half of the twentieth century brought on the video renaissance. Movies and television took charge of our eyes and our minds and the movement, the special effects, the soundtracks, the cinematography, and the overwhelming video captivity made ponderous preaching look dull. Still we all felt it was our duty to listen even when listening left us dozing in the pew.

But seeming dull wasn't preaching's only problem. Unwittingly, the show-biz society had turned up the lights and the amplifiers. So the church did too. Most people weren't at first turned off by the marriage of technology and theology. But they were turned off by its dull insistence that when you strobed things up people ought to listen merely because you said God was in favor of PowerPoint.

The preaching they first abandoned was that which flew at them in a highly propositional style. The preaching they cheered on was that with a highly narrative style. By the dawn of the third millennium, the sermon as mere lecture was on the ropes. But the sermon which picked up on Augustine's word *narratio* was alive and well. The *narratio* was the story-saturated, image-driven sermon.

All of this talking about being image-driven was not a new idea. Jesus himself told lots of stories, and his sermons were full of images—image-driven, to be precise. We still remember the images that drove Christ's preaching: wildflowers, shepherds, fig trees, weeds in the wheat fields, a despised Samaritan that turned out to be good, and a goody-goody Pharisee that turned out to be bad. And this is just the beginning of the images that drove Jesus' sermons. Think of leaven, chaff, foundations, cheap sparrows, poor widows, barn builders, bridesmaids, vine dressers, lost coins, lost sheep, lost boys, thankless lepers, pipers and dancers, dishonest judges, reeds shuddering in the wind, houses on sand, white-washed tombs, scorpions for fish, right-hand-sheep, left-hand-goats, and beggars at the rich man's gate. On and on the metaphors rise to define the preaching of Jesus.

But the hurdle that many evangelicals have not yet crossed is the final barrier of biblical exposition. Does expository preaching have to be totally precept-driven and logically set forth, or can a far more inductive, artistic mode play a role in exposition? Can biblical narrative, as a style of preaching, be expository? Can preaching—narrative style—really be expository?[13]

Jesus thought so.

When asked, "Who is my neighbor?" Jesus in effect does not say, "Let me give you three Hebrew roots on the word *neighbor.*" What he does say is, "A certain man went down from Jerusalem to Jericho. . . ." In other words he follows the question "Who is my neighbor?" with an immediate "Once upon a time" and then launches into a story. He never does come back with a precept, but ends his highly expository story with a great inductive conclusion, "Who do you think was neighbor to him who fell among the thieves?"

Throughout this book, I will be arguing for preaching as craft. Preachers are not only professionals in their field, but the best of them are artists who can make the Scripture come alive with metaphor and image. I will also argue that metaphor and story is not only a legitimate form of exposition but is a preferred style of exposition mostly because it is so much more memorable than mere precepts-driven homiletics.

So the force of this book will be centered on narrative exposition. In the video-oriented world in which we now live, this is the way the modern church-goer listens. Many preachers are terrified by the fear that they cannot learn to preach in this manner. But I believe that while all preachers cannot tell stories with the same ease, most all preachers can learn to communicate in a narrative style. It will require some work for those not naturally blessed with the talent. But it also will be worth the discipline. Narrative preaching begins talking where the world begins listening: at the point of narrative exposition. If only this ideal is achieved, this volume will have been well worth the writing.

Conclusion

The Bible will be the primary text upon which the argument is based. But I will, in speaking of being a true "herald of God," call upon many of the books of note I have read. The authors of those books all stand about my word processor as I write, and their integrity and commitment to biblical preaching inform these pages. I am not great at soloing. I like living in the company of the committed. My small logic is not a grand river of truth. It is just a brook that feeds that stream from which we all may safely drink. For the water of life is kept pure and safe for all generations by the filters of sound doctrine, a guardian community, and a fearless commitment to truth.

In this book I hope to encourage the preacher to preach as God intended preaching to be done—in both a narrative and expository manner. It's the only kind of preaching I have any interest in.

Part 1

Analysis:
The Exegesis of All Things

1

Who's Talking?

Exegeting the Preacher

The best preachers are heard before they preach, not during their sermon nor because of it. Did St. Francis really say, "Preach the Gospel. If necessary use words"? Who can say? Clichés, when they live long enough, become adages. Still, as old saws go this is a good one. Far more important than what is said is who said it. "Fire!" spoken even by a blackguard and charlatan will clear a theater. It is the shortest of speeches that may be uttered by a villain and liar and still be heeded by those who, given a choice, would prefer to be saved by a person of good character. But generally speaking, preachers who preach the Word will only be heeded if their manner of life convinces their hearers that they believe there really is a fire, and that they hold the extinguisher.

No reasonable book on the subject of preaching can begin with what is said. The force of preaching must begin with who's saying it. The collapse of many religious cable empires in the '80s points to the fact that what is said makes very little difference when compared to the character of the one who is saying it. In those bygone days, evangelistic kingdoms came and went. These multimillion-dollar video icons rarely told the truth in any profound way, but none of them lied in what they actually preached. Why didn't they survive? Because the world will not accept truth—even redeeming truth—that arrives through flawed channels. But they will readily hear an honest herald whose life backs up what the lips set forth.

The Ethics of the Persuader

The passion of the sermon and the honor of the sermon-maker are codependent. Most of us want sermons to fly at us with passionate urgency. If there is fire and fury, we seldom think of asking about the preacher's affair with God while the fire burns and the fury rages. Rhetorical arson can delude us into feeling that with that much fire the herald must be for real. Even such sermons, falsely esteemed, tend to be rated well by the congregations who attend them. They can be interesting and occasionally even inspire. What they cannot do is entice the Holy Spirit to get involved. They also are poor at effecting change, since they do not come from a prophet who is living out the kind of transformation that is being called for.

"Man he can preach!" is an accolade often given to those passionate and fascinating preachers who build megachurches. These churches have often not gotten on well with the academy. Why? No scholar I know is opposed to the "mega" in megachurches, only to the preacher's love of the prefix. In such churches, it is often the case that the gospel gets shuttled in favor of what works. Real study dies. A "lite" preachment often proceeds out of the starry status of preachers. But light or not, these sermons charm the needy and seem glamorous and successful. Then too it is often buttressed by casseroles and softball games. All too often popular pastors challenge their needy accusers (who want more), saying that their sermons are "lite by intention" so that those outside the fold who are "lite by lifestyle" find a little haven where they can play the outfield of discipleship until they get a yen for diving into Leviticus. The bottom line is not yet drawn on "lite church," but I feel that when it is, we will be abysmally ashamed that we excused those prophets we called exciting without requiring more substance from them. The world was too sick to be healed by their congenial placebos. Merely to build a big hospital is a lame dodge for practicing real medicine.

Who's Doing the Persuading and for What Reason?

Great expositors succeed precisely because they refuse to trade honest exposition for congregational popularity. They have never been intrigued by the wonder of becoming mega influences by preaching minisermons.

Twice in my life (and likely much more often) I have been privileged to know modestly great preachers whose greatness didn't come from how their sermons looked in print. Yet there's joyous response to who they were more than what they said. Their communities noticed that they were unswervingly committed to truth but lacked the flamboyance of the megachurch prophets.[1] Their churches are large and healthy, two adjectives that don't always go together. By odd coincidence they are both named Dean, and in an odd sense do not seem to notice that they are committed to getting the truth out. Neither would call himself a "prophet" for it is too grand a word for them to paste across their genuine modesty. All they do is "preach the Word" and their churches grow. They do not really explode. No mushroom patches are their churches. They tell the truth, cherish the truth, and would be ashamed to live honoring anything else. They are intelligent and influential, largely unpublished, but authentic. Everyone they serve hears their words but only because their lives shout louder than what they say. As Emerson observed, "Don't *say* things. What you *are* stands over you the while, and thunders so that I cannot hear what you say to the contrary."[2]

I was in India when Mother Teresa died. I was struck by a Hindu city of eleven million raising billboards to her honor all over that vast sea of poverty the world calls Calcutta. Her sermons—if they were that—were not reputed to be great. It was her life that called for transformation and conversion. Teresa proved that persuasion does not have to be confrontational—at least in the sense of conflict and an aggressive spirit. She kept pressure on Calcutta to examine the Christian faith at the starting point of her life. She had a message of hope and preached it till she became the very embodiment of hope.[3]

Long after I had returned from India, her life haunted me. I found myself asking, "Why has only one person tried her lifestyle in such a gentle and a persuasive way?" There is no easy answer to the issue. But I have come to believe that what lies behind the effective persuader is an indefinable love for Christ that always issues in hope. That hope and that love keep tension on the world around the sermon until the world is so overwhelmed by the godly life, it must pay attention to the sermonizer and the sermon. I believe many of these preachers exist, and have achieved authenticity by caring deeply about the things of God. I cheer on all who have made their eye single and left their sermons so full of light. We make a mistake in always trying to write better sermons while paying so little attention to the life of the preacher. Yet I know of few sermon makers or sermon readers who feel the issue important enough to call the world to reverence around the authentic life of their preacher.

Richard Baxter's Axiom

We have lost that reverence for the godly life. Puritan pastor Richard Baxter was convinced that no pastor should have more people in his congregation than he could personally know. Groomed by megachurch madness as so many of us are, this now seems a tedious way to go about church growth. Indeed it seems a very odd doctrine to us—one totally out of sync with the church's basketball tournament ladders and ceramic classes. It seems the church must be big to be called a real church. And if it gets big enough to get written up in the journals, it must be a whirling mass of nameless people led by nameless staff members, who love the faceless ones to whom they minister. But Baxter believed that sermons preached to strangers were no sermons at all, for no preacher deserved to sell God or transformation to others if his life—observed daily by all who heard and knew him—added no force to his words.

What then are the keys to analyzing the sermon makers? First, the preacher must be in love with God, and second, he must be in love with all those whom God loves. This seems too simple a conclusion to occupy space in a textbook on preaching. But the world comes to church looking precisely for a sense of significance, and we who preach tell them week by week that God loves them. It's a truth we tell to give them that sense of significance for which they sought us. But it is a truth that can only be told by those who sense that the preacher also loves them. There is not the slightest chance that they will get hold of the first truth, unless they feel the second. The current crowd of worshipers has been brought up beneath the libertine pall of the secular city. They do not know what has happened to them. Like the frog in the kettle they have been warmed so gradually in the kettle of secularism, they are all but cooked and have not had the wit to notice the rise in their own secular temperature.

The answer is not to shout down their secularity or scream at them for being so secular but to role model what's missing in their lives. What's missing is a spiritual heritage and destiny. But generally when they are led to address their secular lifestyle, they often look at the preacher and fail to see any contrast in the values he cherishes with those they hold.

Analyzing the Persuader

The Preacher as a Person of Faith

The preacher, to beat the bum rap of secularism, must see that pulpit effectiveness is built on four things. First of all, his congregation longs to see their pastor as a person of faith. Only the truly otherworldly have earned the right to speak of the other world. Faith is the sine qua non of all who preach. If the preacher cannot squint the eyes and see something of what John saw on Patmos, the proclamation is but a marked-down book in a secondhand store. Most people will only hear what a preacher has to say if that preacher has caught sight of the land to which the congregation is being led.

The world is tired of hearing pulpit "how-tos" that have arrived to take the place of genuine transcendence. How-tos seem to skate on the wheels of relevance. And no one wants to be accused of irrelevance in the pulpit.[4] But if there really is a heaven and—God forbid—the hell that Jesus so frequently spoke of, never to mention eternity in favor of telling people how to handle their finances or relationships can hardly be called relevant.

Megachurch is all too often a congenial discussion of how to succeed, based on tiny exposition of a hidden verse deep in the bowels of Proverbs. What the world is clamoring for is not "the gateway to success" but a window on the universe next door. Alas, sermons too often study the floor of existence with no eye to the ceiling. And of course, most sermons come without literal windows. So do the churches, believing the light we create in huge concrete boxes is somehow more interesting than the light whose intensity burns the heart with a greater reality than the most clever worship team can create.

In this sense the sermon must be bound up in the lifestyle of the preacher. The preacher is not an answer man. Preachers are God-lovers. If they are robust in the vitality of their faith, their love will appear to be romantic. Romantic? Yes, there is something exotic in God-love. As in any other kind of love, preachers can't quit thinking about it and serving it.

In some ways the prayer life of preachers is like two teenagers caught in the grip of puppy love and talking on cell phones till the batteries die. Their conversation bears the mark of immaturity about them, for neither of them can bear to hang up first. So to keep the conversation going each of them insists—"You hang up first"—"No, you hang up first"—"No way, you hang up first"—and so on ad infinitum, ad nauseum. Sure it's immature, but it does speak to the fact that they have narrowed their world concerns to the two of them.

In a way people want to catch their pastor being romantic about the world he is trying to tell them about. Evangelicals have been bad about faking the distance between the two by using clichés: "Here there or in the air," or "I'm on a roll and Jesus is my rock," etc. And their immature response is best received by the spiritually immature.

But here and there, one meets real preachers of faith. They are not so angelic they abstain from popcorn, but they live in their communities as believers who keep an eye on the world that holds their affection while they preach to the one where they must serve. Such ministers are the essential persons of power.

I am reluctant to speak of this otherworldly romance for fear that reverencing preachers too much will turn them into inflated psychotics who believe they *are* God just because they speak for God. The meek not the blowhards shall inherit the earth. But when pastors keep their own humanity in sight, and still speak for God out of the love they bear him, a wondrous thing is born.[5] God has found among such servants his best lovers. These preachers write sermons that are full of light.

Preachers are people of faith, but they are not oracles. They have too little wisdom and often make dreadful mistakes even while they are preaching. But their confidence in God leads them not just to confess their humanity; they can actually—if occasion demands it—ask their parishes to forgive them. They don't take their preaching lightly, but they are never severe even in insisting that all who hear them must pay them heed as though their words are the final words of God.

Preachers are incarnational souls, who want God to inhabit them, for they long to be like Christ. They want to face the crosses of their lives with a resolution that their courage is a part of their identity in Christ. Yet they don't want to magnify their own troubles in sermonizing or cast their leadership as a martyrdom merely to gather the congregation's commiseration.

But when they speak for God—when they say, "Thus saith the Lord"—they mean to be heard, and their love affair with God endues them with the confidence that they are not just lobbyists for virtue, they are faith-filled servants. They are in love with the world that's one world away. They are gripped in a divine romance, with no intention of disappointing their wonderful distant lover.

The Preacher as a Person of Information

Second, the congregation wants the pastor to be a person of information. No one who speaks all the time—as preachers do—can be right all the time—as preachers aren't. Still the people in the pew want us to be right, and not just about the Bible either.

I well remember a pastor who preached a sermon in which he included a story from the life of the hymnist George Matheson. According to his sermon, Matheson wrote "O Love That Will Not Let Me Go" shortly after losing his sight. His fiancée, learning of his condition, snapped her fingers, flung back his engagement ring, and shouted dramatically (don't they always shout dramatically in sermon illustrations?), "Really George, you can't expect me to be married to a blind man for the rest of my life!" Matheson's heart was broken by her rejection, and through streaming tears (aren't they always streaming in sermon illustrations?) wrote the lyrics to "O Love That Will Not Let Me Go." The story was so emotionally wrought that it inspired me to retell it in a sermon of my own. People wept at my repetition of the tale. It was a real sermon clincher and seemed to go so well with "Just As I Am." I had used the sermon and the story many times before I found myself challenged by a church musician who said, "That was a beautiful story! Too bad it never happened."

Smart aleck, musician! I hated having my beautiful fancies bludgeoned by facts. I almost wish I had not been informed. But the truth must be told, even when it ruins a great sermon clincher.

All of us who preach have bloopers to confess. Back in the '70s, I commented on Esau and Jacob and their continual quarreling by mentioning that even today, three and a half millennia later, the descendents of these adverse twins were still quarreling, only now they did it with F-15s and rocket-propelled grenades. Then I said—thunderously, of course—"This is exactly why Menachen and Begin can't get along right today." After the service, a kindly layman gently informed me, "Pastor, I think Menachen and Begin are the same person." I immediately reddened. He had me, and while many in the congregation probably thought they were two different prime ministers of two different countries, alas, the two were but the first and last name of the same Israeli prime minister.

There are many other foolhardy statements I have made. But for the moment, I choose to confess nothing else. I will say that people expect the pastor to be a person of information. I once heard a concert artist say that the Holy Spirit had led him to comment on that passage where the "angel sprung Paul from jail, in Acts 5, he went immediately to the gathering of Christians in Jerusalem, and they rejoiced to find the glorious ex-con at the door." The event happened to Peter not Paul, it wasn't Acts 5 it was Acts 12, and if the Holy Spirit actually had really led the concert artist to be that confused, he was probably only trying to help the poor artist set a new world record for pulpit ignorance.

I have a preacher friend who often mocks the kind of arrogant ignorance of those who eschew seminary educations or as some would say "cemetery eddy-kashuns" by praying, "Lord, make me ignoranter and ignoranter for thy glory!" This is a day when people expect their leaders to be sure of themselves. No one can do it perfectly, but everybody ought to take the issue as far as they can.

Preachers can avoid some of those moments when they look ignorant for God's glory, just by developing the habit of footnote and reference. Sermons shouldn't sound like the preacher is always quoting from other sources, although a few oral footnotes jammed into a lot of pulpit fluff can actually add an aura of authority to what's being preached. But the note sheet, sermon brief, or manuscript—however preachers prepare—would help preachers be sure of their material even as they preach.

For years I've tried to furnish my sermons with insight by being what I call a "middle reader." To hold peoples' attention you don't have to know the itsy-bitsy ins and outs of all schools of knowledge. But the center of world thinking should be a matter of continual observation and study. When you say anything that comments on the current world events, you ought to be trustworthy.

Middle readers try to read from the center of all disciplines. I don't read monographs or articles from the *American Psychiatric Journal* (is there one?). But I have read and annotated Rollo May, Sigmund Freud, Abraham Maslow, Thomas Harris, Eric Berne, Viktor Frankl, Karl Menninger, etc. I don't read the *Harvard Historical Review* (again sorry, but is there one?), but I have read all of Barbara Tuchman, Herman Wouk, Thomas Cahill, David McCullough, etc. I have read most of the Nobel Prize laureates in literature (there are not hundreds of these). Same goes for Pulitzer literary laureates (I once ran across a list of these prize winners in the *New York Times Crossword Puzzle Dictionary* and have used the list to inform my reading across the years).

I pay attention to the newspapers. I think Karl Barth may have been divinely inspired when he said preach with a Bible in one hand and the newspaper in the other. I like the metaphor, because holding the Bible suggests that the preacher is not captive to this world, but holding the newspaper says the preacher at least knows where the world is. The sermon should not be an intellectual documentary. But it should be an informed homily. People like listening to a preacher who knows the Bible and understands the culture.

Yet there is a caveat to reading widely: the more we know, the harder it is to keep hold of the central, simple tenets of our faith. It is hard to build a heart that burns for God while we develop minds that are informed and incisive. Rarely are big heads and great hearts found in the same body. It is hard to believe much and know much. Yet the power that comes from living in the stretch between the two is immense. People like hearing brilliant preachers who fully understand their world and yet still retain a depth of love for God. The answer to how to avoid the dilemma is not to remain naïve for God's glory. The answer is to accept the ambiguity of unresolved conflict and to teach by example that great sermons do not exist to harmonize all truth and knowledge but to find a richness that comes in holding both of these values as important.

The Preacher as a Mystic

Third, congregations have a right to expect their pastor to be a mystic. I use the word advisedly but with the best of intentions. Mystics are those souls who walk with one foot on the solid path of humanity and the other in the real world of the spiritual. They are those who resent themselves for not being able to cross the threshold into the reality of things too wonderful to be practical or reasonable. They huddle around the things too awesome to be told, so miraculous they stop the breath. But when heaven is in the wings, breathing is too earthly a virtue to be esteemed. Mystics believe all things are possible. Even if they have never moved a mountain, they are convinced that it can be done. They just haven't found the right moment when they were hand in hand with the Almighty who has called them to get the job done. They believe the blind can be touched with sight. The lost can change under the spell of an invading reality to become the saved. Fire and wind are possible. Dead churches can become incendiary fellowships. The stifling, dead air that gathers around gossipy old sinners can leap to life when the breezes of Pentecost bristle into the gales of life.[6]

Homiletical mystics are positive thinkers. All good things are possible, but most of them are probable. This positivism pervades their sermons. The good dreams that God has in mind for the congregation get pulpit time. Their sermons are more than words; to be near such preachers is a reminder that too much of the world is earthbound.

When Moses came down from the mountain, the big party that had formed during his absence suddenly broke up. His face shone said the Scriptures. The exact kilowatt measurement of a shining face would be hard to tell. But there was something ethereal in the leader, which they had not experienced before.

I hesitate once again to speak of this as a virtue to be coveted. To experience the mystery of godliness may or may not be a blessing. To crave it above all else is to live a Christian life that admits it is lacking. The pursuit of the Spirit is like the pursuit of happiness: those who pursue it most give very little evidence of having captured it. Chasing mystery is not to be done with a trident and net. In the Broadway play *Agnes of God*, the playwright sees the mystic as a person who didn't just achieve the ability to snag mystery but was given her mystical hunger as a gift. I hesitate to see the play that way, for it seems to indicate that those who want to experience this exotic state of relating to God must be some sort of lama in saffron robe. I think not.

Paul confesses to being "caught up to the third heaven." In this wonderful and electric experience he could not even tell whether he was "in the body or out of the body." Since he felt the experience worth space in his epistle, we can only say that the ordeal had a part to play in his spiritual life. Great preachers are positive purveyors of the wonder of God.[7] They sometimes preach with an aura of power that is beyond what they learned about the art in seminary. They are "caught up" in a better vision of God, and the power of their hunger for the holy blesses all who hear them.

Wherever such a pastor is found, life is found. The sermons may lack the ability to be published, but they become the anointing that raises the dead, heals the sick, puts divorcees back together, and calls the weary soul to sip a new elixir; it sets the crippled dancing in the streets. No wonder Theodore Roszak said that the effective minister has for a role model the shaman, for it is through the life of this exotic person that the people of a primitive community can sense strange powers at play. We ought never to champion psychotics just because they are wild-eyed or otherworldly, but the church should also not be anxious to sanction leaders who have grown too heavy with doubt to dance alive the dead souls to whom they minister.

The Preacher as a Shepherd

Finally, the preacher is a shepherd, a *poimen* (the New Testament Greek word for *shepherd*) whose task is to shepherd (*poimainō*) and feed (*boskō*) the sheep. Sermons are food, sheep food, and sheep who are not regularly fed become restless and, in the furthest reach of the metaphor, begin to devour each other's wool. Only the Bible, regularly preached, can stay the wave of malnutrition that in our day leaves the sheep emaciated, wandering from suburban fold to suburban fold, seeking an adequate meal and bleating out their hungry condition.

These sheep are not only unproductive, but they are often quarrelsome without actually understanding that they are merely hungry. But they have been fed too little of the Word to grow toward maturity in Christ. Their immaturity results in a kind of ecclesiastical dyspepsia. Paul warned the Galatians that if they continued to bite and consume one another, they might actually eat each other up (Gal. 5:15).

The evangelical churches of America are losing members every year, often in devouring quarrels. Are they entirely to blame or have the sermons been only the dry fodder of their nonscriptural fare? We who preach need to take seriously Peter's advice, "Feed the flock of God!" The congregation longs for such a feeding. The congregation needs it. The congregation deserves it.[8]

Good preaching feeds the flock, and nothing else will do it quite as well. Churches, to avoid a great deal of inner turmoil, must have a raison d'être. For all my years as pastor, I considered that reason to be evangelism. If I kept reminding the church of the Savior's commission to go into all the world and make disciples, things tended to go pretty well. If I failed to remind them of that, the people didn't do as well. It was easy to see that my sermons emanated from this centerpiece of my convictions.

But the sermon that feeds brings the agenda of God to the congregation. Without this, God does not have the direct input he needs to keep the people focused on his plan for their lives. Nothing but a regular diet of the Word of God can nourish the congregation on God's intention. Nothing but a regular opening of God's Word can really feed the flock of God.

In Genesis 49:25, the patriarch Jacob seems to make an interesting connection between the words for *God* and *breast*. The Hebrew word for *breast* in the passage is *shad*. Jacob's benediction says that Joseph prospered in Egypt despite his brothers' treachery

> because of the hand of the Mighty One of Jacob,
>> because of the Shepherd, the Rock of Israel,
> because of your father's God, who helps you,
>> because of the Almighty [*Shaddai*], who blesses you
> with blessings of the heavens above,
>> blessings of the deep that lies below,
>> blessings of the breast [*shad*] and womb.
> Your father's blessings are greater
>> than the blessings of the ancient mountains,
>> than the bounty of the age-old hills.
>
> verses 24–26

It may be more than a coincidence that the word *shad* is also the word stem that is included in the name for God *El-Shaddai*, according to Robert Chisholm in the *New International Dictionary of Old Testament Theology and Exegesis*.[9] When you put these two together you get an interesting alternate root meaning of the ideas.

The human breast (*shad*) is where we first go in life for that nourishment that enables us to thrive as we enter life. But our need for God's nourishment never ceases. Well aware of this, Jacob says blessings and bounty of the Almighty, El-Shaddai, are greater than the age-old hills. When David asks, "I lift up my eyes to the hills—where does my help come from?" in Psalm 121:1, could he have been thinking of Jacob's El-Shaddai connection in Genesis 49? There is no way to know for sure, but he does seem to be giving us a picture of the God who nourishes and succors us—the El-Shaddai God of the breast—the God of the hills.

The nourishing of God is the imperative point of our preaching. When the apostle Peter teaches and encourages us to "feed the flock of God," he has in mind the idea of feeding our sheep from the Bible. The Word we bring in our sermons is there to feed the flock of God, lest they go undernourished.

It is easy to catch the tone of two ideas here. First the word *pastor* is the most appropriate name for the preacher. Shepherding takes into account a whole range of compassionate skills that belong to the pastor. Shepherds guard, heal, tend, and maybe even shear, when the care of the sheep require it. But of all these activities nothing is more critical than feeding them homiletically.

A second idea inherent in the word *pastor* is the act of "knowing" them. Jesus makes so much of this idea in John 10. He said that his sheep knew him and he knew them. Who knows all the applications that might be made of this idea, but one thing must be said: we can only preach to them—really preach to them—if we know who they are, the burdens they carry, where they work, and the heaviness of life that has gathered about them.

We will shortly have a lot to say about audience analysis, but in reality this high-sounding idea means nothing more than understanding your congregation. Baxter's axiom became the center of my pastoral care, and as our church grew from ten members to three thousand, I grew increasingly uneasy with the nonfamiliarity that seemed to haunt my sermons. I really believe that had I stayed there, I would have started some strong young mission churches filled with youthful sheep-feeders who could know their sheep and take seriously the job of caring for them.

Conclusion

Preacher analysis is not just a predator sport for laypeople, it is an art for every true proclaimer. I have not talked much in this chapter about self-studies or for that matter self-perception. But I believe that there is no knowledge quite so important as self-knowledge. Perhaps this is what lays behind Socrates's great proverb, "Know thyself."

This kind of knowledge can be gained by listening to our critics. They are not always right nor always fair, but they are more prone to tell us the places that we are weak than our friends are. Our friends—often because they realize we live in a fish bowl of criticism—are reluctant to be honest about our weakness. But not our enemies. Many of them find delight in pointing out our faults to us. When those criticisms come, sift through them to determine which words are valid, then use them to guide yourself into becoming a better person. Bless your critics for their honesty. They do not criticize you to be a blessing to you, but the end product may be the same.

By the time most ministers reach the pulpit, they have been Myers-Briggsed to death. Still there is great value in self-analysis. To know who we are while we seek to learn who they are is a rock-solid foundation for preaching. While we never really finish this conundrum of self-study, we can issue a certain sound for the gospel only if we have some certainty about who we are.

Whatever is done the preacher must live a life that authenticates the sermon.[10] This proclaimer has been called to make the world real, not because of what he says but because underneath of what he says is a persuader . . .

whose faith is real,

who is a person of information,

who is a mystic, longing for the inward glory of the mystery of godliness, and

who feeds sheep, sheep who find his sermons nourishing and who long to understand the Bible that the preacher expounds—who want to find the way into that world the preacher adores.

No person of God does all these things perfectly, but every perfect parson serves those longings that in time redeem the world through Christ-centered preaching.

At the conclusion of each of these chapters or sometimes earlier within the chapter appears a section such as the one below, which I have called The Sermon Journal. Take time to study each of the questions or exercises in these sections and answer them in turn.

THE SERMON JOURNAL

What acts of spiritual formation have I engaged in this week that I must never mention but that give me a secret walk of faith that allows me the right to be heard by those who attend my sermons?

_____

_____

_____

What can I say to remind them how much we are alike?

_____

_____

_____

What can I do to individualize and personalize the text?

_____

_____

_____

_____

What things in my personal experience and study give me the right to speak persuasively about this text?

_____

_____

_____

_____

_____

What elements of insight can I draw from this text for "sheep feeding" and growing my congregation in Bible knowledge and Christian growth?

_____

_____

_____

2

Who's Out There?

Exegeting the Audience

The Sunday service is a gathering of troubles. Half of those who enter the church and take their seat before the pulpit are moving in a privatized fog of their own ills. In the words of Thoreau, they are living lives of quiet desperation. They are the dying anonymous. Their ills are real to them, yet they can confuse the untrained pastor because they keep up the appearance of having life in tow. The music, the liturgy, and the sermon may gang up on their sullen inwardness, trying to force them into the real world. But having moiled through the past 167 hours of their 168-hour week, their private doubts have numbed their hearts. Sunday's single hour of God-talk does not last long enough to lure them back into the world where the sermon would have them live. Given the choice, they would never choose to be mummified in the bandages of their own ills. They want to be free, and that's partly why they first came to church. They are usually too fogged to care about when Leviticus was written or whatever happened to the Hittites. They are the wounded, reaching out to snare the God-words that fly at them between eleven and twelve o'clock. They are pew sitters, trying to remain anonymous, while they cry out to the sermonizer, "Hey look! I'm here! I'm bleeding." They do not want us to bring a set of ancient commentaries against their injuries of heart. They just

want a counselor to stop the hemorrhaging of their souls, and
if that can't be done they would like some life-survivor to show
them a set of well-healed scars so they can leave the service
believing that healing is possible.

The first thing to be done to this section on *exegesis* is to define
the word. It comes from the Greek *exhēgeisthai* (*ex* "out of";
hēgeisthai "to lead, guide") which means to lead out, just as *exodus*
comes from the Greek word *exodos* meaning the "way out." *Exegesis*
implies a gaining of understanding by taking a thing apart to see
into the nature of how it works. There is no ending to the study that
must be done to complete the exegetical work of preaching.

Although we generally apply the word *exegesis* to the text itself,
every element of preparation and delivery must undergo its own
exegesis. If only the text and preacher are exegeted—however noble
the study, however devoted the preacher—there still is no sermon.
So let's begin our analysis with the exegesis of the audience.

Audience Analysis

I spent my first thirty-five years in ministry as a pastor and
have spent the past decade and a half as a teacher, lecturer, and
evangelist. But the hardest exegesis I do—the exegesis that pre-
cedes in importance even analyzing the text—is the work of analyzing the audience. Now almost every Sunday (and at myriads
of conferences and lectures between them) I speak to complete
strangers, people I have never met before. From the moment I
enter a hall or church, I find myself engaged in the most rigorous
study of the audience gathering before me. This is an excruciat-
ing labor of trying to figure out who these strangers are. What
are their values? Are they dreamers? Demagogues? The wounded
arrogant? The spoiled indulgents? I feel that I must get answers
to these issues, for only as I form some idea of who they are can
I really speak to them.

The effort requires everything. I am spent by it. For I know that
if my audience exegesis goes awry, my exegesis of the text—however brilliant—will not help much. And these days, I lecture a
great deal to pastors, who have in some cases spent years in the

same parish. Still I always remind them that audience exegesis is not just a concern for itinerant preachers like me. Audience analysis is also the most formidable work of the local pastor.[1] Just because the pastors have preached hundreds of sermons in one place does not give them the liberty of skipping the work of audience analysis for even one single Sunday. The best of them know that their congregation will not be the same this coming Sunday as it was the last. Their world and their community have changed daily since last they preached. Every parish is undergoing constant renovation.

People are being born and dying within any given week. Terrorists made everything in late September different than it was in any early August. Whole communities suffer shock and blessing from day to day. Oncologists have suddenly laid a terrible prognosis against some key member of the church. Stockbrokers sometimes ruin a lovely week or lifetime with horrible announcements that truncate the future. Fortunes are lost, lotteries won, children break their parents' hearts, engagements die, Super Bowls are won, elections lost, all in a single week even within the smallest of communities. Only the preacher who sees his flock undergoing constant change has the right to preach. Every parish pastor must analyze his audience Sunday by Sunday or the sermon will miss the mark because the expositor, who may have thoroughly exegeted the text, has gone asleep at the business of people, the first business of God. To set the issue straight there are four questions that must be asked.

Question #1: Who's out there?

The first question is, "Who's out there?" The high work of audience analysis is more than just noticing what has befallen the world since last Sunday. It is the prayerful work of the ongoing analysis of who will be hearing the sermon this week. No public speaker other than a pastor is ever called upon to speak to such wide emotional needs and maturity levels. Children, adults, families, seniors, incurable grumblers, and naïve romantics are all there with their little beaks turned up and opened, waiting for their particular appetite to be fed. Each of the hearers have come to the church, needy in their own way. They all need God to reply to the cramp of their own existence in different ways. Enter the preacher! Armed is this healer with a Bible full of Band-Aids and sutures and medicines for all the wounded who attend the sermon. But best of heralds can only heal if the preacher is good at the diagnostic work of audience analysis.[2]

Question #2: What do they believe?

The second question is, "What do they believe?" This question was once answered in denominational ghettos where doctrines were firmly implanted at confirmation. No one doubted openly in those days. The province was secure. We all believed the same things, and if we didn't, we didn't dare mention it. The amen corner was full of "amens!" and when the Bible was held up we all cheered one solid orthodoxy together. But today's congregation is composed of a highly eclectic and diverse group of believers. Some believe a lot. Some believe a little. Orthodoxy here and there has been compromised by heterodoxy. People who attend church have no forum for expressing their diverse views and none are given polygraph tests to be sure they agree with the creeds. But many of them don't.

It is not that these variants have studied widely and become honest critical thinkers. It's just that *The DaVinci Code* makes sense to them. Dan Brown and Paul Tillich (whom they have never heard of) are coequals, and the novelist they see as more interesting than the theologian. They've picked up a lot of their theology from Oprah Winfrey's guests because it seems so right to them. They do believe in the resurrection, but they also believe in reincarnation. They are pro-life with a tendency toward pro-choice. They are for the sanctity of marriage but think gay weddings are alright if groom and groom are really in love. Tutored by secularists, they want God on their own terms, and prefer a worship service in which there's a lot of smiling.

So when the time comes to stand up and preach on Sunday, the pastor may be well assured that all those smiling faces are not schooled on doctrine, but they believe fervently what they believe. They do not have a lot of convictions, but they never run out of opinions. Their last appeal for what's right or wrong is their own ego. Like Hollywood stars, they believe their opinion should be honored as widely as possible. The idea that God should have the last word from his Word seems restrictive. Any idea that there are commandments or a Messiah that everyone should take seriously seems to circumvent their own desire to see themselves as right—totally right—with the right to define what is right for them. And to relate to them from the pulpit, we've sometimes tried to speak with less content because that is the theological snapshot of their lives.[3]

Question #3: What do they know about God?

The third question, "What do they know about God?" has for its answer, "Pretty much nothing." The question also is how we can get them to come to terms with a requiring God who sets his agenda somewhat in the mouths of his sermonizers. Preaching has for its best definition—in my opinion—this very special cliché: Preaching is one beggar telling another where to get bread. The problem with the definition is that it in effect lowercases the word *humanity* and uppercases the word *divinity*. And gone are those sermon auditors who want to be lowercased for any reason.

The problem with preaching, as many secular churchgoers see it, is that it is preachy. "Thus saith the Lord" seems ultra-pushy to the secular sermon hearer. The Ten Commandments are really the ten suggestions. The Beatitudes are all right in their place, but to suggest that it's good to be persecuted for righteousness' sake totally eludes the postmodern comfort index.[4] To get people to church is a matter of pampering their idiosyncrasies, keeping the pews padded and the sermons short.

Question #4: How can we help audiences come to terms with who they are?

The fourth question is, "How can we help audiences come to terms with who they are?" The first job of the preacher may be to see things as they really are. With God's help, after we've done that as best we can, we must ask ourselves what's to be done with these increasingly secularized pew sitters. I visit a lot of churches and see myself dealing with three pastoral myths that need to be cleared up.

Myth #1: There are still rural churches filled with old-time believers. Not so! It is true that there are still country churches, but the farmers—whether they've been to Texas A&M or not—are often as secular as their urban relatives. Every cottage on every unpaved road has a satellite dish, and the contemporary exurban, like the here-and-now suburban, has taken up philosophy and reasoning. Farmers are both as studied and as likely to doubt the virgin birth as high-rise condominium owners.

Myth #2: Once secularians have been discipled they'll become orthodox. Wrong! The church only gets them for an hour or two a week and television (depending on their age group) gets them for thirty hours a week. They are being secularized at a greater speed than they are being orthodoxized. The media has made the millions of opinionated souls, one large cacophony of self-expression.

Myth #3: Most preachers are free of the secular current which has swept their congregations into the river of relativistic theology. This too is false. Still, pastors also suffer from the illusion that they are heresy-free. The odd thing is that while "thus saith the Lord" once permeated their preaching, now they're getting their salaries for telling their people what "they and God" think about things. They still read the Bible just ahead of their sermons, but the part of their sermon that really counts—in their opinion—is what they think. Their sense of calling to be true to Scripture matters much less than it did to preachers in former generations.[5]

I have no intention of being harsh in this matter. I only lay it all out to talk about what is to be done sermonically in the church. Every sermon must continually do two things. First, preachers must never forget the chasm that exists between secular thinking and what the Word of God says. Further it must always keep in mind that the distinction between these two understandings is easily blurred. Pastors are at great risk. They swelter under the daily temptation to marry the spirit of the age and beget an odd spiritual genre of offspring that can never really become the children of God in the New Testament church.

Second, the sermon has a bifold task. It must first carry on its time-honored work of preaching the whole counsel of God. But it must also carry the burden of informing its hearers about the single reality that lies at the heart of Scripture: God has a word for us, not an opinion. The kingdom of God is not a discussion club. The church doesn't gather on Sunday to invite opinion. It gathers to hear the Bible—the Word of God—the wisdom of ancient saints and martyrs comes down to the current calendar after a march of centuries.[6] Preaching the Word lays down that one great argument that invites no dissent. Still, putting steel in a flabby sermon is a daunting task. For postmoderns, discussing the Word is always to be preferred over obeying it. But unless the Word is set forth as incontrovertible, week by week, over a long time, opinion will at last win over commandment, and we who preach will be largely to blame for the loss.

The church—in its finest definition—has always been seen as the bride of Christ, whose zealous Groom prefers her to be chaste in every respect. *Chaste* means that through the centuries of rising and falling heresies, the preacher and the church have stood between the ancient truth and the giddy, eclectic ages. Did sermons in earlier ages never cave in to the shallower philosophies of the times? Some did. Maybe even most did. But there has always been a remnant which seemed to take the word *orthodoxy* seriously. And those who did so have stood against the gates of hell to defend the faith. Their shield and buckler was the sermon. The faithful witnesses to the Word made flesh have lived on through every age because the sermons of the godly defiant were determined to tell the truth.

What Sermon Hearers Don't Want

Long Treatises on the Ever After

In a simple word sermon hearers don't want to hear about transcendence, and they particularly don't want to hear about hell. It does little good to remind them that Jesus spoke more of hell than of heaven. To them hell is a bygone notion no matter how often Jesus spoke of it. Even among the most conservative churches I visit, I rarely hear the word brought up. It's not that I have some morose need to hear a lot about it. It's just that its absence in sermons triggers in me a huge doubt about the continuance of the faith. Hell is on the opposite end of the teeter-totter with heaven, and things have gotten so light on the hell end, that the heaven end is flat on the ground and being nibbled at by nuances of all kinds. It was bound to happen. Nearly all great truths are bipolar (in the best sense of the word) and to eliminate one pole is to destroy the other.

It's not really hell that is missing from the modern sermon. It is transcendence. Modern preachers rarely talk about anything mysterious or mystical or redemptive. "How-to" is a more popular sermonic crowd getter. Stuart Barton Babbage said that the emerging society he knew spoke guardedly of sex and openly about death. But the secular society of today has reversed the poles. People in the youth-dominated, secular megatemple just don't want to hear about death. In our protected society we have not been asked to deal with it all that often. Disease has been inoculated out of existence, and between Zocor and Lipitor the great either-or of "repent or perish" seems overserious. Heaven has become a popular but fuzzy notion, which like the populist intrigue over angels has everyone writing vague books on the subject.

Comtemporary pulpits feel that to bring up dying is just not as relevant as telling people how to live, marry, succeed, relate, or become a winner.[7] Sermons that say, "Repent and believe!" usually don't do well for three reasons. First, in this gospel-saturated society, virtually everyone from network anchorpersons to garage mechanics knows the "get saved" lingo. Billy Graham and Christian bookstore bumper stickers have done their national work. Everybody generally feels they have repented and been baptized, and so the great evangelistic texts designed to convert pagans do not apply to them. In the Bible Belt the flood of clichés is so engulfing that evangelistic Christians wear tags to "keep from winning each other to the Lord." So all attempts to save a world grown weary of the "get-saved" clichés have become a dull art.

Second, the word *repent* just doesn't apply to the secular hearer. Repentance is a doctrine for people like Adolf Hitler or somebody who has done something really wrong. People believe they are Christians: they say the pledge to the flag and give to the United Way. They have done a lot of good, and what they do that isn't good just isn't all that bad. The idea that anything in their behavioral pattern had anything to do with Jesus being crucified is just plain weird. Psychology has taught them well: they're OK, we're OK, the preachers are OK, and it's OK. If they listen to any sermon on sin, they feel that the sermon is for somebody who isn't as OK as they are.

Third, sin has been redefined as sociology run amok. Most evangelicals still are sweltering under old definitions of the subject. Legalisms like no dancing and no canasta still linger among the older faithful, while sleeping around lies more central among modern singles who want to define sin more tolerantly. It's not sleeping around that's bad, they would say, it's being promiscuous that's really bad. Most of us who have lived through the lost decades of evangelicalism agree that our legalistic petulance needed to go. Still as we lost our nit-picking definitions of sin, the general conscience seemed to go with it. Now, like Karl Menninger, the last psychologist to really consider personal evil, we all are lamenting, "Whatever happened to sin?" For all practical purposes it has disappeared from the self-congratulating millennium we have just entered. There may or may not be sin, but the question is prosaic and, frankly, contemporary sinners find little interest in the subject and find the whole idea a drag on their self-esteem.

Long Sermons on Doctrines Unapplied

All real preaching is doctrine. Everything we cherish, all we believe and trust, is doctrine. It isn't just the virgin birth or resurrection. Grace, redemption, confession, salvation, the sinlessness of Christ, heaven, hell, the church: all are doctrines. But the key is for the preacher to be committed to the truth that doctrine articulates, and be able to preach it without always having to stop to label it. To say, "This morning I want to preach to you a doctrinal sermon," is to hear the loud report of a thousand minds clicking off at one time. The church cannot be the church without preaching the important truths, and the important truths are all doctrinal.

Still, there exists a notion that doctrine is dull. The error needs correcting! Doctrines are the high-voltage center of the faith. Doctrines are the faith. Nothing is more riveting than a sermon on confession or more exciting than one on the resurrection. What is dull is a lecture sermon that tells a great truth in drowsy ways. So what if Jesus is sinless? What does that have to do with a UAW employee bolting Fords together on an assembly track in Dearborn? So Jesus is coming again; will you please tell me when or how? I could use this information in building my long-term stock portfolio. Why in the world am I sitting here listening to you tell me why being a Calvinist is such a life-and-death matter? I'm over my credit limit on Visa and my boyfriend just walked out on me and left me no forwarding address.

Doctrinal preachers often fall into the trap of giving their congregations the notion that the Bible is something to know but not necessarily to live by. This is particularly the case of the congenitally left-brained expositor, who loves pursuing all things cerebral, for the sheer joy of knowing them. Such preachers get excited over new ideas and love the speculative and exotic facts that they discover while they read or listen to other smart people talk. Without realizing it they sometimes get so excited about learning, they forget that what they most enjoy—sheer insight—is a difficult habit for others to acquire. Then they really cease to preach and begin merely to spout unapplied information. It's not just that it's unapplied, it's not applicable! Or, when it is applied it changes little in the listener's world.

If they are dedicated students and thrill at the very sight of an Aramaic verb, they often lose all touch with their more right-brained, more relational brothers and sisters. I have seen the phenomenon many times. There are precept-driven preachers who have such a great time preaching that they seem strangely unaware that no one is listening. Such preachers have a kind of seminary drone they learned from their uninteresting professors in the M.Div. wonderland of tidy theology.[8] They are not generally aware that their congregation is thinning year by year. I know some of these preachers who are killing their churches with the dagger of dull homiletics. I stand utterly amazed that they can't seem to see that their sermons are gradually dividing them from their flocks.

The trick is to be a scholar-pastor who preaches doctrine but who will not take a drudgerous course into a dry gulch of arid homiletics. Such a pastor finds a way to make a sermon on the sinlessness of Christ exotic stuff. Such a preacher moves slowly, illustrating, storytelling, metaphorizing, until the congregation can see clearly that Jesus was sinless. People count themselves fortunate to hear the preaching, for without this great virtue the kingdom would not be possible. Without this truth every sermon hearer would have no real hope of the life they enjoy because of this joyous doctrine so utterly relevant to their living.

The difference between a dull lecturer and a glorious preacher is all in the application. In this book we will pay a great deal of attention to this element of preaching. Application is where the rubber meets the road. The rubber is the life of the sermon hearer.

The road is the truth of God, glistening, enduring concrete in the life of the creative expositor. Truth either plods or flies and the effective expositor knows that even the most exciting truth can be dull and pedestrian when it can't be applied to a needy world.

Below I have offered an audience analysis inventory in which I set at the first of the sermon "the speech before the speech." This is what you say when you stand to preach, that is, what you say before you begin preaching on what you intend to say in your sermon. The speech before the speech is a reaching out to those who will soon hear your formal propositions. But before they do you have a few "off the cuff" remarks that say to them, "I understand who you are and what we're doing here together. Let's agree to be friends."

AUDIENCE ANALYSIS INVENTORY

How are we alike?

   a. From what part of the country does the audience come?

   _____

   b. What denomination do they belong to, or which one has nourished them across the years?

   _____

   c. What great common doctrines do we share?

   _____

   d. What important differences do we esteem in each other?

   _____

   _____

   _____

   _____

   e. How does the average age of the listeners compare to mine?

   _____

How are we different?

   a. In gender _____

   b. In marital status _____

   c. In educational background_____

   d. In vocation and calling_____

   e. In spiritual or economic need _____

What can I do or say in my "speech before the speech" to create a feeling of relationship? (Don't outline or write this out. Speaking extempore is the key to identifying authentically with the audience.)

_____

_____

_____

In what ways do I need to alter what I have written down to say in order to tailor my remarks to this audience?

_____

_____

_____

What the Sermon Hearers Do Want

A Sense of Significance

The American writer Henry Miller said we are all neurotics down to the last human being. I'm confident he is right. I am equally convinced there are only two kinds of neurotics: those who admit to it and those who live all their lives in the pinch of cover-up. One reason I believe we are all neurotic is that all of us suffer from time to time with feelings of inferiority and therefore lack a sense of our significance.

People come to church with their hearts on their sleeves. They are longing to be told that God loves them.[9] They want to be told that they are special to God and the very fact that he loves them means they have significance. Often preachers get so involved in the mechanics—sometimes the brutal entanglements—of running the church that their sermons reflect a negative spirit. Perhaps even a spirit of rebuke. Nothing I suspect is worse than a napalm Calvinist, or for that matter an abusive Arminian, who feels like the world needs to be dressed down and whipped into humility. The urge to beat up on people is never legitimate. There are some biblical examples of ancient prophets who excoriated the rebellious, and flayed the self-willed. But a great pastor feels for the broken souls who come into the fellowship weeping inside, looking for any reason to feel they have a right to continue on in the world. Think upon them. Try to see that anything from the pulpit that further damages the damaged is ungodly.

I must confess I never rebuke a child for being noisy in church, for I suffer the distinct impression that if I were more interesting, he would be less rowdy. I once heard a famous preacher rebuke a retarded child for playing in the aisle next to where her parents held a pew. I cringed in sympathy for the family, as did the rest of the church. I had the sneaking suspicion the sermon was so bad that we all would have preferred playing in the aisles had they been wide enough to hold us all.

Not long after that I was at a service where a famous evangelist was preaching, and right in the middle of his sermon a little girl broke away from her parents and ran right up onto the platform, grabbing hold of the preacher's leg and holding on in an affectionate but unrelenting grasp. Everybody smiled as the preacher reached down and pried the little girl off his leg and held her up and then hugged her saying, "I don't know whose little girl you are, but they have fifteen seconds to claim you or you're mine." Here was a preacher who had learned the meaning of people and had built into his homily a way of being sure that while he was preaching, no one's significance would be insensitively buried beneath his own ego needs—or for that matter even his own need to be hailed as a great expositor.

Sermons that celebrate the broken are healing homilies. I suspect this kind of preaching does not come from heavy research and long nights with the commentaries.[10] I have a feeling such sermons are born in the quiet moments of formation that great pastors rely on. These heralds cherish the quiet place where identity with Christ puts authentic counseling at the center of every sermon. Jesus modeled this for us in the great tale in the allegedly spurious section of John's Gospel when he said to the woman taken in adultery, "Neither do I condemn you." What a powerful affirmation of the half-naked woman who stood cringing before him. The Son of Man may have understood that he would one day be naked and seen by most of his world as significant. It was not a part of his sermon, but even during his sermons, Jesus picked up some little tots who were deemed by the apostles to be in the way of Jesus's popular ministry. Stopping his sermon midpoint, he said, "Unless you change and become like little children . . ." well, you know the rest. The point is that Christ's sermons did not complicate people's need to feel they had some worth. No great preacher or sermon ever does.

Instructions on Coping with Pain

Pain comes in all types and sizes. Most of those who sit in a chapel, waiting while the Word is preached are either enduring it or shut down emotionally. A preacher that I much admire wrote of a time when his daughter was very ill with a condition that would soon take her life. He confessed that these were very dark days for his family and that during her illness he never went to church casually to hear the casual preaching of a casual parson. He went to church desperately because his needs were desperate. Most of the time he heard three-point sermons filled with lots of information about the Bible. But what he really wanted was not more biblical information but a pastor who would bleed with him.

I am convinced that people in some sense visit a church like they visit their doctor. Something is hurting when they walk in. They want the pain to stop, and just as they would not recriminate a doctor merely because his prescriptions didn't stop their pain, neither will they recriminate the preacher because the tears they brought into church with them are still flowing as they leave. But if the sermon cannot heal them, it should at least ache because of their pain.

Sermons are not placebos prescribed to make people feel good. But they are a stab at kingdom togetherness, and they are a balm for the broken. Audience analysis reaches its heights when something like 9/11 happens. For one brief, shining moment, sermons all weep from church to church, nationwide. We have no answer for the great pain, but not to offer the hurting a God-word is sermonic shame.

After a church reaches any reasonable size, some enter the Sunday service bewildered by circumstances. A sermon which bleeds is better in this case than one which merely offers biblical information. Preaching a cold Bible steals the life from those it wants to inform but has not the compassion to touch.[11]

Three Common Needs for which Souls Seek God

When the audience has been analyzed there are any number of other needs that surface. The sermon probably cannot know or heal them all. But let's for the moment consider three of these common congregational needs.

ADVICE ON GETTING AHEAD

First, there is the very practical how-to subject of getting ahead. In some ways this does not seem to be the kind of issue that dealing with personal pain might appear to be. But most young career-seekers are coping with these kinds of issues. They want to know how to succeed and how to pay the bills before and after they reach that elusive threshold they call achievement. It has never been preaching's first agenda to inform people as to how they are to get on in this world. Still, getting on in the world for many is their first agenda. And if the pulpit can offer them no rules of engagement, it should at least remind them that they are children of a kingdom where ethics and obedience are major considerations in what makes living beautiful, which it ought to be even if it never becomes successful.

I have had to take a rather apologetic step backwards on this issue. Sometimes offering advice on how to get ahead seems too Dale Carnegie to be allowed a place among the noble themes which preaching addresses itself. Still at the heart of the secular society in which preaching now has to do its work, there is an ache and cry of financial fears and job insecurity. I have come to believe that where the Scriptures and the concerned pastor can allow the sermon a voice on this important matter it should. A family's livelihood should be a concern of the church. It is the number one concern of so many wage earners in the church that strong preaching must allow God a voice in the matter.

HOPE

Second, hope is ever in short supply. I realize how many people are being kept alive just by the routines that keep them going to work and coming home feeling trapped in a vocation they hate. Many empty workers serve a boss who makes their lives a daily hell. They are up early going about life in a constant zombie state. They are suffering from a huge hope deficit. They are trapped with no way out of the grim predicament in which they are forced to live. These come to church desperately hungry for a word that will make the day worth it. If the Word doesn't flow freely from the pulpit, they have no counsel of hope.

Besides, hope is hard work. It can't be done by oneself. It is best done when two or more hopeless people get together to talk themselves into hoping. For many a quiet soul who has no one to help with the hoping, the preacher becomes the counselor in this difficult work. I once saw a bumper sticker that read, "I'm having a better time since I've given up all hope." It is really a hollow proverb for the hollow people that T. S. Eliot lamented were as empty as straw-filled men. The whole world is interested in the subject of hope.

An Experience of Grace and Mystery

A third item sermon attenders listen for is the possibility of mystery that comes in any experience of grace. Sermons sincerely preached are the red carpet down which the Spirit strides to make any ordinary day a day of jubilee. People attend church to feel the coming of the "other." They want to bump into what the apostle called the "mystery of godliness." Sermons that are only about the practical things of this world are often too bound by this world to help them. And this world is too weak to heal what is wrong with most people's lives. People see great sermons as rooted in a transcendence that becomes their entry point into a better world. It is a world which is more than just cause and effect. It is a world where the disenfranchised don't have to believe that their lives are controlled by normal, predictable rules. The predictable can be shattered by something honest and enduring and otherworldly. Preachers who care about God care passionately about the real realms that lie beyond the workaday, stifling issues that trap their flock in a "no-exit" world.

The three common needs for which people seek God must, of course, be related to the biblical text you have chosen as the "master direction" for your sermon. The chart below is designed to harmonize the two.

Aligning Textual and Audience Analysis

The Drive to Achieve

Note the part of the text that might allow you a legitimate digression into this area.

Hope

What in the text and in your message will allow you to make your preachment a document of hope?

Mystery

How does the text and your sermon call into play the visitation of the Spirit and transform your sermon from words to a godly encounter?

This is a lot of weight to be borne by the preacher. Wouldn't it belong more naturally to the church musicians, who can make us feel and laugh and weep? Isn't the musical center of worship better suited to bring us into the world of grace and mystery than the homily? Not necessarily. If the preacher is in love with the Christ of heaven and lives life in touch with the unseen realities that authenticate and make the sermon real, maybe the preacher and the sermon are indeed the best place to bring the entire audience in touch with what one theologian called the "numinous"—loosely translated the spiritual realm. People want to be impacted by "the great beyond of the Holy Spirit." The best chance of this happening is when the Spirit thrives in the secret devotion of the God-hungry pastor.

What Sermons Need to Talk About

Sermons have a need to talk about those items which remain God's agenda for the church. These are not things the church generally cries out to hear preached. In fact they may find something easier and more congenial that they would rather hear preached. But whether they want this kind of preaching or not, they need it. The pastor in some cases becomes parental, giving the children what they need not what they want. What they want of course is all sugar and cream; what they need is good instructional protein and firm didactic fiber. There are lots of these kinds of needed themes, but let me mention just a few of them which will show up consistently in the Sunday-to-Sunday preaching of the gospel.

How to Continue in Reconciliation

First, people need to know how to continue in reconciliation. Most of the congregation, to whom every preacher speaks, has been converted or confirmed for a very long time. The subject of "how to be born again" is not nearly so important as "going on to maturity in Christ." I grew up in Pentecostal and Baptist churches where a huge amount of the preaching was given to converting the lost. I am convinced that evangelism is an important task of preaching. But I also believe the best preaching addresses the spiritual need of the majority of people in attendance. I am reluctant to bring up the whole subject of reconciliation because I am afraid that in all but a small percentage of the churches the crying need is for more evangelistic preaching not less. Still, most people need more information on how to become conformed to the image of Christ than they do on how to be converted.

The levels of immaturity in the church are astounding. These "never-grown" adolescent members in some cases run grasping committees, moderate the mayhem, and generally visit the pastor with more negative evaluations than are deserved. So it isn't just Jesus who would like them to grow up, the preacher's own mental well-being has a share in the matter. The members need to hear regularly about how they are to go on to maturity in Christ.[12]

The Eden-Life God Intended

Second, the Eden-state is out to be restored in Scripture. As I mentioned in the introduction, Bryan Chapell has set this forward in his FCF—the Fallen Condition Focus. We were all created to live in harmony with God, but what has happened? And what will it take to get us back all that we lost when Adam ate the forbidden fruit? Only preaching sets itself to the task of getting us back to where we all started.

An Anchoring Theology

Third, what the church needs to hear is an "anchoring theology." The world has been set adrift in a broad, meandering sea of secular values and "anything goes" worldviews. This area of preaching is especially important to the youth. I for one have always been in favor of the youth staying in the main worship service rather than having a service of their own. A part of this is just plain selfishness on my part. When the youth are present there is always a better possibility for God. Youth are more often vitally interested in the dynamic subjects of God's will—far more than their parents are. They are more eager to know and please God than their more weary forbears.

But the youth live in a peer-driven culture and they need the anchors that hold them in place between Sundays. Services which offer an anchoring theology are inevitably honest about the dangers of conforming to the secular onslaught. And the preachers who preach the sermons that drop these anchors have weighed the culture and made up their minds that the ship of faith must not lose its moorings or all is lost. Theology isn't a drag. It was once called the queen of the sciences. Theology is there to anchor both the church and the Christian.

An Eager Expectation of the Final Hope

Finally, preaching needs to preach on the second coming of Christ. This is a day and age when premillennial thought has dominated eschatology. Second-coming novels have furnished an entire age—Christian or not—with a worldview. It would seem that any further mention of the fact that Jesus is coming again would be unnecessary. The truth is this: God is the keeper of the end of history. And there is so much about the *eschaton* (last coming) in Scripture that the subject has stood at the center of all the ages. It must stand also at the center of ours.

Further, the second coming is all bound up with the church's definition of hope. To preach Christ's return is to keep his ascension from being the end of all things. No funeral should be preached without some reference to our ultimate hope. After all, our eternal existence is wound very tightly with his coming again, when the "dead in Christ will rise first." Put more starkly, there is no religion without destiny. A faith without a God-confident conclusion is no faith at all. Since the current age will end in glory, the theme validates all sermons and keeps God at the center of all our futures.[13]

Conclusion

Audience analysis faces every sermon with the complexity of understanding. A predictable set of questions always arise. Who are these people before me? What are they doing here? What am I doing here? What right do I have to address them?[14] But along with these predictable questions there is an immutable set of propositions that belongs to every pulpit opportunity. Here's who will hear me. Here's what they want to hear. Here's what they need to hear. Here's what will fascinate them. Here's what will transform them.

Knowing the audience is everything. Being fuzzy about their identity will foil the work of the Spirit, and the sermon will fly as scattered as buckshot. Truth will then be strewn all about the hearers, having touched no one. The scope on a rifle is the metaphor of audience analysis. Get a good gun, aim carefully, and the Word made flesh will fly directly to the heart of every matter on which we ought to preach.

3

Whadda Ya Hear Me Sayin'?

Exegeting the Sermon

Great sermons gather about a narrow range of subjects: Christ, the Bible, life. And from this narrow list the average pew sitter wants the preacher to extrapolate a prescription for their healing. But preachers are not chemists—not even alchemists—brewing up healing for every hurt. Preachers are physicians who, having found that the Spirit's healing arts have worked for them, are trying to take the cure to the world. Still, most people rate their doctors on the basis of how seriously they take their patients' hurts. Preachers are compassionate clinicians who don't dodge congregational pain. The best of sermons have never been a belch of information or piety. Good homiletics are wellness reports that take seriously the cure of souls. Great preaching is not a busy mouth, spewing forth answers. Great preaching is an ear. But real listening begins not so much in the ear as in the epidermis. The noblest of prophets should feel before they advise. Preachers, however eloquent they are, are rarely heard as readily as pastors. After all, shepherds are sheep lovers, and the sheep are dependent upon their shepherds, who love them even before they listen. Perhaps God really did give us two ears and one mouth so we could listen twice as much as we speak. The prophet must feel so that the sermon can listen. The sermon that will not listen cannot speak. The deaf expositor is mute as well.

After we hear the sheep we must speak to them, and what we say must be carefully measured so that no words fly at them that we have not analyzed and commanded. We analyze to be sure we have picked just the right word to carry our message. We command the words not to hurt or bruise the hearers. Thus we become gentle and yet direct, kind but clearly understood.

Substance Analysis

To analyze the central focus of the sermon is to ask ourselves three questions. If any of these three issues go unanswered, some vital function of preaching will not be present. These are not questions that relate properly to sermon preparation. But they are equally important issues if the sermon is to be both biblical and relevant.

The questions are these:

Is the sermon about Christ?
Is the sermon about the Bible?
Is the sermon about them (the listeners) and the present moment?

The sermon must arrive at the listener's hearing through a channel of intensity and interest. The first two of these questions will give the sermon intensity or passion. Without passion, the first two questions will arrive at the listener's ears as a drone of no importance. The final question is the issue of relevance. Until this last question is answered, sermons inevitably degenerate to boredom because to the hearers such sermons seem to contain no information they need, nor can they apply what the preacher is saying to the "right-now" predicament of their lives.

Is the Sermon about Christ?

But what does it really mean to ask, "Is the sermon about Christ?" To preach Christ means that the sermon must attend to three homiletical linchpins.

First, preaching Christ is a matter of getting Jesus across as a worldview. When I read books like Bryan Chapell's *Christ-Centered Preaching*, I realize that the author wants to be sure that each reader understands that every sermon preaches Christ only as it allows the Lord's presence in what is being preached. But it is more than just saying Christ inhabits the sermon by metaphor or isolated references. Preaching Christ is the purpose and intent of the sermon and comes from a preacher whose life is captive to the momentary presence of Christ.[1]

But what does this have to do with Jesus's own worldview? Well Jesus obviously believed things about the human race. He believed things about God, life, and the changing of the seasons and political systems. To preach Christ is to be sure that Christ's value systems on all these subjects permeate the exposition of that text which houses the central presupposition of the sermon. This virtue of preaching Jesus causes the hearers to want to imitate Jesus. It encourages Christlikeness just by telling the world in the sermon what Christ is like.

But the second issue in asking whether the sermon is about Christ goes beyond exposing his worldview to the sermon hearers. Preaching Christ is not about merely informing the listeners what he believed or how he saw things. To preach Christ is to place—here and there—within the sermon the preacher's own affirmation of love and respect for Jesus. The idea here is not to expose Christ's worldview but to praise him for who he was. This aspect of preaching Christ lays down a tone of worship celebrated by the text. The delivery of the sermon acquires a tone of high esteem and great praise.

Most of those who hear the sermon draw in close to the devotional pulpit, for how the Christ-affirming preacher feels about Jesus is exactly what they are feeling or at least want to feel. Nothing cements a devoted congregation to a devoted preacher faster than "bragging up Jesus." This common point of great love emanates from the sermon and falls fully upon both pastor and hearers. This, after all, is the best of public worship: a sermon that is personally about Christ creates a oneness of adoration, and it imparts to biblical preaching a huge amount of togetherness and warm emotion.

Third, preaching Christ means that we build within the sermon Christ's own altar appeal. By this I am not saying that every sermon has to end with an altar call. I am also not saying that it shouldn't.[2] I happen to come from a denomination where invitations and altar calls are frequent, and I have observed that those sermons which talk about Jesus tend to have a much greater response than those that remain theologically correct—and are maybe even morally challenging—but do not center around Christ.

All sermons should, in my opinion, move between the text and the altar. The altar may be a "Just As I Am" and a "Yes . . . yes . . . I see that hand, and is there another?" kind of altar, or it may simply call upon the listener to meet God at the inner altar of the heart for a renovation of dead ideologies or selfish agendas. But whichever kind of altar (maybe both) that the sermon addresses, Jesus is a better motivator to draw listeners to the altar (whether inner or outer) than logic alone. People will change sooner when challenged with the requirements of Christ than any secondary rationale.

In the sermon focus inventory below, I suggest four questions that help the preacher make sure that the sermon is being developed in such a way that the text, whatever it is, is tied to Christ and his requirements for the listener. Of course, there may be some texts where the teachings of Christ do not relate at all to either the text or the theme of the sermon. But where a good concordance can establish a link between the text and the authority of Christ, it should be done.

SERMON FOCUS INVENTORY #1
IS THIS SERMON ABOUT CHRIST?

Text _____

Sermon Theme _____

What did Jesus have to say about this theme?

_____
_____
_____
_____
_____
_____

Is there any one of his parables that focus on this?

_____

_____

_____

Where did Jesus act on this?

_____

_____

_____

What do the epistles say about what Christ did or felt about this?

_____

_____

_____

Is the Sermon about the Bible?

Before we look intensively at the question, "Is the sermon about the Bible?" let us examine the nature of the text that lies at the center of the sermon's argument. The issue of what sort of text the sermon should be built upon can be determined by considering which of these three forms the sermon's text is like: Is it *preceptual*? Is it a *narrative* text? Is it *poetic*? (Within the gamut of these three broad selections there are lots of other categories of genre such as Gospel, epistle, history, Pentateuch, prophetic books, etc.) It usually enriches the sermon to some degree to mix the various genres together. Mixing them together also educates hearers by helping the people understand what a literary form is so they learn to distinguish between the different genres. If a text is preceptive, you may want to include support from a correlating narrative text. If the text is poetic, you might want to support it with a highly prescriptive text.

Why mix genres in such a deliberate way? Because every congregation is a collage of both right- and left-brained people who each receive biblical truth in different ways. The more left-brained our hearers are the less likely they will gravitate toward the poetic or narrative style.[3] Since we all learn in different ways, writing and preaching with those differences in mind is a good way to make sure we are preaching to the whole congregation at once.

What are the relative strengths of preaching in each of these three primary modes?

First, let us look at the strengths of preaching in a propositional style. Preaching a precept-centered message has for its best advantage the fact that it is concrete and can be stated in a brief form. The motif that we spoke about earlier is generally an easily held precept. Consider these actual sermon titles:

"Where You Go Hereafter Depends upon What You Go After Here"

"When the Going Gets Tough, the Tough Get Going"

"Trust God for Heaven's Sake"

All of these are precepts. Yet each of them are going to become more memorable as they receive support from either the poetic or narrative categories of supporting Scripture.

Why do propositional preaching at all? Because precepts are the best way to build the skeletal structures that good sermon outlines require. You can hang poetry and story off precepts but not vice versa. Good sermons are built upon categorical statements of truth that form the sermon's framework and illuminate it with the more artsy (and usually more interesting) categories of poetry and story.

Precept Preaching

Precept preaching has a clear-cut and incisive appeal to sound reasoning. Narrative and poetic texts hold interest but build fuzzier transitions and more formless arguments than are shaped by strong precept-driven reasoning. "Give me the facts, just the facts!" is a way to keep a case on track but is usually the most boring way to arrive at interest.[4]

Three-point sermons are sometimes one-two-three body slams that are easily traced but just as easily forgotten. There is little about precepts that hold enduring interest, for once they have been stated their force is spent. The Ten Commandments are precepts—good ones. But once you speak any one of them their force is spent, and if you expect to hold the audience in tension, you must quickly illustrate them with a story or poem or metaphor of some sort. "Thou shalt not commit adultery" is a powerful one-liner, but like all precepts it is out all at once and not baroque enough to engage the mind for any length of time thereafter. But if you can follow the short precept up with a longer tale of where the wayward deacon left his bicycle on Saturday night, the sermon gains fastidious interest. Precepts need narrative to enforce communications with memorable lessons.

In my preaching classes, I rate sermons on two words: *flow* and *fix*. "Flow" is how a sermon moves; if it does not move it will hold no interest. Streams are more interesting than ponds. Streams move. Ponds stagnate. Sermons also stagnate when they refuse to move. Illustrations put movement into more stolid precepts.

"Fix" is what listeners take home with them once the sermon is over. "Fix" may become "fixed" by a story, but the take-home is usually stated in the precept. For instance, here is a list of precepts ("fixes") inspired by stories ("flows").

Fixes	Flows
Ugly duckings are swans in the making.	A story by Hans Christian Anderson
There is power in "I think I can."	A story about a little train engine
We're not in Kansas anymore, Toto.	A story called *The Wizard of Oz*

NARRATIVE PREACHING

The second of these three forms of Scripture is narrative. Narrative preaching has only to be created (and rehearsed) to engage an audience. The Bible is so well written that the narrative passages have a built in power within them to hold attention. The most wonderful thing about these narrative passages is that they not only hold attention, they also are a form of exposition that makes the text clearer. Story also makes a text more interesting.[5]

For years I have had students debate me in this matter of narrative exposition. There exists within evangelicalism a philosophical fetish that claims narrative is not expositional—not real preaching. Nonsense! Lest Jesus be accused of not being an expository preacher, it needs to be pointed out that he often followed a precept with an expository story that exposed the truth of his precepts. And the nice thing about narrative exposition is that it—unlike precept-driven exposition—sticks itself in the mind and is remembered long after the sermon's outline, which gave it birth, is forgotten.

POETIC FORMS

The final of these three forms of texts is poetic. These texts have for their most positive virtue the fact that they are seedbeds of worship and praise. They do a great deal to make the sermon more artistic and elevating. Indeed, they give the sermon that feel of craft and art, gifts that the more prosaic genres of texts cannot do as well.

But best of all, poetry invites decision. If the ending of the sermon is the best place for motivation and persuasion, poetry has its best work to do in the final arguments of the homily. The reason why is because art and craft—indeed all creative and right-brained functions—are far more motivational than precepts. People can be drawn aesthetically to a place of change far more easily than they can be compelled by reason alone. Bible poetry really is a stronger motivator than even the best of the secular poets, because with biblical poetry the sermon becomes a purveyor of biblical authority, a force lacking in more secular kinds of creativity.

In the second sermon focus inventory below I have provided a schedule where the expositor can list correlating genres that support the master text. This form should be completed before the sermon brief or manuscript is written. Once this form is filled out the manuscript can be created with far more "flow" and "fix."

SERMON FOCUS INVENTORY #2
IS THIS SERMON ABOUT THE BIBLE?

Text _____

Sermon Theme _____

List a correlating, supportive precept-driven passage:

_____

_____

_____

List a correlating, supportive narrative-driven passage:

_____

_____

_____

List a correlating, supportive poetic passage:

_____

_____

_____

Is the Sermon about Them (the Listeners) and the Present Moment?

Good exegesis isn't content with digging word studies out of commentaries but with getting truth into the listeners. Interesting sermons are easier to ladle into souls than dull ones. Sermons should be delivered with an involving exegesis. But the best preached sermons don't try to write the Bible on the lives of their hearers, they write their hearers into the Bible. To do this, one important kind of mind-set must occupy the preacher during the delivery of the whole sermon. Preachers must always be thinking of the application all the time they are dispensing information.

This sense of application lies in the use of pronouns. "Ye must be born again" is an ancient, second person way of saying, "We must all be born again." *You*-preaching can seem overbearing in an *us*-culture. Most of the imperatives in all kinds of communication have moved to the indicative. But it is very important in preaching that the pastor applies the sermon by describing—from the Bible—what hearers ought to do. Then the preacher points out the outcomes—such as heaven or hell—and asks the auditor to make a choice. Older styles of deductive preaching tell people simply where to go and what to believe. Newer forms of communication let the audience make those decisions on the basis of information supplied in the indicative sermon.

The *you*-sermon must make God the speaker. If it sounds like the preacher is saying "you"—even if what is being said is true—it will not be well received. I grew up in a denomination that grew radically in the 1950s because it preached such imperative sermons: "You must turn or you will burn! You must be born again!" All that was said was true, but the contemporary church attender will be slower to heed such second person threats. This is a day of individual sovereignty when listeners are better attuned to propositions. Therefore set the proposals before them in indicative language. The choice over what to do with the information is their own as is the responsibility to choose.

Still one thing must be made clear: they must decide now. The biblical text must be preached in such a way that they who listen see themselves like Ahab, or Aaron, or the Pharisees, or Alexander the coppersmith. If the preacher cannot write the listener into the text, and if no urgent appeal is of the moment and for the moment, the sermon will not succeed in seeming relevant. The sermon must be about the listener and it must offer them options on what they need to do at this present moment.

In the third sermon focus inventory, the issue of relevance is addressed. For many people a text cannot be relevant unless it can be stated in the present tense. Its relevance will not motivate very well without a narrative base. And it can be neither inductive nor innovative unless it can be preached in a conversational, first person plural mode. This focus inventory is therefore most important if we hope to set the sermon in the here and now—if "relevant" is our adjective to be cherished.

SERMON FOCUS INVENTORY #3
IS THIS SERMON ABOUT THEM
AND ABOUT RIGHT NOW?

Text _____

Sermon Theme _____

If the text is a past tense text, rewrite the text in the present.

_____
_____
_____

If the text is written in the third person and in a didactic style, write in a supporting narrative text that can be applied in the second person, but let it remain free of imperative statements.

_____
_____
_____

Finally, once you see how the text applies to the second person, put your own paraphrase of the text in first person plural. This will keep your sermon from being preachy and instead put the whole thing into an indicative mode.

Relational Analysis

It is possible that older textbooks on preaching did not need to deal with relational analysis, but modern sermons do. For most of Western history, truth was widely separate from those who believed it or preached it.[6] Real truth is still constant and unalterable, but we have now arrived at a place in time where people buy or sell truth largely in reference to the peddler who brought it to them.

Relational preaching is everything. The herald may not be good at one-on-one relationships, but while on the stage before the masses, one must appear to be good at these things. Nobody buys truth from someone they don't like, and if they do buy it, they do so with reluctance. We are the world's most alienated society. Most of us, from time to time, suffer from low self-esteem, and we have an absolute fear that we are unloved.

Most who show up in a service are saying, "I came here looking for a friend, beginning with you, preacher." Most people are intent on building a silent case about how the communicator feels about them before they really tune in.[7] Insomuch as the entire community has often failed them, they enter asking first, "Does anybody here like me?" And they are far more interested in making a friend than they are in understanding the Pentateuch.[8]

But how do we go about building this relationship upon which so much hangs? First of all we have to understand what's at stake. In this regard formal worship services have a long way to go to help the potential listener hear. In very liturgical churches, the structure so dominates all that is about to be communicated that the first-time visitor is often bewildered by why so many people have gotten so involved with such a dreary, timeless dance. Words come and go, hymns drone on metrically without feeling. Ad lib is dead. No one says anything not written in the worship folder.

Evangelical churches have generally had a little edge here. They are usually a tightly wrapped package of koinonia, waiting to erupt when the cork is snapped. They bubble like a witches' brew, and while their worship may not be well thought through, to the lonely visitor seeking a friend, they seem miles ahead of their liturgical brothers. But the big issue is the sermon itself. How formal is it? How widely does it reach? Is it full of hard logic or does it take time to reason with listeners? Is it all stated forms of reason, or is it filled with rhetorical questions that involve the "poor little lonely me" visitor who wondered what he was doing there until the sermon made it seem that the pastor wanted to involve him and maybe even really liked him?

In an earlier chapter we referred to the "speech before the speech." This "ad lib" part of the sermon is intended to furnish relational clout to what will later be said. Remember, this is the part of the sermon that isn't really a part of the sermon. It receives only minimal "human" preparation. It is an on-the-spot reference, or series of references, to life in general—the war, the courts, the Super Bowl, Valentine's Day, the weenie roast last Thursday—whatever is current. Should such trivial things be allowed to nudge the all-important exposition of the Holy Word a few seconds toward the rear of the service? I believe so, for what may be lost from the sermon's time might be gained in making the preacher seem warm and believable.[9]

Sermon hearers are not good at separating their feelings about the sermon from their feelings for the preacher. Plus the individual listener—say for instance some guy who works a pretty stressful full-time job—may listen with a chip on his shoulder. He sees his time at church as a kind of gift he gives to God and he sure hopes God appreciates it. He may sit there smiling like a happy saint but inwardly he is thinking: "Look buster, I consider my weekends part of my annual vacation, and I just don't want you to forget that I'm on this two-day vacation that the world calls the weekend. My freedom ends on Monday morning. I'm giving you one precious hour. Don't waste my time."

Underneath this unspoken vitriol, he never quits asking, "Is your church friendly? Are you, preacher? I'm not here for my health. In fact I'm looking for a place to fit in. I sure hope it's here. But talk to me, and while you're talking, let me know whether or not you consider us to be friends."

The pastor who is committed to pastoral care—the cure of souls we earlier mentioned—has the best chance of making the sermon a relational document. In the new management echelons of mega-church duties, we have preaching pastors who often state they are just "no good at working with people" and have therefore hired others who they believe can take up the slack in their relational weaknesses. But in all honesty, such "preaching pastors" can only thrive where there are listeners willing to say, "Even though my pastor isn't interested in people, I'm just crazy about his sermons." Unfortunately, the pastor who doesn't care for people has missed the heart of God.

One of the most powerful messages I ever preached, I preached totally without words. At the beginning of a service, one of our fine men had a heart attack just as the choir was filing in. When I saw him fall to the floor, I immediately left the podium and went to where he lay and began to embrace and pray for his wife, who almost at once knew that she was a widow. We both prayed and cried together, while our sensitive minister of music asked the congregation to go to prayer.

This was done in a supportive manner and punctuated by the coming and going of paramedics and the rescue squad. The man's sudden death occupied the greatest part of our service. The orchestra did not get to perform their offertory anthem as they had rehearsed. The choir also did not get to sing their long-studied choral work. I, of course, did not get to preach the sermon I had written. But God visited us all with a sobering sense of Psalm 90:12 though the text was never read.

There would be other Sundays for performing. In the meantime, being real was the order of the day. I suspect in that congregation of 2,500 souls was at least one visitor looking for a sermon that spoke louder than words, but if so, surely it was a good day for being human, right up to the gates of the next audible sermon I *would* preach. We were just home folks that Sunday. We were there—not preaching, not pushing our gospel wares—but we were saying, "Test our motives and decide what kind of fellowship we really are."

Spiritual Formation Analysis

But a relational style is not just for the skeptical believer, it is also for—and perhaps mostly for—the company of the committed who are there to try the sermon, not to see if the preacher loves them. These members have needs too and those needs are not primarily evangelistic. Yet sermons have some tasks that are not immediate and must serve in ways that build rapport across a great many years. Not all of those who hear us from week to week are going to take our sermons to heart. Nonetheless, the sermon must furnish members with the ability to be spiritually formed in the fullest possible way across the years. There is a developmental way in which sermons should serve. They should move those who are at lesser levels of spiritual maturity to ever greater ones.

In the spiritual formation inventory below, the various levels of spiritual maturing are addressed in terms of what can be done to help everyone grow personally.

SPIRITUAL FORMATION INVENTORY

While I may not be able to crunch the major theme of every sermon I preach, is there something I can say about these important issues in this particular sermon?

_____

_____

_____

_____

In what way in this sermon have I included the question: "Is Romans 12:1 possible?"

_____

_____

_____

_____

In what way in this sermon have I taught the deeper Galatians 2:20 issue of identifying with Christ to the point of being crucified with him?

_____

_____

_____

_____

In what way have I made it clear that the Christian message of the incarnation means we are not in this alone, and we are winning?

_____

_____

_____

Let me cast the issues raised in the spiritual formation inventory in three different and ever deepening modes.

IS ROMANS 12:1 POSSIBLE? CAN ORDINARY PEOPLE BE CONFORMED TO THE IMAGE OF CHRIST?

First, sermons should reckon with the issue raised when we ask, "Is Romans 12:1 possible?" Can people really be conformed to the image of Christ? Can this be done by the nine-to-five layperson, who finds her career and possibly her home life ever more demanding?[10] I believe it can but the preacher must take all long-range sermon planning seriously. Further, pastors must be able to believe that what they are doing for others is not a wilderness they have never crossed. It is dishonest to desire a level of spiritual formation for others we have never owned for ourselves.

Since our preaching cannot take people where we have never been, the issue is that we must commit our own lives to the issue that is always two steps forward and one step back. Spiritual formation is not a destination to which we arrive but a hunger of heart we long to satisfy. I believe preachers have lost a great deal of credibility in the ministry because they project that they are living in a spiritually satisfied state rather than living in a wilderness of hunger for closer intimacy with Christ.

IS GALATIANS 2:20 POSSIBLE? IS IT POSSIBLE TO BE CRUCIFIED WITH CHRIST?

The second issue a sermon must reckon with is to ask, "Is Galatians 2:20 possible?" That is to say, can we really be "crucified with Christ," and what does the crucified life look like in the church? Most of the time, the church does not wrangle so deeply with spiritual issues, but that is to our undoing. In the Roman Catholic Church there is always a gathering of deeper monks and nuns who never let these issues die. But within evangelicalism there is none to answer these questions except those pastors who have taken the issues of spiritual formation deeply.

Is Philippians 3:10 Possible? Can We Gain This Threefold Relationship with Christ?

Third, Philippians 3:10 speaks of the fellowship of Christ's suffering, and the best preachers would find a way to apply this to all suffering as it rises in the church. The church has just as much pain and suffering as are experienced outside the church. Sermons must deal with why bad things happen to good people, or for that matter to any people. The gospel redeems but it also is the energy behind a huge Spirit-driven coping machine. People need to know what to do with their pain, how to live after being "gutted out" by the circumstances of life.

I know of no way of preaching on *coping* except by preaching the cross. Only when sermon hearers really understand the word *incarnation* are they able to cope at all. Jesus did not leave the world a get-well card, he got sick with it. He didn't exempt himself from the pain he would later have to heal. He is in this hellish life with us, and further has guaranteed that his victory over all things negative has foreshadowed and guaranteed our own ultimate victory.[11]

Joy of course becomes the mode of such preaching. If the sermon constantly says, "No matter how things look, we're winning!" then the church ultimately becomes a center of joy. Great churches understand this. The best of churches do not wink at ripping pain, but they never forget to preach the whole point of the gospel: WE ARE WINNING! Sermons that serve their hearers with the finished work of Christ insist on loitering around every grave with the good news. When everyone believes in such sermons, spiritual formation has not only formed a solid community of faith, it has become an anthem in a tuneless world.

Conclusion

Let us now consider the content analysis form below. See this as an important inventory because it will take the fuzz out of your preparation and fill it with definite content and conclude your sermon with a specific challenge.

CONTENT ANALYSIS FORM
GUIDES TO SERMON PREPARATION

What points in my sermon are about Jesus?

_____

_____

_____

What points of my sermon can I connect a supporting biblical text?

_____

_____

_____

_____

What am I specifically asking them to do in this sermon?

_____

_____

_____

_____

What am I specifically saying they can apply here and now?

_____

_____

_____

_____

What reminders am I giving them about our relationship as preacher and listener?

_____

_____

_____

_____

In what way does my sermon promote listeners' spiritual formation?

_____

_____

_____

_____

4

So What's to Be Done Now?

Exegeting the Call of the Sermon

Application is the science of what's happening now. Without it the sermon is at best a diagnostic device in which the preacher points out what is wrong with the world and then says the benediction. Diagnosis is analytical. Application is prescriptive. Without application there is no sermon. Application is what gets the Sermon off the Mount, and down in the valley where the toilers live out their days. Once people know what the Bible says, their next questions are: So what? How to? Where do I start? Sermons must take the information they dispense and tell the church what to do with it. A man was arrested in Tokyo some years ago for walking down the street and crying, "The world is round like an orange." Nobody disagreed with the hapless psychotic. But his preaching was irrelevant because his hearers were not told any meaningful way to make use of his truth. I remember a certain preacher who told me (for I had no idea when the world would end) that the world would soon come to an end. I didn't disagree with him, but he left me no clue as to how I should occupy my time till it did. I found his description of the great harlot of the Apocalypse interesting, but she's not nearly as much a contemporary danger to the tempted as prostitutes on the streets of their hometown. Good preaching can do great things but only when it deals with life in the moment.

The riskiest single sentence that appears in a sermon is, "Here's what you do with what I've just told you." It sets the listener on edge and sometimes drives the preacher to the ledges of courage to bring up the issue of application. Why? Because it seems to the hearers that application is where the sermon ceases to be biblical and begins being meddlesome. It often seems that way to the preacher as well.

Yet application is the money on the game. It's where the indicative sermon seems to leave its inductive style and takes an abrupt turn into the imperative. Even if the preacher does not say, "I told you so!" at the point of application, the tone of the sermon shifts in the direction of "I told you so," or "I'm telling you so," or a least "here's what's to be done about what I just told you." Application is where the sermon turns prescriptive and if the sermon fails to prescribe, it is only a speech and probably not a very good one. Application is the place at which the preacher leverages the strongest influence.[1]

The rules of application are not difficult, but they can be very dangerous to the preacher and hazardous to those to whom the sermon's prescriptions are given. Just to make clear the atmosphere of preaching and the danger of being too passive or aggressive with the application, let's examine what's at stake.

The Three Axioms of Application

Axiom #1: Most people would rather listen to sermons than act on them.

James reminds us that we are to be doers of the word and not hearers only (James 1:22). But there's something in the psyche of those who attend sermons that says sermons are mostly for the hearing. With the advance of so many new books and approaches on preaching, this problem has only compounded. Once again, I repeat the hazard hidden in the new homiletic: that sermons have "interest" for their chief purpose. Such scholars feel that if a sermon is fascinating, then it is a success. As long as this view pre-dominates, application will seem less important in preaching.

I attend—and preach at—a lot of pastors' conferences, which in many cases are preach-a-thons where speaker after speaker comes before the same audience with a bundle of hyped homiletics. These long processionals of polished oratory become vast competitions of sermonic fireworks. All of them depend upon the best use of stories and dramas, pauses and staccato repetitions, silence and thunder. Nobody who pays money to hear these sermons is expect-ing any dramatic changes in their lives. They are merely paying to hear. The question is: what *is* preaching? Is it entertainment or impact?[2] A kind of entertainment is the chief reason they attend. To the vast majority who prefer a concert to a preach-a-thon, it may seem odd entertainment, but preaching well is vastly important among evangelicals. But overall, preaching is losing its reputa-tion. Sermons are getting shorter and in some cases are only brief moralisms tacked on the end of rock-based praise.

Sermons in the burgeoning evangelical churches of the 1950s and '60s (during my adolescence) were quite another matter. The artistry and form of preaching were far less important during those years than they are now. In those days (possibly the good old days of application), people went to church expecting to be challenged by the daring applications of the daring preachers who owned the times.

Sermons are preached to effect change. The unsaved were more openly honest in those days, liberally confessing that they were sinners. The saved had hang-ups and freely and openly ad-mitted they were in dire need of change. Everybody seemed to be working on their soul's sad state and knew that they went to church both fearing and hoping for a massive firestorm of per-sonal transformation.

And change we did, just as the sermon called for it. In my little Baptist church, drunkards teetered forward and laid their bottles on the altar. Smokers laid their vile Lucky Strikes on the altar. Snuffers laid their snuff. Chewers, their Skoal. All of this sounds funny now, decades later. But then it was serious stuff. Preachers in those days told us to get closer to Jesus and then actually told us how to do it.

Every worship service in the mid-twentieth century was aimed at some kind of challenge. So we who went to church quailed before each sermon. The pulpit was a fortress of fire, and we loved and feared it. The preacher though dressed in polyester was no Pollyanna. He read his text, and we cringed before the leisure suit prophet, "Oh, oh! Here it comes!" Then the truth flew at us and we dodged the pulpit grenades and clung to the pew ahead of us. The sermon began to wind down just as the preacher got wound up. And then the preacher told us what to do right before we sang "Just As I Am." Our nerve ends were exposed! We all knew who needed what sermons, and we waited to see who would break free and dash down the aisle first. We hated to see other people get honest because we knew their honesty would point out our flaws. Our neuroses were on edge. Our destiny was on the line. The sermon's application fell heavy upon our integrity. We could either apply it, or remain "dirty rotten skunks." So we applied it and left church on Sunday greatly relieved that we wouldn't have to face a new volley of fire for another week.

The application point in most evangelical churches at that time was called "being under conviction." I suppose none of us would want to return to the guilt-ridden gospel churches of those lost decades. We have all seen that love empowers change, and the preacher who orders change is less effective than those who set forth a gentle counsel of love so that listeners want to change.[3] But we have arrived at a glistening, smug day when nobody much sins, and those that do are prone to call it something else. In some churches we still sing "Just As I Am" after the sermon, but everyone leaves pretty much just as they were, too. Sermons have come to be listening points not change points. The missing factor is application. Preachers preach without telling us what to do about what they have just told us.

Axiom #2: Most people don't mind preachers stating the ideal, but they shun the rigors of reformation that would make their world ideal.

There is no harder work than change. This is why the number one reaction to change is resistance. Social reformation is hard work. A single sermon is not likely to effect much change. This is probably because sermons are typically seen as group information, not necessarily something that needs to be acted upon. But the preacher must never sell short this ancient form. The sermon can be a powerful agent for change, especially when coupled with pastoral care. Sermons grow robust in the soul of the listening servant. The best prophets listen before they preach—they reason before they rage. Their ears are always larger than their mouths.[4]

In my thirty-five years of pastoring I have seen in my microcosm renovated men and women who have taken the gospel seriously and made enduring changes in their lifestyle. I remember a man who told me that at the end of every workday, he stopped at a particular lounge on the way home and had two martinis. In candor with a little bit of pressure he admitted to having three on some evenings (and four if it was Friday). When he finally agreed to enter a detox center (a step which brought healing to his marriage) he was in church listening to a sermon on conformity to Christ. I believe he opted for the suggested application of the sermon because of long sessions of counsel and much pastoral care. Still, giving the sermon its due, I believe that the important demands of Scripture can settle on a soul during the courageous application of a text. The church may be the last place souls are cured by someone, somewhere, drawing a line in the sand and saying, "There are still scriptural constants that heal behavior and ancient truths that correct bogus philosophies!"

I once had a young atheist in my circle of acquaintances who allowed his daughter to attend our congregation. In the course of time, the girl decided to be converted and baptized. And so she was. This step by the daughter that he so loved began to effect in him a softer attitude toward me, and soon he also began attending our church. At the end of our services I often gave an invitation where application was the mode of the appeal. When I preached the gospel I laid down what was to be done to gain the approval of God, and in time his solid resistance to Christianity melted into faith. It did not surprise me. I expected it. Over the years I had told the congregation what God required. I tried to remain neutral in the business God had with his church. It was his business not mine. It was the hearer's responsibility to obey and not mine. But as his proxy, I asked the listener—on behalf of God—to comply.

But what if they had not? Would there have been any slur against me? Would I have felt thwarted by their noncompliance with the Scripture? Of course not. I had no real stake in this matter. Application isn't a requirement created by preachers to magnify our own sense of success or acceptance in the church. Application is laying out the terms of God. Human transformation is the Spirit's work. When people yield it is his work. When they don't it is still his work. We who preach the Word are not to congratulate ourselves when people take God up on his purposes, nor are we to feel bad when they don't.

But the contemporary mind-set is that religion is private and that people are going to come slowly to any declarative statement about how God is requiring them to change. Changing summons fear. This dread of openness precludes the possibility of real revival in the church because until we shed our fear of openness, confession is not a possibility, and without confession, neither revival nor change is possible. In actuality there is no real hope of spiritual authenticity of any kind without a renewed respect for sermon application.

Axiom #3: When told how to apply sermons specifically, most people over-congratulate themselves on how biblically they already live while thinking of others who could really use the sermon.

Beginning with the new congratulatory psychologies of the 1950s and '60s, self-esteem began to flourish. In the succeeding decades it became what Robert Schuller called a "new reformation." From that point on the whole thing got out of hand. Even at the present moment, the source of all well-being is in every person's right to think well of themselves.

As was mentioned in an earlier chapter, it was Karl Menninger who asked, "Whatever happened to sin?" And it was a fair question. Sin was just gone. Evangelicals at the moment still retain the category, but they are uncertain just what they mean by it. Yet most of them agree that Jesus died for our sins, and some even go so far as to accent the old adage that it was our sins that nailed Christ to the cross.

But you can't live honestly in a world where you feel that sin just doesn't exist. With the whole world congratulating itself for good behavior, most Christians just gave up on the idea, at least on weekdays.

This was all a major problem for sermon application. When everyone is glisteningly pure, who do you really apply the sermon to? Rapists, Hitler, and terrorists were about the only categories that remained. So sermon applications began to be hard to apply. They just never seemed to fit the new guiltless generation.

There was an anecdote that surfaced in the '80s about a woman who left every service saying to the pastor, "Well, you really told them how the cows ate the cabbages today" (i.e., "you told them like it is"). On a particular Sunday, a terrible blizzard prohibited anyone from reaching the church for Sunday services. The only ones who actually got to church on that Sunday were the pastor and this self-excusing woman. The pastor saw this as his big chance to personally apply the sermon to his lone parishioner and so he preached as fervently as he ever had. He described in detail the woman's hypocrisy. When the sermon was over he sang several verses of "Just As I Am" but could not budge her from her lonely pew to come forward and confess. Still, on the way out of church she said, "Well, it's too bad they couldn't get here today, 'cause if they had been here, your sermon would surely have told them how the cows ate the cabbages."

This is the milieu in which the current preacher is to be found. Sin exists but other people do it. Application is a difficult art, especially when it tries to rise above the barricades of defiant self-esteem.

Making the Application Honest

To make the application seem natural and real and thus honest we must do these three things:

First, we must tell the listeners what the text says.[5]
Second, we must reinterpret the ancient meaning for the current moment.[6]
Third, we must make abstract ideas concrete through metaphor.[7]

All of this may be best done by setting out an example of how to arrive at a contemporary focus through examining the ancient text. So from this point on in the chapter I would like to discuss how we are to deal with the three axioms listed above by working through a paradigm text. I have decided to pick a text for which the application might be difficult to push, simply because the text upon first reading seems so remotely connected to contemporary life.

> [21]Balaam got up in the morning, saddled his donkey and went with the princes of Moab. [22]But God was very angry when he went, and the angel of the LORD stood in the road to oppose him. Balaam was riding on his donkey, and his two servants were with him. [23]When the donkey saw the angel of the LORD standing in the road with a drawn sword in his hand, she turned off the road into a field. Balaam beat her to get her back on the road.
>
> [24]Then the angel of the LORD stood in a narrow path between two vineyards, with walls on both sides. [25]When the donkey saw the angel of the LORD, she pressed close to the wall, crushing Balaam's foot against it. So he beat her again.
>
> [26]Then the angel of the LORD moved on ahead and stood in a narrow place where there was no room to turn, either to the right or to the left. [27]When the donkey saw the angel of the LORD, she lay down under Balaam, and he was angry and beat her with his staff. [28]Then the LORD opened the donkey's mouth, and she said to Balaam, "What have I done to you to make you beat me these three times?"
>
> [29]Balaam answered the donkey, "You have made a fool of me! If I had a sword in my hand, I would kill you right now."
>
> [30]Then the donkey said to Balaam, "Am I not your own donkey, which you have always ridden, to this day? Have I been in the habit of doing this to you?"
>
> "No," he said.
>
> [31]Then the LORD opened Balaam's eyes, and he saw the angel of the LORD standing in the road with his sword drawn. So he bowed low and fell facedown.
>
> [32]And the angel of the LORD asked him, "Why have you beaten your donkey these three times? I have come here to oppose you because your path is a reckless one before me. [33]The donkey saw me and turned away from me these three times. If she had not turned away, I would certainly have killed you by now, but I would have spared her."
>
> [34]Balaam said to the angel of the LORD, "I have sinned. I did not realize you were standing in the road to oppose me. Now if you are displeased, I will go back."
>
> Numbers 22:21–34

This text is one that challenges the biblical expositor in several ways. First, the text strikes at the credulity of so many hearers. Second, while the point of the text lies in the issue of obedience to God, the stern judgment of the angel seems severe, probably too severe, to the modern churchgoer. Third, the events occurring in the passage seem too unrelated to the grand themes of love and redemption to be of much consequence. Fourth, to apply this passage is to bring it out of its setting in the Pentateuch, reinterpret the donkey, and speak in a relevant way about God's punishment for our disobedience.

When you read what was back then, you must tell listeners what this means now.[8] The story in many ways is fascinating, and as to the types of passages that could be picked for a sermon, this one would rate higher than average in sustaining interest. Still the strength of the story is not enough to make the passage a good sermon text. The story is essentially about the importance of obedience, and this is the most likely theme for the sermon. Therefore it is easy to fix the most important part of the text for focus.

Focal Text

[31]Then the LORD opened Balaam's eyes, and he saw the angel of the LORD standing in the road with his sword drawn. So he bowed low and fell facedown.

[32]And the angel of the LORD asked him, "Why have you beaten your donkey these three times? I have come here to oppose you because your path is a reckless one before me."

The meaning of the original language in verse 32 is uncertain. My own feelings about textual difficulties is that they are important for the expositor to know but any attempt at ferreting out textual criticism in a Sunday sermon is not wise. It diverts the audience from the point of the text and usually confuses the call of the sermon.

Now the task is to pick a motif, a brief motto or slogan which will define the text and therefore set what form the application will take.

Motif

[32]And the angel of the Lord asked him, "Why have you beaten your donkey these three times? I have come here to oppose you because your path is a reckless one before me."

Motif: Disobedience to God is a reckless path.

Now the theme of the sermon is set in a phrase that can direct and channel the sermon. At this initial stage of sermon preparation, the application can and should be set. This means that from the earliest stages of the sermon's preparation, the preacher knows what the sermon is going to ask the people to do. If disobedience is a reckless path, as the motif suggests, the application is going to ask the hearer to obey. But this kind of requirement is too abstract. Of course they ought to obey, but obey whom, by doing what, and in what course of action? "Be obedient" is too general to make an application specific.

First, to build a specific application we must turn to the text itself. We notice that Balaam beats his donkey at first (unmercifully it would seem) to get her back on the road (v. 23), second, for crushing his foot against the wall (v. 25), and finally, for failing to move through a narrow place, walled on both sides (vv. 26–27). So whatever else the application says, it says that anger obscures good judgment and causes us to forget the gentler requirements of God.

Second, the application must point out that Balaam cannot be healed until he hears God point out to him the error of his ways: he is indeed set upon a reckless path (v. 32).

Third, before he can reestablish a path of obedience he must repent: he cries, "I have sinned" (v. 34). Every sermon we preach ought to bring every listener to the point of responsibility for doing the will of Christ.[9]

Now all that is left to do is to get the action out of 1400 BC and into the present moment. To do that I would probably change the metaphor. I would cast Balaam's anger as resulting from his attempt to escape his call. He is trying to run away from the requirements of God when he knows clearly what God requires. He is being self-willed and therefore cannot please God while he tries in vain to make life work by doing what he wants to do in the face of all that God has asked him to do. When he finally

comes face-to-face with the angel who points out his disobedience, Balaam admits he has sinned and decides to return to God's
primary agenda for his life. If I set the previous paragraph up
visually, doing so shows me how I "contemporize" the text to
set it before the application to which I hope to lead my hearers
(see outline below).

Body of the Sermon in Outline Form

Balaam's futile attempt at escapism

a. Here include other biblical examples of people who tried to get out from under God's
   heavy requirements: Adam, Jonah, Gideon, Moses.

b. Find a good illustration of someone who in the current day and age did all they could to
   keep from obeying God.

The dangers of self-will

a. Discuss Balaam's outcome had he never reckoned with the angel.

b. Get some statistics on how many ministers now leave the ministry.

c. Find three supporting passages from the New Testament where the issue of self-will is
   the focus.

d. In the final analysis, where does self-will lead?

Reckoning with God over spiritual willfulness

a. Was there a time in your own spiritual life when you were self-willed and had a face-
   to-face experience with God? (Remember, confessional preaching is the most powerful
   kind of communication.)

b. Outline clearly your steps back to the obedient life.

Repentance

Discuss the steps in returning to obedience and usefulness.

Application

Ask hearers to inwardly acknowledge their willfulness.

Ask them to inwardly agree with God about the sinfulness of
disobedience.

Ask them to silently offer him the original content and meaning of the word *Lord* as they used the word when they first
began to serve him.

Ask them to enter, at their own pace somewhere in their Bible,
the moment of this inward confession and return to the
commitment every day for a week in their private prayer
times.

Now we have essentially outlined the text in such a way that all factors in the preparation lead naturally to the application of the text in a specific way to the hearers' lives. In this sample outline we determined to do these three things:

First, reading what happened in the book of Numbers, we set out to tell the listeners how they should apply the importance of the text in the current moment.

Second, taking time to describe Balaam's sins, we then reinterpreted how those sins in the biblical yesterday should be translated now.

Finally, in terms of the abstract incidents of the text, we made them concrete with contemporary metaphors.

The Relevance Analysis

The Apologetic Factor: I Don't Believe in Talking Donkeys!

While it is true most people who come to church have enough reverence for the Bible that they are not likely to balk at difficult texts, such an assumption is not altogether certain. Very often any text dealing with a miraculous event needs to be set forth in a declarative manner so those who hear it understand from the preacher's firm words that the Bible is to be depended upon. Texts having to do with Jesus walking on the sea, or Moses dividing it, raise huge questions in the minds of some hearers. The authority of Scripture is an absolute essential in applying a text to the lives of the hearers. If they are not altogether convinced that the Bible is telling the truth, they will be far less likely to apply that truth to their lives. But can a sermon really preach the truth and try to defend it at the same time?

First of all, the preacher's attempt to defend any single passage as the truth might create a sense of doubt in the minds of the more credulous among us who had no tendency to doubt the Bible until the preacher started defending it. One of the top dangers of expository preaching is that preachers sometimes hammer their exposition home so hard, their hearers may doubt that they really believe what they are saying. Screaming our affirmations can make us sound like we're in doubt ("The lady doth protest too much methinks," said Hamlet's mother). Further we have this false idea that expository preaching consists primarily in a style of delivery—a form of passionate delivery—as though the Word has to do only with content and disclosure.[10] For this reason (and I'm in favor of the vast majority who do believe the Scriptures) I personally would not go to great lengths defending a passage which has no real defense except that it originates from that central core of truth that we call the Bible.

If, however, there is some outstanding archaeological evidence or philosophical school that corroborates the text, then the point may actually strengthen the Bible's already strong position on the text in question. The point might be made during the preaching of any miracle-centered passage in Isaiah that the Dead Sea Scrolls have helped to certify the integrity of the passage.

Whenever I preach on any passage involving Troas (or Troy) as mentioned in the New Testament, I always corroborate the once-doubted veracity of the text by those who long ago insisted that Troy was a fiction of Homer that Luke used. The actual city may never have existed, but archaeologists have discovered that Troas as a region did exist.

But talking donkeys are harder to substantiate. Since this is the case, I believe that any reference to whether or not the story can be proved only injures the sermon at that point. The issue is to preach the entire Bible with a kind of authority that leaves no doubt among the potential skeptics in the audience that the preacher at least believes it. This kind of preaching should be the norm for all preachers who want to build strong congregations who approach the Bible as a great answer that overrides the questions.

But a final caveat must be sounded. The effective preacher in the decades ahead will be one who understands the importance of apologetics and unhesitatingly preaches the whole counsel of God (Acts 20:27). Such preachers have a confidence in the Scripture that is undergirded by their ability to care about what the ancient text says and what evidence from the world in and around that long-ago day serves to corroborate the text at the present moment. Every good preacher is one who is always ready, as Peter urges, to give a reason for the hope that is in us (1 Peter 3:15). *If* the reason is strong enough, Balaam's donkey will speak to them as surely as it did to Balaam.

The Personal Factor: I Don't See How This Applies to Me

This particular part of the relevance analysis depends on how well the preacher has contemporized the point of the text. Describing the action of the text makes the text real enough to apply. To preach on brimstone so realistically the listeners can sniff it requires some excellent sermon writing. Still, even when the writing is excellent, the listener may not be able to apply it unless the message of the text is made personal.

Jezebel's perverse reign may seem a difficult thing to personalize. She is a sort of Cruella DeVil, the villain in *101 Dalmations*, in most caricatures. Yet R. G. Lee in his great homily, "Payday, Someday" preached her sad story more than a thousand times and great crowds heard of her evil life and came to Christ. Why? Were they trying not to be like her? No. Was eighth-century Israel so vital to their American heritage they could not escape the connection? No. The story captivated them and the transference was immediate.

Remember that all application when done well is little more than a kind of transference. The preacher is almost like a psychiatrist transferring the burdens of one person onto the psyche of another. When the transfer is complete the application is over. It is much like the viewfinder of old cameras. The pictures are taken at what is called the parallax moment. The two out-of-focus images are cranked together in the viewfinder and when they coalesce into one, the shutter is depressed. The parallax moment has occurred.

Biblical application in preaching is a matter of parallaxing: of cranking the exegesis into a single image over the hearer's psyche. When the two become one the shutter is depressed and the application is made.

Russell Conwell's famous "Acres of Diamonds" was preached hundreds of times. In his case the text was the story of a poor young man who went out fruitlessly seeking for diamonds, only to find as an old man that there was a diamond mine right under his house. Henry Drummond's *Greatest Thing in the World* was found in 1 Corinthians 13. He spent the entire sermon showing the audience that what they had was what they were seeking. Martin Luther King Jr.'s "I Have a Dream" was applied to the heart as a reasonable cry for equality in an unreasonable world. But what he conjectured was in fact a possible world, only it had to come from its dream status to application.

Most of the time the application is not something that requires the Bible to be contorted or forced into a fantasy mold and shoved into tightly fitting minds.[11] Most of the time it is an easy leap of faith, requiring the obvious similarities between Bible and life to be pointed out, without having to be tediously retrofitted.

I remember that my first sermon I ever preached, I preached on Naaman the leper (2 Kings 5). I delivered the skittish homily in the Garfield County "old folks home" (as they called it back then). In some ways I could hardly have preached on a less relevant subject. There had never been an outbreak of leprosy in Garfield County, and in fact, none of us knew anyone who had ever had the disease. While I took some time to discuss the symptoms and cures of leprosy, my diagnosis was of no real import, especially in an area where an outbreak of leprosy was impossible. But the sermon was hugely successful because I managed to describe the disease in terms of current things that all of us knew and struggled with. The sermon worked because as it progressed, we thought less and less about leprosy and more and more about our personal struggles with sin.

This is the key to dealing with the objection "I don't see how this applies to me!" The passage must be set in the moment at an increasing intensity as the preacher moves through it. If the biblical text is to do its best work, it must be slowly laid aside as it is replaced by an intensity of current concern. When the Bible has served best, it has been forgotten as it has been replaced by the acute concerns of the moment. Application is most relevant when it is so personal that the hearers are pulled from the crowd and stand alone as individuals who are forced to reckon with the text on their own.

The Urgency Factor: Do I Have to Make Up My Mind about This Right Now?

The world is a place of procrastination. Sermons fit into lifestyles. Preachers preach them with regularity and hearers hear them the same way. In this predictable, repetitious cycle of preaching, nothing seems like it has to be done right now. So many of the invitation hymns of the church are rooted in this plea for "do it now." "O Why Not Tonight," begs one. "Why not come to Him now," is a line from another. "Time is now fleeting, the moments are passing," pleads "Softly and Tenderly." It is difficult to make the application seem so imperative that it cannot be forestalled till later. There has always been a next week and a next year. So the issue of urgency, when seen over the probability of a long, long life, doesn't seem so critical.

Almost any phrase we use could legitimately end with "later!"

Be a better father . . . later.
Come to Christ . . . later.
Start tithing . . . later.

In many ways this procrastination syndrome has all but limited the immediacy we used to feel when the invitation was given. Billy Graham seems to be the last person who actually pled with sinners to "be saved, now," and get the job done.

As is true with the other factors, the urgency factor works better with an extended amount of pastoral care. As preachers circulate through the ranks of those to whom they preach, they are able to pray on an individual basis with those who need to make some decision. This is not to say that direct, one-on-one confrontation with those who need to make decisions actually prompts them to do so under hyperindividual pressure. But they are more likely to make such decisions when pastoral care has individualized the urgency, plus many people are just not able to respond to public invitations to get it done. One of the real difficulties in an increasingly privatized world is that invitations just cannot be done in such a powerful mode that people will shuck their anonymity and make an open decision. Application works best when what the sermon asks them to do can become an affair of the heart.

Another answer to the objections of people who resist instant application is to deal with a subject over a whole series of sermons. This gives the hearers plenty of time to deal with what is being asked of them and to work through some area of personal reformation over a longer period of time. If people are to reply in the future to the call of the sermons preached in a series, their response is often more secure. This may be why pledge campaigns can be seen as models of sound application. Usually there is a period of weeks when sermons point to the final application where a name is actually signed on a card. Such a mode of arriving at an application moves at a pace that works well with anyone's reluctance to come to quick-fix decisions.

The Commitment Factor: I Was With You Till You Said "Lord."

Application generally has for its most fearsome quality the idea of submission. Gaining the approval of God almost always requires submission. Whatever the application calls for, most people are ever so reluctant to give God the control he wants over their lives.

Balaam, in the Scripture above, is most anxious to cast himself in the best possible light with the nobles of his country. He also wants to obey God. But in his mind he feels that although Israel will soon have passed through his nation and be gone he must go on living in the land. So it seems to him that to lose favor with the local nobles will in the end not be in his best political interest.

In most cases obedience is not what is involved in the toss-up. Balaam would not have admitted (in all likelihood) that he was being disobedient to God. He would merely have said that this seemed the best way for him to get along in the world. God, however, speaks his rebuke through the mouth of Balaam's donkey. And considering both Balaam and his donkey, the donkey is the most reasonable. He all but threatens to report Balaam to the SPCA (Society for the Prevention of Cruelty to Animals) when the Lord shows up and gets Balaam back on track.

All application comes to rest on the hearer as one basic conundrum. Shall I be the lord of my life or shall I have a Lord for my life? As ludicrous as this sounds, the ego ever seeks the upper hand in all our relationships and is most reluctant to abandon control to anyone, God notwithstanding. So "signing on the dotted line" of God's agenda for our lives is the key place where the hearer must meet up with the existential demand of the sermon text.

The key words of Balaam's submission are "I have sinned!" What this means of course is that the prophet has already reckoned with the word *Lord* and decided he isn't that word. And then by saying, "I will go back with you," he has acquiesced to the state of obedience to which God earlier summoned him.

It is almost never possible to sell lordship on the short haul of one sermon asking for everything all at once. Therefore all application works best when the pulpit continuously lobbies on God's behalf for all to follow Christ. If this is an ongoing theme—and it very well has the right to be—asking people for utmost commitment, sermon by sermon, made real by the Word, will always seem reasonable. No single sermon rings very far in what it asks for. Good application is always asking for the entire will of God to be done in manageable bits and pieces, day by day, week to week throughout the life of the church.

Conclusion

In speaking of application we have established that only its presence gives preaching its name. No application, no sermon. Without application, preaching is at best a lecture and at worst entertainment. We have determined that the application must be marked out in the first steps of sermon preparation, for only after it has been decided will the sermon find a clear channel of communication.

A sermon must ask something of its hearers. In the last analysis, however, it is not the sermon which asks, nor is it the preacher. It is God who is using the parson as a spokesperson to plead his case for his ongoing renovation of the world, one submissive soul at a time. Therefore the preacher must ever make it clear that the day does not belong to the one preaching. It belongs to God, and the hearer must pass up the Sunday lecture and reckon with a mightier force than the preacher. Surrender is the only option when God is the only subject.

The note sheet below is a call to clarify the issues of application and relevance. This is one of the most important work sheets in the text. If these issues are not clearly decided, the listeners will likely be befuddled as to why you selected the text you have chosen.

SERMON NOTE SHEET
ON APPLICATION AND RELEVANCE

On Defining the Text
Here's what the text says:

_____
_____
_____
_____
_____

On Contemporizing the Text
Here's what the text means in the here and now:

_____
_____
_____
_____
_____

On Applying the Text
How will heeding this sermon require you to alter your lifestyle or worldview?

_____
_____
_____
_____
_____

On Dealing with Your Fears Concerning Applying the Text
Here's how you, the auditor, can overcome your fear of being different:

_____
_____
_____
_____

Part 2

Writing
the Sermon

5

Dealing with the Text

Title, Theme, Pacing, and Preparing

The Word of God is like a garden, says a celebrated hymn. In this garden grows an ultimate number of texts. And the preacher who cares about his flock will want to nourish them on the fruit that springs in the verdant rows of life between Genesis and Revelation. In this garden the texts demand their right to serve as counsel to the needy. To the lonely, the sermon may rise from a text of Jeremiah the imprisoned prophet, an outcast in a time of desperation. To those facing death, the text might rise from the psalmist who in Psalm 116 admits that the cords of death have entangled him. To those at the marriage altar, Ruth offers her constancy to Naomi, crying, "Thy people shall be my people, and thy God my God." The Bible is God's Word which we stalk for the sheer sake of its splendor and authority, its counsel, its promises, its covenants. But a sermon cannot be called a biblical sermon unless it gathers its fruit from this garden of the ages. If there is no Bible in the preachment, then all that is left is the word of the speaker, and that word is too weak, too sterile to beg for wind and fire. Sinai is silenced, Golgotha holds no sacrifice. The textless sermon is a stammering talk by a prophet whose amnesia will not allow him to cherish the call. Such a prophet has never made friends with the Author of the Word. Still the sermon must not speak for God, it must allow God to speak for himself. When the preacher is willing to be such a channel, heaven falls like a welcome rain over the parched fields of human need.

All artists begin a painting with the picture they intend to create already hanging in the gallery of their minds. The painting is not only finished in their minds, its mental existence becomes a carping critic of the painter's outer work as it materializes on the easel. It remonstrates with the artist who struggles to get it just right: "That's too much umber. . . . The foreground is too dark. . . . That stroke is too rigid. . . . Wipe off that oil and try this portion of the painting again."

It is the intention of this noisy inner image to clone itself in the outer world. Adulterations do occur. The outer image is rarely as good as the inner image wanted it to be. Then the mental image either shuts up, or says to the artist: "Well, it's not exactly what I had in mind but let it live." Preachers are artists—their sermons are their art. So remember this: if you move too far afield from the lovely image sitting squarely in the center of your soul, what you're bound to preach will be an amateurish, garish piece that will be neither persuasive nor interesting.

Further, the mental sermon is never really happy with what the preacher has produced. Even if the parson alleges that the sermon is somewhat good, it makes the sermon maker feel bad that it wasn't better. In this allegory, preachers become neurotic bards and artists.[1] So the preacher lives in a world of pulpit anguish. Why did I do this or that? The sermon would have been so much better if only I had . . .

Preachers live in the agony of Prometheus. They write and preach wonderful sermons in their minds, but when they actually start their delivery, the inner sermon, which was so beautiful and forceful, begins to remonstrate with the less superior one that is gushing out over the congregation: "Why did you say that? It was stupid. What you wrote down to say is so superior to what you are really saying. Look at the big guy in the choir, he's sleeping and you haven't said enough so far to give him a reason to wake up and listen."

Most of our disappointment comes because we have mishandled the text. How then do we deal with the text? In this chapter we will not focus on how the sermon emanates from the text but how we select, present, and structure text so the rest of the sermon relates to it. We will talk about titling the sermon to reflect the text as well as fixing the thesis and motif to help present the text. We will also talk about pacing the sermon in such a way that the text doesn't get buried in all the clever rhetoric that the preacher spins around it. In the final sections of the chapter we will talk about how your long-term and short-term preparation should enforce the central power of the text.

Title: It Ain't Nothin' Till You Call It

The famous cry of the baseball umpire Bill Klem is foundational to good preaching: "It ain't nothin' till I call it." A new sermon—even one in embryonic form—needs a name, just like a new baby does. I recommend that just before you allow the sermon to begin forming in your mind, you name it.[2] When you do name it, allow that name to rise from the text. Russell Conwell named his famous sermon "Acres of Diamonds," a title which derived from the key illustration that provided the sermon's focus. The same could be said of Martin Luther King Jr.'s "I Have a Dream" sermon. Peter Marshall's story of the "old romance ranger" who kept the streams clean and free of silt became the focus of his mother's day sermon, "The Keeper of the Springs." There are countless other examples where the sermon's chief illustration or motif became the name of the sermon. This is not bad, especially when the sermon is famous as literature or has great historical significance. But I generally like the title to be related to the text, and I believe the text becomes better fixed in the hearer's mind when this is the case.

In most cases the sermon begins forming in the preacher's mind well before a full outline—complete with points and illustrations—has emerged. Indeed, the text may be all that is fully in place to provide a basis for naming the sermon at its earliest conception.

Still, the homily should be named even in its earliest state. The sermon becomes real when it is named, and once it becomes real, it gains the inner force to direct the crafting required to bring it from the embryo to full maturity at eleven o'clock on Sunday morning.

The sermon title's ability to keep the preparation time in focus is enhanced when the theme of the sermon and the text of the sermon are both served by the title. Let's return to the passage on Balaam's donkey (Numbers 22:21–34), which we discussed in chapter 4 on application.

Title Study

What the text is about: ***Obedience***

PLUS

What the sermon's thesis is: ***Honoring the command of God***

EQUALS

The strongest title: "The Folly of Self-Will"
                      or "You Can't Run from God"
                      or "When Your Donkey Speaks, Shut Up and Listen"

In this bracketed focus the first two titles relate to both the text and the point of the sermon while the third relates only to the story of the text. It may be more clever, but the fact that it leaves no clear-cut relationship with the text weakens it as a title for the sermon.[3]

Propriety must guide you when you are seeking a formal title. Let's assume your church has a marquee sign in front of it on which you can list your sermon title for the coming Sunday. A guide to whether a clever title is best will be your best assessment of what those who drive by the church will have to say about the sermon title you have posted. If you imagine the passersby smirking quaintly at (what you hoped would be) an attempt at clever creativity, you might actually want to change the title before you post it. Further, if you have (over the years) posted too many hypercreative flops on your marquee board, you might actually have become a smirking point, if not a laughing post, in your community. A church near my home was gaining a reputation for ninnydom just because it consistently put silly, farcical things on its marquee. I always felt a little cheated when they came to their senses and gained enough propriety to communicate something besides their latest wacky brainstorms.

Remember that these posted titles serve in two ways: first they whet the interest of those who drive by and hopefully lure them inside on Sunday for a paragraph or two of your insight. But second, before they serve the public they must serve you, giving you a reasonable focus that keeps your preparation always before your inner eye as you assemble your homily, verse by verse, precept by story. Naturally your preparation will be enhanced as your title touches base with your theme and the text.

The Thesis: It's What the Sermon's About

Every sermon issues from the text in what Haddon Robinson calls "the Big Idea." The big idea is the thesis. It is a short statement that expresses what you're going to talk about and what the sermon will call the reader to do about it.[4] Almost all homileticians call for this approach. While they call the big idea by different names, all of them agree that the guiding thesis should be a short sentence—twenty-five words or less—that keeps the sermon on track during its preparation and delivery.

In the next section of this chapter, we'll discuss how the motif should originate from the thesis, which may actually become a verbal directive, often repeated in a planned redundancy during delivery. Of course, not every sermon has to have a motif to succeed, but motifs can be immensely helpful in keeping the congregation and the sermon together during preaching. Regardless whether or not a sermon has a motif, the thesis is essential.

Let's turn again to the passage about Balaam to show how the sample thesis statement is developed from a common text such as Numbers 22:21–34.

Sample Thesis Statement from Numbers 22:21–34

The sermon's thesis: *God expects obedience in every aspect of what he asks of us.*

How does the thesis relate to the text: *The text is an example of how we can stray from honoring God's commands and therefore dishonor God's expectations*.

What is the sermon's task (its application): *This sermon exists to call people from a lackadaisical or disobedient lifestyle back to a walk of faith*.

The theme may be contemporized in this way: *In the current secularized culture, how does the believer practice godly obedience in the marketplace, classroom, or the arts?*

The difficulty of achieving clarity when we preach most often lies in failing to adequately answer the question, "Why are we preaching?" It would seem that this question of purpose would be an easy issue to resolve, but it is not.[5] To be sure there are those moments in every preacher's life when the crises of life or personal ministry stir us to the point of precision. But far too many times the issue of why we preach refers only back to the lectionary or some less strategic whim of why we are up in front of some group talking about God. To offer an honest testimonial, I feel a need to confess that after twenty-five years in one pulpit I was too little motivated by a sense of great compulsion when I preached and too often not motivated by an inner passion on the importance of the text, the thesis, or a real burden for contemporary application. It was Sunday. I was the main guy who said religious sorts of things on that day. Impertinent or passionate, faddish or sage, I was the preacher and so I spoke.

But let us establish this: arriving at the sermon's thesis is not a mechanical exercise that can be blocked out in the sort of schematic contained in the sample above. In fact the best thesis is one that could never be arrived at so mechanically. Great sermon theses are powerful acids that etch themselves on the "have-tos" of the speaker. They are rarely written down. They don't need to be. They have already been written boldly on the preacher's soul. When they flame forth, they are a consuming fire of compulsion.

I do not hold the following model up for well-roundedness, only to make a point. The preachers of my Baptist childhood preached regularly on John 3:16. The Bible for such communicators contained only John, along with a thousand other inconsequential pages no one cared much about. It was years before I knew that

Ecclesiastes was in the Bible, and even when I found out it was, I couldn't understand why. Whatever was to be said for their narrow range of preachment, their sermon theses always arose from the central passion of their souls. "Turn or burn" may not be the cleverest of theses, but it did fly at us with conviction, and when we left church it was easy to tell others what the sermon was about.

So often these days it's hard to tell others what the sermon is about.[6] I recently heard a preacher wax eloquent on the need for world evangelization. At least I think that was the intent of the sermon. But all of us who heard him had to ferret out the thesis. What he said was, "Global enterprise is the lingua franca of evangelicalism. In light of the impending parousia, we must not neglect our mandate nor lay aside our soteriological imprimatur." He came close to being a blessing, and when he was through I walked up to him and said, "I'm guessing this was about Jesus." He looked at me oddly as though he couldn't believe I had not understood what he said, for it was abundantly clear to him.

A great thesis is kindergarten in its clarity and Harvard in its force. Practice ahead of time writing out your theses for all of your long-range sermon plans. This discipline will help you both prepare and deliver. Over time it will become the bridge between what you first decide to preach and actually do preach when the time comes. It will inform your words with passion and a sense of importance that your hearers will feel and attend.[7]

One final word about contemporary application: the word *contemporary* comes from the Latin (*com-* + *temporarius*) which means "with the times." Modern and postmodern worship leaders have often put the word in "contempt." Perhaps you have caught the truth that *contemporary* and *contempt* both have Latin roots, though not the same roots. *Contempt* also comes from the Latin (*contemnere*) which means "to hold in scorn." It's not the contemporary that should be scorned, however.[8] Contemporary is good. Contemporary is where the world is at the moment. And while we don't want to sack the great hymns and liturgies of the ages, we can only speak to people in the here and now when we begin with the current moment—indeed, the current age. It is this task, this place that ought to furnish the thesis of every sermon. When sermons face their times with a challenge to transcend them with an everlasting gospel, the sermon will have come to understand its role in the world.

The Motif: A Redundancy of Fours

The thesis tells what the sermon is about and what it set out to do. But the motif is a kind of rhetorical call that keeps the sermon on track. Motifs are best when they are simple, short, and somewhat dramatic. I once heard a great preacher preach on 1 Thessalonians 5:17; the thesis drawn directly from the text was "pray without ceasing!" In the context of the delivery, near the start of the sermon, he told a great story about flying through a storm with a competent pilot. The clouds were close to the ground and thus blinded the pilot from seeing the runway. So the pilot had to depend upon instruments to safely land the plane. He had, according to the preacher's tale, to "report to the tower" without ceasing. The hope of landing the almost doomed and hopeless plane was emphasized over and over again as a matter of trusting the instruments. The wary pilot had to remain in complete dependency upon the tower—to survive the fog was a matter of constant communication. It is easy to see the metaphor of praying without ceasing, which was the thesis of the text. But the motif was "you must report to the tower" to avoid wrecking your best intentions in the low and blinding ground fogs of life.

Throughout the ensuing sermon, the motif came at every critical homiletical juncture.[9] "You must report to the tower!" shouted the preacher.

> Can't figure out why bad things happen to good people?
> Brothers and sisters, report to the tower!
> Caught in the middle of a fierce emotional storm?
> Report to the tower!
> Is your heart broken by false starts and the loss of a dear friend?
> Report to the tower!

Recently this wonderful pastor lost his wife and when I read about it in the papers, the first thing that came to my mind was his sermon motif. I think I know what he did in his crisis.

Take the case of our paradigm text:

The Theme of Numbers 22:21–34

The sermon's thesis: *God expects obedience in every aspect of what he asks of us.*

A possible sermon motif might be: However God speaks to you, listen up!

This phrase—"However God speaks to you, listen up!"—is to be used in exactly the same way that the phrase "report to the tower" was used in the previous sermon example. Here's how it might go:

> Do you find it hard to believe that your wife's counsel could be the voice of God?
> However God speaks to you, listen up!
> Do you get tired of the preacher telling you to open up your hand to the poor and give liberally?
> However God speaks to you, listen up!
> And if you ever find yourself so out of fellowship with God that you, like Balaam, find your donkey talking back to you . . .
> However God speaks to you, listen up!

How frequently should you use a motif within the sermon? This is a question of art, and the answer is a matter of artistry, not mathematics. A few times, or maybe less or more, or perhaps many or some. You're in a conversation with your people. The same rules apply as those that would govern your conversation in a tea room. In either place, whether in the sanctuary or the bistro, when you feel like you're starting to overdo it, stop. The motif is a selling stratagem, not a club. If you catch yourself thumping the pulpit and screaming the catch phrase, you are no longer a herald, you're a hack: the redundancy is only that. You're but a deaf cheerleader before deaf fans.

The motif has another wonderful function. It adds a dramatic finale to bring the curtain down on a wonderful homily. Just as the motif surfaced at the first of a sermon, its use near the end can become an artistic sign-off and evidence to all your hearers that the drama is closing. The rhetoric has furnished your hearers with a round-trip ticket. You have dropped them off where you picked them up, and the motif is there to label the spot. The motif is both the *bonjour* and the *bon voyage* of your sermon.[10]

Pacing: Reaching an Effective Rate of Delivery

This word *pacing* is a kind of unintentional double entendre. Pacing the floor from side to side, around and around the pulpit is a dead giveaway to nervousness and an open confession that we have lost charge of good rhetorical style during our delivery. Later we will deal with how to correct this affectation, and it must be corrected for it is destructive to real communication. But for the moment let us consider pacing only as it regards the rate of communication and those functions of preparation and delivery that influence the pace at which the oral communication proceeds.

The key to great communication has to do with vitality more than velocity. When sermons become a holy spew, preachers are usually confessing that they are not able to get control of their nervous system. After my first sermon, which was preached at a nursing home, I gave up preaching for a long time. Most of those who heard me breathed a sigh of relief that I had voluntarily left the ministry after a single sermon. The reason for this rejoicing was that I preached my entire sermon in three and a half minutes. In Oklahoma, this was a clear sign I had not been called. Preachers with no education could stand without notes and for an hour or two lather their shirts with huge underarm circles of commitment. There was little excuse for my three-minute burnout, for I had typed out three pages of single-spaced notes. Alas, my adrenaline address spewed forth and spent itself in a violent eruption. When it was over I sat down humiliated by my hasty homily.

A huge part of my difficulty lay in my conception of the sermon as a written document. How false my view was then. The sermon is an oral document. Learning to see yourself in the task of delivering the sermon will be of immense help as you create it.

In this sense a sermon is rather like a Shakespearean play. When my wife and I were first married, I decided to go to the Shakespearean festival in Stratford, Ontario, which of all the festivals I have been to is still my favorite. I ordered the tickets because my wife felt that she couldn't in good conscience spend our money that way. She really didn't want to go. She had never liked the Shakespeare she had read in high school, and thoughts of those beastly English classes had severely prejudiced her against Othello. But then she saw Othello the jealous Moor, driven by the conniving Iago and supported by the plaintive Desdemona, suddenly she saw that what was dead in high school English became powerful when performed. When she heard and felt Othello, as Othello was meant to be heard, she was converted to the Bard. At last she overcame her high school bias and discovered the enchanting world of the theater.

Sermons are oral events. Writing them to read is unnatural. When they are read they lose their colloquial lure, and this amounts to death in the community where they are spoken. This is a conversational culture! Preaching works, reading doesn't. The worst function of reading is that it couples with the neurosis that we've got to keep things moving so the audience won't abandon us. We are afraid of the silences that mark punctuation. We get so nervous that we feel we must hurry lest they be bored. So we fly past periods and hurtle past commas and, like an Olympic luge, we rocket past the sluggish minds of those who try in vain to grab at our gospel gush. So went my lamentable first sermon.

My next public sermon lasted longer. I rehearsed it in a mirror, looking into my own eyes as I went. Soon, I became interested in what I was saying. I slowed the adrenalin engine and actually listened to myself. For my first years of preaching, I found rehearsal a must. I had to get the sermon fixed as an oral document to get it slowed down. What had happened was simple. I simply found that the same people who enjoyed a leisurely view of Pikes Peak fled in fear before Mount Saint Helens in eruption. I learned to pace my delivery by thinking about my sermon in a new way.

The Functions of Pacing

INTENSITY

Intensity is both the communicator's best friend and worst enemy. To really hold an audience, they must sense that what you are saying is important, at least to you.

Passion is the soul of intensity. The speaker who truly loves God may or may not lead others to believe it, but the speaker who doesn't is only a philosopher whose ideas are too bland to be important.

Intense feeling sets the blood astir and often causes the communicator to be agitated in voice and gesture. How should the importance that preachers feel about a subject cause them to interact with a passage emotionally? Again the answer to how much intensity is good and how it comes out is a matter of artistry. My rule for this I discovered in one short little phrase: "Excess within control." Intensity of feeling is always accompanied by the urge to "let it all hang out." As a young Pentecostal I noticed that our preachers and evangelists were very athletic when it came to religious intensity. So to some degree I grew up with the feeling that Billy Sunday was a better role model on the subject of preaching than the Archbishop of Canterbury.

But the real key lies in never saying anything we don't believe and then saying it in such a way that we keep our excessive emotions within control. Often the sign that our homily has gotten out of hand is the number of religious interjections that we allow to interrupt the delivery. A predominance of "Hallelujahs" and "Praise the Lords" may be a sign that we have lost control. But an even stronger sign is drooling, hopping, or barking.

Most of the time these outbursts of heavenly psychoses come from a loose spontaneity that has never opened a commentary nor read a book that might slow the saliva and cool the uvula. If you are given to hyperintensity, a simple rule cures all. Write down what you want to say, and then practice being normal a lot.

MODERATING YOUR CONTENT

The exhortation issues of the sermon often become so glandular and loud that it is hard to settle back into a conversational mode once the spell of our own pulpit passion is spent. Psychologists refer to this emotional bondage as cathexis. Cathexis is our emotional attachment to our moods. When we "really get to going" we can find we have a great deal of trouble disconnecting from our moods.

I have seen a great many people captive to this fault. The bonding we establish when we speak fervently creates a huge connection between the preachers and their hearers. This ethereal communication results in a kind of religious rapture. It is a delightful closeness we are often loathe to interrupt so we can get back to being normal. Unfortunately, to try to stay in the state forces us into a pseudo-persuasive mode which goes from looking earnest to looking forced. Remember, conversational style is the best state; it is never too glandular and hyper to be regulated.[11]

Pacing is a conscious act that we must agree to force upon ourselves. Then we can preach, teach, wax eloquent or profound, whisper or shout, all because we have *not* lost control. From the moment we open a sermon we are in charge of a teaching mode, a cerebral moment, or a thoughtful, reflective suggestion. Best of all we look like our blood pressure is being regulated by a huge dose of humanity.

Pacing therefore is the regulator on the velocity of the delivery. It holds the braking system which moderates your speed, direction, and insertion of content or emotion. If your control mechanism gets "out of whack" and you allow your rhetoric to go unregulated, you may have a few dramatic, even coherent moments. But by and large, you will have lost command of your sermon. In such a snit you are likely to say things you didn't write down to say. You will later wish you hadn't let your emotions cause you to look like a stem-winder whose stem just broke off. The homiletical adrenalin dump can make you look prophetic for a couple of seconds but it is rarely a stable state. Stay in charge. Pace yourself.

The Balance of Passion and Relief

Balancing passion and relief is rather like the balance already established when we talked about pacing. The difference is this: pacing relates to the preacher's self-control to allow staying on track. Balancing passion with relief relates to the audience so they can stay on track. It is like the eye of the hurricane which gives the afflicted a lull in the category-four sermonic storm. During this lull they can assess where they were before the storm began and how they hope to ride out the last half of the storm.

Eugene Lowry in discussing his famous narrative "loop" speaks of preachers intentionally letting up on the tension, and creating a moment of relief in the tension. Dramatic and passionate preaching may establish a tight bond between preacher and listener but it doesn't do much for the humanity and relationship that ought to characterize the best conversational style. Only when passion and relief are interchanged and juxtaposed does the sermon achieve its best rapport with the listeners. All scream and no cream is not good preaching. Nor is a namby-pamby, droning conversational style. The sermon, like life, must come at us in a variety of modes. The teaching aspects may arrive quietly in a gondola whereas the exhortative aspects may roar in on a hydroplane. But only pacing allows every part of the sermon to hold its own characteristic mode.

To stay in charge of the pacing means that we must learn the ropes of style. We must learn how to use humor, the pause, good oral interpretation, induction, story and artifice, character development within our illustrations, word studies, statistics, etc. The more that we vary the constitution of the sermon, the more we will automatically pace the sermon as we move from one sermonic form to the next.[12]

Finally, the *sermo corporis* (the speech of the body) will play its part in pacing. To wildly gesticulate, move in ardent circles of athletic delivery, blam the pulpit, stamp and snort, may let the body become too active in the delivery. But this kind of wild style often rockets outside the range of our ability to control it. Nonetheless, the body must be allowed its own energy to fit the words we speak. Pacing is a consciousness that will not allow any part of the sermon's delivery to break free from our important mastery. Pacing always consorts with propriety, and sometimes muffles volume with velvet.

Pacing is a march cadence. To quit counting is to wind up out-of-step with the rest of the band. To keep the discipline going is what makes a half-time performance a moment of wonder. It all depends on who's in charge, that's all! When the preacher is, the emotions and the delivery speed are serving an obedient and a powerful master, whose sermons dare not become self-willed for they have a mighty task to do.

Preparing

Preparing the Mind, Readying the Soul

The numinous half of a Sunday sermon is far more elusive than the mechanical half. Getting ready to preach: this is the mysterious work without any one-two-threes or bulleted how-tos. Reaching the soul of the preacher in preparing to preach is a work more mighty than readying the mind. It is a life absorption in the call to preach, a daily walk, a sensitivity that is not born in a hurried lifestyle or a fit of rapture. It is far more than psyching up the soul. It is a love of God and an unending fascination with what he has made and how gloriously he orders our lives. It is a love of his Book and a joyous saturation of the life in the Scripture.

It is a life of wonder rising from a love affair we cannot learn in seminary and we cannot nourish on self-help books. But it is so important that to have it is to abrogate much of the need for this book. Not to have it will render this book powerless to make of the sermon that unstoppable force that only rises from a passion for inwardness.

To prepare a great sermon begins with a greatness of being that comes from a magnificent obsession with the Savior. In such a soul, pencil and paper preparation is a kind of interruption of that state of heart that renders every sermon a work of grace. Why? Because the preacher who belongs to God is powerless to stop worshiping him just for something as cybernetic as sermon planning.

I first discovered this nonteachable sine qua non of preaching when I was on a missionary assignment in Central America. I was working for the missionary board within my own denomination when I stumbled upon this truth. The denominationally trained, seminary-educated missionaries with whom I worked were models of conservative, homiletical excellence, but their churches were small and there were yards of pew per attendee at their services. Across from one of these sparsely attended churches a group of Pentecostals had "claimed an old movie theater for Jesus" and had retrofitted it to make it serve as a kind of church. Notre Dame it wasn't. And as for the preachers in the old cinema-turned-church, Henry Beechers they weren't. But these preachers were the very models of the kind of "Jesus-obsessed" souls that marry adrenaline to naïveté.[13]

Now it is at this point I was filled with confusion. Those who know the least about theology and the Bible often out-preach—or at least out-fascinate—those who are well studied. And once you become an educated professional, are you still better off in serving the Lord as an informed mind than as a zealot, whose mind seems less essential to his listeners than his passion? Still, I came to see that to add educated understanding to the practiced art of homiletics is the best way to live life. Zeal alone will not change the world in any important way. Adrenalin will speak to adrenalin, like cheerleaders who resonate noisily and cheerfully with the fans during an intense game. "Two bits, four bits, six bits, a dollar! All for Jesus stand up and holler!" Everybody's so titillated, they may for a moment forget that there are such things as the

Apostles' Creed, Aramaic, and exegesis. Under the sheer force of passion all honest *didache* can be swallowed up in "Yes, yes, I see that hand, and is there another?"

But here and there great preachers arise whose minds have been honed by an insatiable desire to understand all things. It is the eleventh Beatitude that reads, "Blessed are those whose love of books and their Greek New Testaments has married their need to live in union with Christ." It is these who hold out substantial hope. Such heralds preach with an informed passion that does change the world in significant ways.

With a single caveat this argument is done. Preparing the mind and readying the soul are but the two sides of a single coin. An unprepared mind has nothing enduring to say. An unprepared soul cannot preach what it has to say in any convincing way. Become devoted before you begin to work at those practiced arts that will improve your preaching. Be what you learn in silence before you stand in public to do it.

The Sermon-Planning Sheet

LONG-TERM NEED OF THE AUDIENCE

Sermons must be planned in two significant ways. First, there is long-term planning. This may be done in any scheduled way concerning any number of weeks. But it can hardly be called long-term planning if it is not done at least three months ahead. This would mean that four times a year you must sit down to block out what the next thirteen sermons will be about, and set about their creation at the same time. As much as you can, create a form for these thirteen approaching Sundays, and write down for each one its text, thesis, a suggested motif, and something of an outline.

Then, create a manila folder for each of the sermons into which you can—over the weeks that remain before they are preached—put notes, anecdotes, statistics, exegesis notes, etc. Continue gathering the "stuff" of the sermon until it's time for the short-term preparation. This way the preparation becomes far less academic and far more spiritual. Prayer and exegesis can begin their disciplined work early then: the heart at last joins what the head did many weeks earlier, and the sermon enters the birth canal.

But is three months of long-range planning enough time? I would advise an annual sermon planning time. For me it always came in the "dog days" following Advent, when the church attendance dropped and the post-yuletide blahs sniped at my moods and my pastoral responsibilities fell to a minimum. Then I got busy and mapped out fifty-two sermons for the coming year. I could at once think through all the congregational needs for the next year and line them up in my preaching schedule. Evangelism, family, stewardship, discipleship: everything found a place. When I added in six weeks of Lent and four of Advent and two for Epiphany, the annual structure took shape rather rapidly in those Sundays that were left to handle other important congregational sermonic needs. Further, I generally preached on the Holy Spirit during the week of Pentecost and the Bible itself on Reformation Sunday. This left me—subtracting my vacation Sundays and special speaker events, which we always knew at least a year ahead of time—to around thirty-five Sundays a year when specific, nonchurch-calendar events had to be mapped out. This does not mean you don't have to plan for Christmas and Easter, but they require a specialized sort of study and preparation that cohere more tightly and remain firmly in place from year to year. Then I used the same method of setting up the sermon file as suggested above on the quarterly system of staying prepared. One of the advantages of either system is that you can give your worship committee the list of topics and texts to keep the choir and musicians thinking in your direction, which helps to unify preaching with the other aspects of worship.

One other thing that must be said is that the lectionary is a great way to stay focused and keep your preaching outlines working far out ahead of you.[14] I consulted the lectionaries from time to time, because I realize how valuable they are in being sure you preach the whole Bible instead of just a few of your favorite texts from year to year. Still, I must confess, for my own preaching I preferred to set my own themes and texts well ahead of time, for it seemed to me that I could never "tailor" these set lectionary themes exactly to what I felt my particular congregation needed.

SHORT-TERM NEED OF THE AUDIENCE

But for all the good things that may be said for long-term preparation, what must be done is good day-to-day, short-term preparation. Getting the sermon done and living close to it during the days just prior to preaching it is essential. Getting the sermon manuscript or brief ready on time is to serve God well. Finish writing it comfortably ahead of Sunday morning and you will live easy with the notion that you are prepared.

But remember, no sermon is finished just because you've lifted it off the printer. Sermons are not merely written. They are oral documents, subject to change right up to and during the moment they are flying forth in challenge. Things may come that weren't there during the arduous, more mechanical days of their formation. Then the spontaneity of the moment may enlarge and sharpen them with ad-lib insights not born until the very moment they are spoken.

Steps to Correlating All Supporting Texts

How do you reinforce the central text of the sermon with good supporting Scriptures? Perhaps just as important is to ask, "Why is this important?" It is important for one very huge reason: supporting texts add the weight of biblical authority to your argument. Good expositors always let the Bible be the primary force that adds clout to their persuasion. Here are five important steps in the process of such reinforcement.

STEP 1: THINK "BIBLE" BEFORE YOU THINK "COMMENTARY."

It is a common fault that all of us pick a text for the sermon and then reach too soon for the commentaries to see what they have to say about the text we intend to preach.[15] To be "quick on the draw" is a mistake. Once you arrive at a text, push your own brain first to isolate all you know about the text you've chosen and then think through what you know about other texts that seem to speak to the issues of your chosen text. Only when you have done all you can on your own should you turn to the commentaries. What you know may not be as thorough as the commentaries, but it will be far more experiential and warm and thus carry a relational clout with your people, which the commentaries cannot furnish.

STEP 2: LET YOUR OWN AFFAIR WITH SCRIPTURE BE THE FIRST GUIDE TO ILLUSTRATING THE TEXT.

When and how did this primary text impact you? Confess how the text at hand has affected your life. Remember, we are not aiming at some scholarly insights here, such as you might find in a commentary, but a warm and experiential encounter with the very text you are preaching. How the text became real to you will be of far more value than how it came to be seen by critical commentaries. For the best part it will be confessional, and as mentioned earlier, confession is the strongest kind of preaching there is.

Step 3: Use only a few supporting texts.

Too much of a good thing is not a good thing. When you use more than two or three supporting texts, you mire the congregation down in a bog of less incisive insights.

Burying people in truth is confusing, much like eating sugar. Overdone, the sweetness is lost.

Step 4: Isolate key words and key ideas that connect the supporting texts.

Be sure that you make it clear how the supporting texts support. What are the words, phrases, and ideas the texts hold in common?

Step 5: Use only the best words, the most textual, the strongest words.

Be sure you keep to only one word or idea. Don't chase the rabbits of scriptural intrigue into sermonic byways that are off the point.

Preaching a Series

I believe that a great pulpit ministry is tied together with series of sermons across a lot of years. We have already established that the seasons of the church calendar—Lent, Advent, and the like—require a group of connected homilies to add focus to coordinated sermons that form the heart of worship during those seasons. But between these "church calendar" periods there are other periods as well when the pulpit can connect sermons together to link teaching and worship values. Such series can build a congregation spiritually and promote community within the church.

Steps for Planning a Series

Here are several steps of preparation to keep in mind as these worship series gather in formation to connect the separate Sundays of the church year.

STEP 1: LET A TEXTUAL MOTIF BECOME THE LINKING, WEEK-TO-WEEK REMINDER OF WHERE YOU ARE IN THE CONGREGATIONAL STUDY.

When conceiving a series find something linking the texts to be considered. For six Sundays prior to Easter I have a "Journey to Calvary" series of six sermons all focusing on the season. I have a certain number of these that mark the Advent season. "The Carols of Christmas" is a series which includes these individual sermons: "The Song of Elizabeth," "The Song of Mary," "The Song of the Angels," and "The Song of Simeon." I have another Christmas series called "It Happened at Bethlehem," in which I have four sermons including people and events that involve Bethlehem: Ruth, the anointing of David, the prophecy of Micah, the birth of Christ. But the title of the series, well published throughout the congregation, connects the busy season into a better whole than the season would have done without the motif.

STEP 2: LET THE ACTUAL WORDS OF THE TEXT BE THE CORRELATING REMINDER OF THE SERIES.

An example of letting the actual words of the text correlate the series is a missionary emphasis series called "Come to the Waters." This phrase from Isaiah 53 titling the series becomes the correlating phrase of the season of world outreach. The actual motif in this case comes right out of the Scriptures and is in some ways much stronger than "It Happened at Bethlehem," the series referred to above where the title is textually dependent but not actually lifted from the words of Scripture.

STEP 3: WHEREVER POSSIBLE LET SOME WORD OR PHRASE BE SET IN A CONCRETE METAPHOR OR SCRIPTURAL IMAGE LINKING ALL SERMONS IN THE SERIES.

"The Journey to Calvary" series mentioned earlier is an example of this kind of concrete metaphor in which the sermons picture the individual sermon attendee on the journey from their current workaday world through the Via Dolorosa and toward the goal of the journey: encountering the cross. Here a concrete image is established and the sermons, which compose the journey, could be illustrated by a banner depicting a pilgrim encountering the cross. A wonderful thing about this kind of image-driven series of sermons is how the graphic of the pilgrimage could be the center of fliers, bulletins, and other promotions, positioning the sermon at the very center of worship during this important season of the year.

The Sermon Study Sheet

I have listed below a suggested sermon study sheet that might be used in two ways, either to pull together a series of sermons or to gather together outlines and titles for a single-sermon, long-range planning file. The purpose of this outline form is to keep the aim or the goal of the sermon before your eyes whether or not you are using the form for the week just ahead or whether you are using it in larger periods such as quarterly or annual planning. Admittedly, it is not an august form. You actually would do better to create your own form tailored to your specific style of study and preaching. But some form like this will certainly enable you to stay focused as you prepare.

Once you have settled on using the sheet below or an outline form of your own contriving, to make its use effective try to keep it to a single page so you can see the whole thing at a glance. This will allow you a one-page visual memory shot at getting the whole thing—like a flat photograph—in your mind at one time. Then this memorized page can serve as a kind of single-sheet teleprompter to keep your outline before you as you preach the entire sermon.

I believe the average thirty-minute sermon will best cohere if it can be seen and memorized as a single piece. This doesn't mean that your sermon will only be one page long. Written out it might be eight to twelve pages for a thirty-minute sermon. But the form of the entire document will have a one-page synopsis that allows you a tight, inner visual control of what you are going to say. Such a visualized, tight outline can keep you from wandering about through a longer, looser outline. But remember, outlining should be as individual as there are preachers to contrive ways of doing it, and finding the best way of being coherent and communicative must ever be a matter of individuality.

That being said let us proceed to the sermon planning sheet and consider how you might best make it serve to help you arrive at your own form for focusing on your title, thesis, motif, and pacing for either a single sermon or a series.

SERMON PLANNING SHEET
PART 1

Text _____

Sermon Title _____

Sermon Theme

_____
_____
_____
_____
_____
_____

Sermon Motif

_____
_____
_____
_____
_____

Focal Text: What is the part of the sermon text on which the sermon's argument is based?

_____
_____
_____
_____
_____
_____
_____

What are the strongest word or words in the text that relate to the sermon's motif?

_____
_____
_____

Correlating Texts

_____
_____
_____

6

Digging for Treasure

The Art of Exegesis

Exegeting the prophet's own soul is the hardest work a prophet has to do. It's complex because it can only be done from the inside out. But it is the most important work to be completed on the study of a text because those who listen to the prophet have far more interest in his God-given message than what the most brilliant of the commentaries would have to add to it. Listeners are needy and want a firsthand confessional exegesis of the text. They want to see inside the preacher's soul. They want to know how the preacher first discovered the text, how it came to mean so much, and in what ways it is found to be true. This depth-of-soul exegesis makes or breaks a sermon. It is likely that in this part of a sermon, welding the parson's soul with the souls of the listeners may be achieved. I grew up in a Pentecostal environment in rural Oklahoma. I was converted when the preacher, who had not attended Yale Divinity School, or even suspected its existence, preached on the text, "Ye must be born again." Even in 1945 no one much said "Ye" except evangelists. The study of biblical commentaries never congested their preachment with what great thinkers had to say about the matter. It would be years before I found out there were Bible commentaries. I doubt if the "King James Only" Pentecostal evangelists had ever heard of them. But they had an ability—still do in many cases—to speak of their personal connection with a text. When they said "Ye!" it sounded to me like they were saying "You Dog, you!" High Church proclaimers have a footnotish habit of sourcing their sermons till they are often too packed with scholarly insights to permit an "as I see it" remark. In being so secondhand about their faith, they leave their listeners aching for a first person testimonial as to why the text is so important to them. So the poor listeners often come and go, baffled as to why they came and went.

Where Does the Sermon Begin?

Where does the sermon properly begin? Those who are largely unseasoned at preaching might say, "In the Bible." And in this day of shallow preachers and surface sermons, the answer does have an appeal. But lest we answer too quickly, we need to find out who's asking the question. The more cerebral and studied the "pastor" *is*, the more likely will be heard this defense: "My exegesis begins in the Bible." But the more outgoing and relational the pastor is, the more the answer might tend to be, "My exegesis begins with the congregation."

My answer was always the latter. This is probably why I have no sixty-six sermon series on Leviticus in my file. Still I did preach a lot of series during my thirty-five years as a parish pastor. In fact nearly all of my preaching was done in series mostly because I could think of no single-sermon approach that met the great needs of the church in an effective way. As I wrangled over what I would preach on in my long-term sermon planning, I thought through an entire year at a time. (See discussion of this issue in chapter 5.) Then I laid out homiletic blocks of sermons that dealt thoroughly with evangelism, marriage, the inner life in Christ, ministry and missions, stewardship, and the like. Advent and Lent were both handled with series of coordinated messages that would help the believer grow through these special seasons as Scripture intended.

Did I preach the Bible? Of course, but my use of Scripture was one of preventive medicine (and sometimes, during a church crisis, of emergency medicine). I wanted to attend to the healing of souls and make the Bible my medical bag for the curing of the church. But just as reading through a volume of medical science is not the most holistic way of practicing medicine, so reading through the Bible in a random manner is not the most healing way to practice the art of ministry.

Digging out just the right text for each Sunday sermon was a matter of taking the spade of exegesis to the needy lives of those who would come to hear me preach that text. Long ago I learned that more than half of any pastor's congregation come to church broken and in the grip of some life issue that is eating at their well-being. Selecting Bible texts without reference to these needs seems calculating and cold. Really, it seems beside the point. Preaching the Bible without consulting congregational need is seeing too much of the Scripture as academic and too little of it as healing.

But "Bible first or congregation first?" is in a sense a question of which came first, the chicken or the egg? And there is probably no good answer. But as a pastor, I never wanted to be guilty of not caring about people, and so in thinking about what I wanted to preach on, I immediately thought of my flock and what their needs and grievances were. Out of my pastoral care, I exegeted the congregation and tried to figure out how the sermon might be of use to win the lost or strengthen the redeemed. Whatever the results of my congregational exegesis were, it was from that launching point that I started into the text, looking for sermon words that were strong enough to do the best work of God in each of their individual lives.

We have spoken of the importance of digging for treasure in every area of sermon preparation. Digging in the text will be the focus of our study in this chapter. The word *exegesis*, which we earlier explored, is the key word for this chapter. It is the *ex* part of the word that most captures my attention, for the *gesis* only speaks of the way, but *ex* speaks of the direction. The direction is important because it implies a "coming" out of the text and even more so implies where our study for preaching properly belongs.

Starting Your Exegesis with Yourself

Life Commentary: Narrate Your Own Affair with the Text

Narrating your own affair with the text as a life commentary is wise counsel for making the biblical text a real ministry. This principle will be an unimportant thing to say to the older minister because this veteran of spirit has discovered that the people who hear him weekly care a great deal more about what he has to say about the text than they care about what the brightest scholar has to say.[1] But the principle is also true of the audience to whom you are preaching. They want to know why you have selected the text and what part this text has played in your life. How did you first bump into it and in what set of circumstances has the text already met your own needs?

All we who preach have a list of favorite sermon texts, which by odd coincidence happen to be their personally favorite passages. Why? Because these passages came to us in some unforgettable circumstance that locked them permanently into our minds. I remember an old man in my first, student parish, who near the time of his death gave me a great gift. "Do you think you will die, Ralph?" I asked this sick old patriarch, rather bluntly. "Yes, but more important than that, I think you will die too." The remark stunned me: I was twenty years old, and he was seventy-eight. "As a matter of fact," he said, "I'm pretty convinced that everybody who is living is going to die—some sooner, some later. And the only people who will really matter, when the dying is done with, are those who were good stewards of the time they have lived. Do you know what Psalm 90:12 says?" he asked.

"No," I said.

"'Lord, teach us to number our days, that we may apply our hearts to wisdom.' There's not a New Year's Day that goes by that I don't quote that to myself."[2]

So I wrote a New Year's sermon on the passage, and whenever anyone brings up the passage, I think of the old man who gave this particular text to me as a gift. It is hard for me to preach on the passage without telling the crowd how I first discovered the passage. There are scores of passages that have a history with me and any one of them came to me from special friends in special moments. At my grandmother's passing, my own mother made me aware of John 14 and its promise of heaven. A church secretary of mine once counseled me on 2 Timothy 1:7 and how she had found the passage helpful in overcoming fear. A friend of mine preached a sermon on Peter's Pentecostal sermon in Acts 2:17, quoting Joel 2:28. He said that most churches have walked away from the Holy Spirit, when what they really need is "A Drink at Joel's Place," which was the title of his sermon. The text became unforgettable to me.

What the Passage Means to You on Both a Surface and on a Deeper Level

Most of us receive any truth that comes to us in one of two ways. We receive it as it first comes to us, in which we hear the statement and say, "That's true!" Then in another set of circumstances when the truth of the statement hits us squarely at the center of our need, we cry, "Upon my soul, this is really true for me!" It is this "second coming" of the truth that our hearers want to hear about. When it comes to scriptural or sermonic texts, the second coming of the truth refers to any later encounter with the same text that adds to the history you previously held with a passage.

I once prepared a sermon on "Bad Foundations for Life" based on 1 Corinthians 3:11: "Other foundation can no man lay than that which is laid, which is Christ Jesus" (ASV). In this sermon I use the substructure of the leaning tower of Pisa as an example of bad foundations. Architecturally, this is true, and the sermon built on the truth very well. After preaching the sermon the first time, I actually went to Pisa, climbed the tower, and upon descending from the top, had a most illuminating talk with my Italian guide. "It's question of bad foundations, you know," he said to me. I thought of my sermon and smiled. He continued, "Most bad foundations can be corrected, you know. Certainly this one could be."

"You mean," said I, studying the famous landmark, which at that time leaned thirteen feet off perpendicular, "that this tower could be saved."

"Yes," he said, "we believe we could pump high-pressure concrete underneath the tower and keep it from leaning any further: we might even be able to straighten it."

"Well, if you can, for goodness' sake, why don't you?"

"Let me ask you a question," he said.

"Go for it," I said.

"Would you have come to Pisa if our bell tower had been straight? You see, my American *amico*, most people would rather be popular than straight."

So when I preach the sermon now, I preach it in light of the second coming of the truth that was added to my history of text just by visiting Pisa. First Corinthians (and the issue of bad foundations) had granted a whole new content for me.

As we learn more, the Scriptures grow ever more pertinent and relevant.[3]

Don't Hesitate to Preach Confessionally about the Text

I can hardly preach from John 3 without including the tale of how I was born again. First of all, I love the telling of this very important story (important to my way of thinking). But second, when I begin any kind of exposition of the passage, I become highly confessional. Anytime our sermons become confessional, they become more powerful. Edward Markquart, a brilliant homoletician, wrote: "People want their preachers to be authentic human beings . . . who experience the same feelings and struggles as the laity, who do not hide behind the role of reverend so and so."[4]

People discover who they are in the context of a preacher's honesty. "Truth and self discovery are the products of openness. Confessional preachers gain the confidence of their audience. . . . The only way we achieve such transparency is by running the risk of self-revelation. Transparency always involves some confessional preaching."[5]

A pastor-to-people relationship is much like a husband and wife relationship. The best way to make it survive across the years is to live in openness with the flock. Are there any rules as to how far our confession can go? Of course, it's okay in most cases to be "gutsy," but letting them "see too much of your guts" can also be counterproductive. How far should we "unzip the viscera" in spilling all our feelings and philosophies? There are three rules which govern confessional sermons.

First, never betray any member of your family or any members of the church with your openness. I had a pastor friend who told the whole congregation—during a sermon on the home—that his wife and he were not having a satisfactory relationship. Their relationship got worse after he confessed it. This bizarre sermon caused him to be forced out of his position. He remains bitter toward his former church and elders, though in all honesty the fault was his own. I have seen (and heard) preachers use their children as dumb illustrations of some point they really wanted to make about raising children. No matter how good a family or personal illustration may be in terms of illustrating a text, if it hurts any person who hears it, it condemns the preacher for being insensitive to the point of cruelty.

Second, any confession which injures the church or the Bible is one that goes too far. I recently heard a preacher say that St. Paul was wrong about some of the things he wrote about. The idea borders on blasphemy, but even if some case might be made for an error in Paul's writings, it leaves the church insecure about how much of the rest of the Bible might be wrong.

Helen Reddy received her Grammy thanking her "Mother in heaven" for the award. In this gender-sensitive world, the church resentments smolder over such a statement as this. I had a professor friend who prayed at our school (a Southern Baptist seminary), "Holy Spirit, come and be Queen of our lives." Not only did the Holy Spirit not come, but the professor soon left the seminary and remained unemployed for a long time. I have no doubt that he really believed his confession, but most of us would wisely refuse to let estrogen and theology pass so close. A very popular televangelist expanded the Trinity from three to seven and—as a result—met universal objections and ultimately pared his sevenfold Godhead back to three. For redacting his theology, evangelicals decided he could go on living, buying white suits, and smiling a lot. But his attempt to make the Trinity a Septinity went poorly. Confessional preaching needs to be orthodox.

Third, when our confession begins to embarrass our audience, we are on shaky ground. This is the easiest and best rule of all. An illustration will help explain why. There circulated a joke the truth of which I much admired. A rustic Christian stood in a revival meeting and began his testimony by telling what "a dirty rotten skunk he had been when Jesus found him." His confession was met with a chorus of "amens!" Then he told how he had been a terrible drunkard and had even danced and smoked. Again the "amens" ricocheted around his confession. Then he told how in his utter depravity he had once romantically kissed his mule. There were no "amens," and the audience looked down and away, clearly embarrassed. To which the preacher said, "Good brother, I don't think I'd have confessed that."

When transparency breaks with propriety, the power of the confessional sermon is lost. But confessing our tendency to doubt, and confessing our idiocy in the whole arena of human relationships beckons the human spirit. And those who hunger for identity will reach gladly toward the confession. Transparency paves the way for the Spirit's advance. And Christ always visits his people on the runways of their openness.

Show How Your Testimony about the Text is Transferable to Your Hearers

Persuasion and salesmanship do have an affinity whether or not they are exactly the same thing. Showing what the text means to you and how it has helped you could be of immense use to your parishioners, if you can show them how to apply it. While all of us turn from how-to sermons, the truth is that people do want to know "how to" live and take care of their problems.

How has become the strategic adverb of the success-driven, entrepreneurial West. It shows up in thousands of book titles, and even when it doesn't show up, it is implied in the many such titles. Take, for example, *Word 2003 for Dummies* or *Chicken Soup for the Entrepreneurial Soul*, or how about *Swim with the Sharks*, *Learn to Negotiate*, and *Climbing the Corporate Ladder*. All such titles omit the omnipresent adverb *how*, but *how* is implied nonetheless, and these titles might as well read: *How to Swim with the Sharks*, *How to Learn to Negotiate*, *How to Become an Entrepreneur*, and *How to Climb the Corporate Ladder*.

The Bible has always been seen as a deep, deep oracle of truth that never lies and therefore holds the answers to all kinds of how-to issues if only we can dig deep enough. Jean Astruc a Royal French physician once sought, through the Bible, to find a cure for King Louis XVIII's gout. The author of a very popular book believed there was a "Bible Code" and if you could get your Ouija board and your exegesis together, you could find an answer to almost everything. This odd fondness for answers still has people reading the Bible for how-tos.

But the preacher does understand the simple wisdom in helping people live fuller, more complete lives by pressing the truth hidden in biblical passages. When this really works well the preacher has found some kind of personal liberation in a text and is anxious to pass on his healing insights to those who still don't quite know how to apply the how-to that the preacher has just discovered.[6]

With such insights in hand, the preacher may genuinely say "how to" with some competence. We are, after all, authorities—or should be—on how to please God, how to win others to Christ, how to walk in the Spirit, how to build a better marriage, how to find peace, how to plan for eternity, how to . . . how to . . . how to. . . . And great sermons take application so seriously that a text which has liberated the preacher is easily transferred to those who are yet unliberated. Just "how to" make this transference is the concern of books like this one. The only reason for reading books like this one is to widen the scope and power of "how to" preach.

Letting the Bible Comment First

What Does the Bible Have to Say about What the Sermon Text Has to Say?

When it comes to adding authority to the sermon, the Bible is the most powerful way to comment on what the Bible has to say. Once a sermon text has been defined, the good expositor will want to add clout to that text by letting other texts with a similar voice make their contribution to its force. A concordance will quickly allow you to find and put all such passages to their fullest use. There is a wonderful interrelatedness to all texts, and the linchpin of all is their relationship to Christ.[7] This is the kind of point that Bryan Chapell has established in *Christ-Centered Preaching*.

There are two ways that correlating texts can add their support. First, they may add insight to the primary sermon text. Second, they may fetch emotional and existential support for the sermon text. Before preaching on any text coming from the last days of the prophet Jeremiah, it would be good to read or quote some passages from 2 Kings, which discuss the fall of Jerusalem. Isaiah and 2 Kings also parallel in a similar way, and a text from either place would fortify the other. Second Peter and Jude have a close affinity, and each might support the other. The synoptic Gospels also corroborate and affirm many of the stories of Jesus.

But there is another way that texts can support each other. They touch the same emotional cords and bear witness to the same agonizing or blessed truths. I recently took Psalm 130:1 as my sermon text and then quickly located two or three other texts that would speak to the primary sermon text. I chose to support this "out of the depths" passage with 2 Corinthians 12:7

where Paul is agonizing and calling out of the depths. I also included the cross cry of Jesus taken from Psalm 22. In this case the insights gained are as transferable as the faithfulness of God is. But whether you are searching for the support of insight or emotion, the Bible is the best commentary on what the Bible has to say.

Differentiating the Propositional Text from the Narrative Text

The shortest way of delineating these two modes of preaching is to say that propositions inform and stories fascinate. Which of these is essential to a sermon? Both, of course. A sermon with no insights cannot be of any lasting help. Sermons with no stories are not interesting enough to pay attention to, even if the aloof verbs and nouns might actually offer help. In the biblical mode, propositional truth tends to be instructional *didache* and stories tend to fall under the exhortative word *kerygma*. Propositions give you the information you need to build a life on, and stories motivate you to want to build such a life.

It does amaze me that highly propositional preachers seem not to understand that stories are the stuff of persuasion far more than propositions. Propositions may tell you what you should do, but stories motivate you to want to do them. Having listened to preachers all my life, I have discovered that those with real motivational powers understand the value of story. If the tale is intense enough, the audience eats out of the storyteller's hand. When the hand-fed meal is done, the next words out of the listener's mouth is often, "What wilt thou have me to do?" F. Scott Fitzgerald wrote of this enchanting power of the storyteller when he said, "Draw your chair up close to the edge of a precipice and I'll tell you a story."[8] I remember an evangelist whom I once heard who spent an entire hour talking about his brother's death and the impact it had on their family. He was not boring. The story was electric; the passion was there. We were ready to do anything he asked. When he was through we sang "Just As I Am," and he asked us to come and avoid the excesses of the wasted life his father once lived. The story was so riveting his persuasion was instant. He was without a doubt a manipulator, and I do not applaud his selfish way of treating his audience, but I have never forgotten the spell of a well-told story and how it readies an audience to commit themselves to whatever a spellbinder asks, whether or not it is ethical.

The preacher who is a manipulator uses high-pressure motivation to take advantage of those brought to tears with his melodrama. It is the fault of such preachers that they seek to build an emotional matrix into which they plunge their audience to drink of their own private agenda. In the case of the evangelist above, he wanted to sell his emotionally moved listeners a book he had written. He had stacks of them in the vestibule, and many of the transfixed listeners filed out of the sanctuary still humming "Just As I Am" and bought the book. I myself went to Barnes and Noble and bought a novel. It cost a little more, but I didn't have to sing "Just As I Am" to get it.

But in the case of Fitzgerald the truth stands: Stories bind an audience into oneness and leave the preacher a special place as an honest motivator.[9] And when the best crafting of the narrative moment has been done, the people who hear it will have heard the truth in two ways. The text of the sermon—properly related to the narrative—will be theirs to take with them a long way into the future. And they will all have felt that special oneness produced by the rapt attention that gathers around a good tale.

Work at Giving Preceptive Texts a Strong Narrative Presentation

Most right-brained preachers delight in the parables or the great stories of the Old Testament and often develop a habit of leaning rather heavily on these stories to create interest. But great preachers—artistic or not—preach the whole Bible. So the preacher who really develops a flock across the years doesn't shy away from the Epistles because of their less narrative character.[10] Still, we have spent a great deal of time considering the importance of story, and it follows that when you are trying to preach a nonnarrative text, you want to find the best, most narrative support for the preaching of it. To make this happen, there are three pieces of advice I would give. In essence these bits of advice suggest that when there is no clear-cut story suggested by the propositional text, the expositor may move first to metaphor, and then to illustrating the sermon with story.

SEARCH FOR WORD STUDIES IN THE ORIGINAL LANGUAGES

First, go to the text in search of word studies, which often will suggest a metaphor that reminds you of a story. This for me is the best of all possible ways to bring narrative interest to precept-driven texts. Take almost any word you wish from the Hebrew Old Testament or the Greek New Testament and you will find those words brimming with life. Very few preachers I know do much with the original languages, and for the life of me I cannot figure out why. Why would they spend thousands of dollars to go to seminary to acquire sermon-making skills and then promptly give it all up when they actually begin a lifetime of sermon preparation? Of course writing sermons is hard work, and it's largely because study is hard work.[11] But the achievement of interest and pulpit clout is surely a worthy reward as well.

No work is richer in pay than digging into a text with the spade of word study. The names for God in the Old Testament and for Christ in the New Testament throw rich and wonderful words at human understanding. Often these images elude us at our first reading where the text appears to be prosaic. The word for *Spirit* in the Old Testament is also the word for *wind* and *breath*, and the richness of the correlation feeds a sermon with images that detonate the dullness with life.

I recently heard a preacher preach on the "breath of God" and the "wind of Genesis" and his own affair with asthma. He described how important breath was, what a privilege it was to breathe. He told a story of being delivered from one asthmatic spasm when his father held him up to the air conditioning vent and allowed him to gulp the clean new air that came sweetly to extend his life. It was a powerful story that grew directly from a Hebrew word study.

I have a story I tell that came from a highly "left-brained" passage in Romans that refers to the *bathos* of God, the *depths* of God. From the word, I tell a story about my venture into the shallows near the depths of the Great Barrier Reef. The problem is I would never have arrived at the story had the Greek word not goaded me into remembrance of something that happened to me that relates to the metaphor. And the image and story were drawn from a very doxological text.

FIND A GOOD ENGLISH WORD

Second, if nothing jumps out of the word study, seek to find a good English word that will push the images of the sermon's thesis forward. This may be even more arduous for the noninventive. But usually the English text will suggest an English word that could become an image-driven word. For example, within the previous sentence there are at least two words which have an interesting derivation. Both the words *English* and *image* come from very interesting roots that might form pictures or stories.

THINK VISUALLY, PREACH IMAGE

Third, try to think visually and preach images. Let's examine what I mean by this. What you actually get people to visualize will be with them for a while. We do speak with words, but we store in pictures. Our minds are not huge dictionaries and lexicons filled with definitions. They are galleries in which hang the images and pictures that we have derived from all we've seen in stories, movies, novels, news reports, sightseeing drives, etc.[12] Jesus' sermons were full of images, which we have already covered in the introduction. But it must be remarked that if the Son of God preached image and picture, it must be a reasonable homiletic method.

In fact, not only is an image-driven homiletic good, but it is not bad occasionally to take some artifact or picture or book which gives the image reality. You can overdo this sort of thing, but occasionally it is a good idea. I have a sermon that I preach on "Treasures in Earthen Vessels." (Doesn't everyone?) But when I preach it, I use an actual earthen vessel at the pulpit. I take an old clay pot filled with the treasures of my life (wedding band, driver's license, ordination papers, etc.). Each of these artifacts has an accompanying story as I draw them from the old clay pot. By the time the sermon is over it is clear that the pot was never as important as the things that it contained, which is of course the point of the apostle's metaphor.

The exegesis study form asks how the preacher's life links to the text. The life narrative connections with a given passage can provide points of contact with the audience. Key words in the text may suggest ways of illustrating the text.

Exegesis Study Form

Sermon's Main Text _____

What is my personal history with this text?

_____
_____
_____
_____

Have I had a secondary encounter (a "second coming" impact)
with the text?

_____
_____
_____

Here is an important "how-to" that the text offers the listener:

_____
_____
_____
_____

If the passage is expository, what are the key words in the original
language(s) that might serve as a springboard to find a metaphor
out of which will spring some illustration?

Word #1: _____

Word #2: _____

Word #3: _____

On the Use of Commentaries

Commentaries and pulpit helps of one kind or another all have
a contribution to make to the sermon. To some extent we have
already discussed the value and use of commentaries, and perhaps with this final word we can put the issue of their use to rest.
There are things commentaries can do, and things they can't.

They can furnish the sermon with substance and insight. They can give preachers a self-confidence that they are in charge of the matter, and thus they furnish the hearld with a ring of some scholarly authority. Commentaries give immediate access to the times, dates, and reasons a part of the Bible came to be, and this will—over a lifetime of study—create for the parson the mystique of a scholar-pastor, which will lead the congregation into a good regard for the preacher's mind.

The word *parson* comes from the notion that the parson was the *person* of the parish. He understood the Bible and doctrine and could help the congregation clarify their questions about it all. Unfortunately, we have come to a sad time when the people of the parish rarely care enough about the Bible to consult the parson. Scripture and doctrine get so little of their attention that no deep issues ever stir in their un-investigative minds. Then too, there are so many religious radio heroes these days that most people would seek answers from their favorite gospel gurus before they take their questions to the "person of the parish." There were members of my flock who would carry into their private church Bible study a stack of sermon books by their favorite "airways" preacher and show little interest in the sermons I preached. These are times when even good pastors are ignored in favor of the latest gospel-glitz hero of the day. Nonetheless, the challenge to be a scholar-pastor is healthy, and the reading of in-depth commentaries will support the communicator's goals of staying informed as he preaches to his flock.

So much for what the commentaries can do. Now let's ask, "What about what they can't do?" They cannot supply spiritual vitality to the flock. The Holy Spirit's visit to the congregation is far more apt to arrive on the wings of good relationships, pastoral care, and the pastor's desire to see Christ formed within his own life. Commentaries cannot supply good pulpit style. They do not teach the value of gestures and eye contact. They rarely inspire a dramatic style or any vestige of passion to the presentation of biblical truth. They cannot supply any whit of expectancy.

Expectancy?

Yes, most of us go to church on Sunday looking for those glorious breakthroughs of godly visitation. In this sense the sermon ought to participate in this wonderful expectancy. Great worship and great sermons contain a wonderful impending, a sense of "watch out, here it comes." People come, thinking to themselves, *God is going to speak, I can feel it. This is wonderful! It could happen, now—at this moment!* If the preacher has been good at the cure of souls we can rightly feel that the Spirit has gathered on the wings of all our needs. The preacher's own life supplies these things where they exist. John Hines said, "Preaching is effective as long as the preacher expects something to happen—not because of the sermon, not even because of the preacher, but because of God."[13] Commentaries cannot generate this expectancy, nor can the how-tos of the most famous lecturers. There are four rules that govern the use of commentaries, so let's look them over to arrive at the best kind of guidance on this subject.

First, read the information, but think application. Commentaries generally inform more than they inspire. In other words it is better to be ready to tell people what to do with sermon information—whether or not it comes from a commentary. Sermons are meant to be prescriptive. Informative is not enough. To spend ten minutes in a sermon on Ephesians telling the people that Ephesus was a great center of commerce and art in the ancient world is to fail them. They would as soon get that kind of information from the National Geographic channel. It is good to offer brief insights that illumine a passage, but the flock simply must have a personal reason to attend to the sermon's insights.

Second, left-brained pulpiteers are generally more excited over pure insight than their audience. Commentaries may lead you into a "verse-by-verse" expositional style that is too mechanical to be really exciting.[14] I believe a better style of communicating the Scripture may be "passage-by-passage," or even better a "truth-by-truth" style of preaching. Commentaries can inspire a mechanical, verse-by-verse look at a passage, which is not all that charming to the more right-brained souls who attend a sermon looking for some hint of creativity which they feel is the signature of the Spirit.

Third, right-brained pulpiteers are generally bored by the merely informative and often fail to communicate the great insights of a text. There is a very great danger prevalent in our times. Sermons void of any commentary insight have spawned a wave of fluff-purveyors, who substitute the clever—or even worse, an attempt at being clever—for the real stuff of the Bible. Tedious information about a text may not be an exciting way to preach, but it is probably better than the "let me entertain you" impulse of a preacher who has forgotten the preacher's mandate: "Do your best to present yourself to God as one approved, a workman who does not need to be ashamed and who correctly handles the word of truth" (2 Tim. 2:15).

Fourth, know the critical commentaries; preach the interpreter's commentaries. In stating this rule this way I have overgeneralized this adage. But in terms of keeping an audience on board for the entire homily, the audience is far more likely to listen to the illustrative than the purely informational. In all four of these rules on commentaries, it is good to remember a single line from Donald Coggan's wisdom: "When true preaching takes place, the main actor is not the preacher, nor the congregation, but the Holy Spirit."[15] In lieu of this truth, it is best not to get the runways of the sermon so stacked with commentary insights that the Spirit has no place to land in the sermon should he be inclined to do so.

Honoring the Textual Genre

A brief word about genre: it exists; honor it. Paul's letters are different from the Psalms, from the minor prophets, from the Pentateuch. Preachers should not handle the Bible as though there is no difference between the various kinds and styles of biblical writing. When preaching any passage, get in touch with the author. When you preach Jeremiah, find something of the melancholy in it and let the tone suffuse the sermon. When you preach Ecclesiastes, do it wistfully. When you're in the Psalms, let there be a hint of melody about it. Let the fire out of the Apocalypse and let courage bleed from Esther; let the wind blow in Acts.

Further, find ways of illustrating every individual sermon text with insights and moods that communicate the genre. T. S. Eliot will better illustrate the Psalms than will Billy Graham. Billy might do better in the book of Acts. Let the poets speak to Genesis 1, and the newspaper to 1 Thessalonians. Archibald MacLeish would do better commenting on Job than a prosaic commentator. Let Shakespeare's sonnets speak to Ruth and Frodo Baggins to the Christ-redemption passages.

Above all put on your touchy-feely wardrobe and pick up the agony and ecstasy and every nuance of form that rings through the various writers of Scripture. To understand this—to feel this—is to give a great gift to your auditors. The gift is one of tone, relationship, and the subliminal. To fail to honor genre is to give your people the fuzzy notion that the Bible, like the Golden Plates of Nephi, was handed down from heaven as a single piece, and all of it is pretty much alike. But the biblical heroes were immensely different. Ezekiel borders on the neurotic, Isaiah on the elegant, Jeremiah on the morose, Micah on the visionary.

The task will not be easy. It is difficult work to make a genre live. It is like the studious work of an actor, who will study for weeks the part he wishes to portray before he ever steps out on stage to portray it. Then when at last he interprets the part, he is captive to it. The role alters the player's complete personality, and the actor cannot easily shuck what he has worked so hard to gain.[16]

Even within a single writer there will be various tones. Moses is a furious zealot in Exodus, but in Deuteronomy he is a reflective old man. Don't preach both passages the same way. Paul is firm and tough in 1 Corinthians, but he is moody and tender in 2 Timothy. Jesus is full of parables in Luke, but full of prayer and philosophy in John. Giving these various moods and tempos, styles and emotions will bring to your people a rich sense of the varied nature of how God speaks through human agency.

Let the Bible become as variegated to you as you would like it to be to them. God does after all speak in various ways his wonders to perform. When the Bible has had its best say, it will be exciting from passage to passage because every paragraph came from a newness that was born of a moment, spoken by an individual, and lived in the separate lives of God's savvy interpreters. Get honest about it: this important task of feeling and connoting genre when we preach will mark the difference between an amateur and a professional. Further, the sermon will be borne by a sensitive expositor who lives well in community and thrives on the kinds of challenge that bring his whole congregation to maturity in Christ.

Now let us turn to the sermon-planning sheet and put into practice what we have just learned about exegesis, confession, and story. These three elements of sermon preparation give the sermon substance (exegesis), heart (confession), and intrigue (narrative style).

SERMON PLANNING SHEET
PART 2

Write a brief paragraph recounting your life experience with the text.

_____
_____
_____
_____
_____

What is the strongest precept in the text (is this the strongest point of my sermon)?

_____
_____
_____

How can I gild the precepts in the text with a memorable form of narrative or metaphor?

_____
_____
_____
_____

7

Imaging the Argument

Developing the Art of Writing the Story

Only a few preachers see themselves as artists and view the work they do as image making. Too bad, too, for all listeners hear with words but store what we hear in pictures. So sermons are remembered only if they contain enough pictures to be stored. And the best, most storable images are those that come from our own lives. Of all the Greek myths, the one which I visit for my own sake is the myth of Polyclitus the sculptor. If the Greek pantheon had been a catalog of saints instead of gods, Polyclitus would be the patron saint of sculptors. To demonstrate the value of originality in art Polyclitus bought two blocks of marble with identical dimensions. He put one of those blocks in the window of his studio, and the other in the backroom. He invited all who came to watch him work to offer ideas and suggestions as to how the statue in the window should be sculpted. The comments were frequent and sometimes major. As each of the critics made suggestions, Polyclitus altered the carving in the front of his shop. But the more people made comments, the more—to use Alice in Wonderland's term—the statue in the front window was increasingly uglified. But all the time this daily process of uglification was going on in the front of the studio, Polyclitus was carving alone on the unseen block in the back of his studio. There emerged from the marble in the back room a gallant rendering of life that issued from his soul alone. The point is that artistic integrity is just plain better off without carbon paper. I have a friend who listens to famous-preacher cassettes as he assembles his own sermons from week to week. He's clearly never heard of Polyclitus, but pieces together a hodgepodge of Swindoll, Lucado, and Schuller. He has built a very plastic congregation who believe him to be a genius precisely because he steals his best sermons in bits and pieces and doesn't credit his sources. But citing sources may not be enough to guarantee integrity. Tony Campolo wrote a book telling of a party he threw for some prostitutes in Honolulu in the wee small hours of the morning, when the girls were "off work" and having a bit of a predawn nosh before they went home "to sleep off their low self-images." The book *Our God's a Party Animal* was immensely popular. Since the book's publication I have heard similar pulpit stories and none of them were quite as good. I can only wish the copycats had a little studio in the back of their public studio where they worked as best they can at creating original sermons in their own voice. Polyclitus would have liked that.

Developing the Art of Story

Preachers are those who are called to be artists of persuasion. They work to set forth the position of God on every issue that Sundays might permit. They are possessed of the conviction that while God reigns from heaven, he has definite ideas about how things should go down here. These artists see God's ideas not as issues of debate but declaration. Yet these preaching artists have read the Bible and arrived at a conviction that God loves stories. Further, they can see that God has encapsulated his ideas about what the world is to believe within that all-encompassing story that we call the Bible.

The Bible begins with those primeval once-upon-a-time words *bereshith bara elohim*: "In the beginning God created." From that point on, for some thirteen hundred pages, the story unfolds till it reaches that simple Greek happy ever after *amēn, erchou kurie iēsou*: "Amen, come Lord Jesus." Between this grand Hebrew *once upon a time* and this Greek *happy ever after* is an engaging, forty-author tale. The Bible has its nonnarrative moments, for it contains a lot of precepts, such as the Ten Commandments and the Beatitudes. But even these structural propositions are contained within the framework of a great story. In other words, Jews and Christians go to this same great story from which to extrapolate their theologies and propositions. The great teachings of either faith are imbedded in a redeeming narrative. We go to the story to find our theology and not vice versa.

In spite of our narratively founded theology, we are all too often at odds with narrative preaching and how it is to be done. There are many who feel that biblical doctrine must not be left as the business of storytellers. Propositional truths can be categorized and footnoted and structured. Then these structured truths spell out precepts that can be memorized and interpreted in the same way each time we meet them. Like blocks in a cathedral they can be made rigid, righteous, and regulated. They form into hard confessions, concrete covenants, and steely creeds and codes.

Stories, on the other hand, are far more prone to end up as art forms and not dogmatics. They seem just too flexible for some left-brained theologians to enjoy. They seem to be more Jell-O than substance. They are high calorie but void of protein. Because they are more flexible they seem to be subject to a great deal of willowy bending by the storyteller. While they counsel us in memorable and intriguing ways, they sometimes appear dangerously wishy-washy and too weak to secure the great doctrines of the faith.

One need only examine the Bible itself to see that thousands of differing denominations have resulted from some great interpretive disasters. When to have communion, how to baptize, what to think of church government, what to believe about capital punishment, or when Jesus is coming again proves that the shades of interpretation on the Bible have splintered the faith. Not all of these dividing lines were spawned by seeing stories in different ways since many of them arose from quarrels over propositional passages also. But stories and storytellers say the more left-brained expositors are not always honest expositors. And propositional preachers in particular have sometimes developed a view that story (because it seems shifty to the rigid) is not exposition.[1]

This book will hearken back to basic biblical form. Story is not just a biblical literary mode but an authentic communication form used first by God in inspiring Scripture and thus making it commendable for all those who later wish to communicate the "Big Story" in effective ways. Storytelling is not only the best form of getting and keeping attention, it is also a great teacher. Storytelling is a great teacher for two reasons. First, it keeps the audience listening so they can learn. Second, it is easier to remember once the sermon is over.

Still, narrative preaching is an art form. But the artistry of the mode need not intimidate those communicators who want to learn to use it effectively. I am often asked, "Can everyone be a storyteller?" My reply is always yes. The issue is like asking a class of eight year olds, "Can everyone learn to ice skate?" The answer is always yes. Not everyone can be an Olympic medalist, but everyone who is eight years old can learn to skate.

What Does the Term Narrative Sermon *Mean?*

Here at the beginning of the chapter, I would like to get this matter of defining terms out of the way. Many of those who espouse narrative preaching have become dogmatic in defining the narrative sermon as an entire homily preached as a single story. To these homileticians the one story comes uninterrupted by footnote, proposition, or any structured theological insight. To these the story is the sermon and is to be told in such a way so the hearers must do their own application. They must also supply their own insights as they listen. When the sermon is over the listeners are to make of it what they can and to live in light of the parable's truth as they can understand it. The biblical text as it relates to this single story may be quoted at the front or at the last of the story or merely printed in the worship folder. The entire sermon as a single narrative diagrammatically looks like this:

Text   Once upon a time . . .   Happy ever after

Once upon a time . . .   Happy ever after   Text

But I want to widen the definition of narrative preaching to a form that more nearly resembles how the Bible itself tells stories. The Bible is a single story that is composed of a great many lesser stories. It mixes its various stories in with other kinds of literary forms and scrambles precepts and narratives in a potpourri of truth. It is not as altogether inductive as the single-sermon narrators would have us believe. Nor is it true that the sermon as a single story is more effective than the use of multiple stories interlaced with good solid propositional reasoning. Jesus's own preaching seems to indicate that he told stories sandwiched in between the use of other forms of reasoning and all to good effect. What effect?

Well, for one thing every congregation and the world at large is composed of two kinds of orientations. There are right-brained auditors and left-brained auditors all listening to the same sermon. Most of us are some combination of the two forms. So merely telling a story without any help in assimilating it is likely not the best way to make the story understood. I learned this the hard way. Once during a time when I had to be absent from my pulpit, I invited a popular single-story preacher to our church to preach. He preached his seventeen-minute story to about two thousand people gathered in three different services of the church. The next week when I returned home to my pulpit, I was greeted by a lot of controversial sermon reviews of the preacher who had filled the pulpit. Some said, "Have that guy back, he was fascinating." Others said, "Don't ever have that guy back, I didn't understand a thing he said." It was clear to me that those who could ferret out a story and apply it on their own loved the narrative sermon; the others left the service confused as to what they had heard and what the story could have meant.[2]

One wonders if the apostles who traipsed about with Jesus didn't have some of the same comprehension problems. In Matthew 13:16–23 Jesus retells the parable he has just told, possibly for the sake of the left-brained apostles who needed a little help. It is not hard to imagine Jesus saying, "The seed is the word" and having some of them slap their own foreheads and cry, "Aha! Now I get it!" only to hear Jesus say, "and the bird is the devil." An incredulous look clouded their faces just before the light came on. "Oh, the bird is the devil. . . . I get it, now. Why didn't you just say so, Jesus?" Narrative sermons are still sermons that everybody should get. They shouldn't play favorites to people who like the baroque and dramatic. If anybody is left behind in a congregation of a thousand, the preacher has not preached well. The left-brained do, after all, have a right to understand those pulpit narratives their right-brained friends cherish. Sermons are for everyone, and preachers should reach out to be inclusive.

The best way to be all-inclusive is to mix the sermon's content with good stories that illumine the precepts and to teach the precepts that apply the stories to the truth of the text. The best model is not so much a linear trail but a stacked sandwich.[3] If it be not too ludicrous, I like thinking of the best mixture of precept and story as a "Dagwood sandwich" of precepts and various sermon forms all stacked together. For more than half a century, the comic strip hero Dagwood Bumstead made comic strip sandwiches. A Bumstead sermonic sandwich would look like this: the bottom sliced of bread is the text, and the top slice is the altar, where the persuader applies the text to the audience and asks them to make a decision on the theme of the text. Therefore, the best model of the narrative sermon would look something like this:

Altar
⇑
Application
⇑
Poem
⇑
Narrative
⇑
Adages
⇑
Narrative
⇑
Statistics
⇑
Narrative
⇑
Supporting Scriptures
⇑
Proposition
⇑
Narrative
⇑
Text

I teach young ministers to preach by constructing their sermons from what I call sermonic forms. Sermonic forms are the basic literary forms out of which sermons can be constructed. There are six of these. I include after all of these the word *text* because I want students to see that all of the forms bear a single obligation to illustrate the text. The text mandates the contents and application of every service form.

Narrative text—stories that illustrate the text

Poem text—poetry that emotionalizes the application of the text

Statistic text—proposition percentages that illustrate the text

Supporting Scriptures text—other places in Scripture that offer further illustration of the sermon text

Story text—a third person story illustrating the text

Personal illustration text—a confessional tale in which preachers relate their own life events to demonstrate the text

The question you may be asking is, "How does your model differ from preaching and illustrating as it has always been done?" The answer is that it differs not at all from great preaching as it has always been done, with this exception: the emphasis on story is far stronger than that traditionally put on the sermon. Further it recognizes that story is as important as the propositions, both in communicating the truth and in holding people's attention.

Great preaching is a mind-set which allows the preacher to see that storytelling is godly and effective, and any attempt to minimize the importance of story as an illustration of the all-important, almighty proposition is to misunderstand the importance of the art given to all great communicators. Precept and story share equally in comprising the sermon's communiqué. Both of them work together in preparing and preaching the image-driven sermon.

Letting the Text Control All Sermon Narratives

But above all else in importance is a controlling text. The controlling text sets the theme and (if the sermon is developed in this way) perhaps sets a thesis above all that is said. This passage or verse, or even portion of a verse, forces all that is said in any one of the sermonic forms to comply in such a way that they fit into the whole. The sermon in no part should ever stray (either to chase a pet theme or some distraction) from where the preacher has set the homily to travel. This text is the sermonic umpire crying "safe" or "foul" to each new verbal entrance into the homiletic show.

Returning to our paradigm sermon on Balaam's donkey, the controlling text in this example is Numbers 22:35: "Speak only what I tell you." Obedience is the theme, and the motif we established was: "Disobedience to God is a reckless path." The idea of grace may be a great theme with you, and you simply love talking about grace. But this passage is not about grace. You may reason that just by bending the idea of "reckless disobedience" you could easily bring the matter up, though you need to be careful. Does this particular passage speak about grace? What does your controlling text say? What does the motif say?

Yes, but you heard a very famous preacher use an illustration you are just busting to use. This is a real lollapalooza that will have them crying in the aisles. The illustration is so forceful it would make your uncle Herman repent. It is so wonderful it will make you feel eternally sorry for Spurgeon for not knowing about it. It is better than anything you could remotely cram under the aegis of the controlling text. Should you use it?

How you answer that question shows the difference between a great preacher and sideshow barker. Show your true scholarship. Keep the illustration for a Sunday when it would fit. Use these sermonic forms in ways that allow your best, most persuasive style. Stick to those things which the controlling text permits.

Moving from Precept to Metaphor by Examining the Words

We have spoken about how the creative preacher can begin with a word study and find the metaphorical content of the word study and then fashion a story from it. But let's examine how it works the other way around. Our motif for the paradigm passage is: "Disobedience to God is a reckless path." This is a precept, and we might look at the Hebrew words which comprise the actual verse and arrive at a word study that would give us the metaphor, and then let that metaphor suggest an illustration.

But to demonstrate how to move from precept to metaphor, let us simply take the motif as it is and let an English word study of the sermon's motif suggest a metaphor that might bring us a story or an illustration to illumine the propositional sermon. The brief words found in the motif are but three: *disobedience, reckless,* and *path*.

Parsing the Sermon Motif
"Disobedience to God is a Reckless Path"

Disobedience

Modern meaning: "to fail to comply with command."

The prefix *dis* negates this strong basic word, which comes from two Latin pieces: *ob*, "in the direction of," plus *audire*, "to hear." In other words, to move in the direction of what you have heard, or to follow a command.

The definition "to fail to comply to a command" might suggest a story about some military officer who did or did not comply with command:

- In the Bible, Joab disobeys the king's command not to harm Absalom (2 Sam. 18:5–15).
- In 1945 the United States gave an ultimatum to Japan to surrender, but Japan ignored the command and the atomic destruction of Hiroshima and Nagasaki resulted.
- On September 11, 2001, terrorists issued an order to the passengers of United Flight 93, and the passengers disobeyed, possibly saving the intended target—the White House. The plane crashed in a field near Shanksville, Pennsylvania, in Somerset County. The White House was spared. This is a clear case that it is better to obey God than terrorists.
- *Obedientiary*, a second-class officer in a medieval monastery with no will of his own, subject to the command of anyone above him. So should the Christian be.

Reckless

This English word comes from the Old English word *recceleas*, which comes from the German base *reck*, meaning "care." The word means "careless." It also relates to another old English verb *reck*, which means "to pay heed," or "take notice." Therefore the word *reckless* basically means "heedless" or "careless."

While the English word study backing up this word is less useable, it is nonetheless a good word to talk about "paying heed."

Balaam should have paid attention to his donkey.

If Paris had heeded Priam's word, there would have been no Trojan War.

If Napoleon had heeded all his counselors who told him not to try to take Moscow, they might be speaking French in Poland now.

Think of all the places Jesus said, "Take heed":

- Take heed in how you give alms (Matt. 6:1).
- Take heed to beware of the leaven of the Pharisees (Matt. 16:6).
- Take heed never to despise a child (Matt. 18:10).
- The New Testament lists forty-one other places where the phrase "take heed" is used.

Path

This word comes from an Old English noun *pæth*, meaning "a course of travel" or "a way of action."

A course of travel is always a course that begins where we are with some end in mind.

President Bush has repeatedly said, "Stay the course!" in Iraq.

Ahead is the course for the brave; to deviate from the path is never to reach the destination.

Jesus called himself "the Path" or "the Way" in John 14:6.

Of course nothing does this with quite the charm or power as working in the original languages of the Bible, but as we see in the word study above, it works very well even if we stay completely in the English.

Going through this word study makes it easy to tell that as a teacher of preaching, I stay very close to words and their meanings. I have simply learned across almost fifty years of writing sermons that words hold the greatest possibility for making sure I properly exegete and expose a text. This should not seem unreasonable. Words are our *métier*: they are to the preacher what the palette is to the artist. Words are what we paint with, and the images that emerge from our paintings provide the congregation with insight and inspiration.[4]

I realize that it is possible to paste more significance onto the word than the biblical writers possibly did. Speech and writing demands come too fast for us to dissect each word we put in a communiqué. When I say that a certain storm was a disaster, I do not think to stop and exegete the word *storm* ("a disturbance," probably from the Old High German *sturm*) nor do I exegete the word *disaster* (from the prefix *dis*, which means "separated from," and *aster*, which means the "stars"). Yet if I stop to examine the phrase, it might suggest any number of things I had missed by not going more slowly.

I once heard a Greek lexicographer talking about Koine Greek, the street Greek in which the New Testament was written. He reminded us that biblical Greek was not just a language in which people wrote books of the Bible. It was the language in which shoppers spoke as they wrapped their fish purchased in the market, and the language base men talked as they conversed with prostitutes. So when Paul says, "We are God's workmanship" (Eph. 2:10), he doesn't think *I'll just put the word* poiema *in here for* workmanship *to help future exegetes write sermons*. He used the words in a far more conversational mode, which we later exegete. Nonetheless, such words become good springboards for building a highly image-driven sermon.[5]

Retelling the Biblical Story

Just a minimal bit of paying attention to the words of a narrative passage can yield rich results. But what is the next step of seeing the entire sermon in a story mode? Just how much can be done in our paradigm passage to enlarge our focus on the story? In the passage considered earlier about Balaam, it is a good idea to write out the story as creatively as you can to simply tell the story already there. The story is fascinating, but in retelling it you want to keep as close to the elements of the plot as they exist in the story. Even so, my favorite adage is: "To the storyteller belongs the art."[6] So much might be done to enlarge upon the story by simply telling it as it actually happened in another way.

There is little use in retelling the story unless there is something to be gained in terms of riveting the story into the hearers' minds, and to do this the story must be told in a quite different way. Retelling the story still will firmly plant the controlling text, theme, and motif in a way that cannot be done as well in simply reading the story once from the Bible. Here's one way the story of Balaam might be recast and retold.

Recasting the Paradigm Story

The day was hot. Flies buzzed at the sweat that soaked the cowl that hung about his neck like a coil of rank rope. Balaam sweltered under an argument of his own making. He wanted to obey God, but that was completely impossible when he considered what would happen to him once the hordes of Israelites were through tramping about his native land. Balak the king wanted him to do one simple thing: curse Israel. As Balak saw it, Israel was the curse! They were three million strong cutting a wide swath of destruction as they passed through the land—not their land; their land was Canaan. But his land! The king wanted Balaam, this chief of all diviners, to curse Israel, for his curses were known far and wide to be effective.

Balaam smiled. He was good at divining things. He could split a frog gigged from the Red Sea at midnight, and from the splay of entrails tell who would rule Egypt for the next one hundred years. He could predict things too. He foretold the collapse of a tower in the Delta of the Nile, and predicted the droughts that plagued the Negev, merely by burning the feathers of a raven which died in the Wadi of Death. He was the wizard of wizards, and the king would pay him major shekels to whomp up a curse and spew it out over the advancing hordes of Moses. He wanted the money, but he just didn't want to tick God off by cursing the people of God. So he saddled his donkey and rode in the opposite direction of God's will.

Bad idea.

The wizard of the day turned out to be the donkey.

As if he didn't feel badly enough, he got into a conversation with the old mare. "Hey! What gives, Balaam? What have I ever done to you to get you to beat me these three times?"

Balaam was so hot under the collar that he was filled with road rage: "You have made a fool out of me. If I had a sword you'd be off to the glue factory."

"Kill me? Why? Haven't I always been a good little donkey?"

Then poof! There stood the angel of God.

"Listen up, Balaam!" said the angel. "You may be good at divination, but you need to take a short course on common sense. When a stupid man gets a chance to hear from a very bright donkey, he ought to listen. God has a plan for you, Balaam. It involves obedience. And right now it looks like your donkey is better at obedience than you are."

"Okay, Okay," said Balaam, "I'll go back with the emissaries of Balak and even if it costs me my life I will obey."

The angel patted the foolish wizard on the head and said, "That's more like it. And you better do it this time. That donkey's got a lot more to say to you, and every word of it comes from the God of Israel. You may be an Arab wise man, but that donkey is God's donkey."

The angel was gone.

Balaam offered the donkey a sugar cube. The donkey didn't move.

"Isn't one enough?" asked the confused prophet.

"Make it two," said the donkey, "and I'll think about it." It was the last words the donkey ever said in Hebrew. She went back to hee-haws after that, and Balaam went back to obedience. He had learned the truth that obedience to God will nearly always shut up a loudmouth donkey.

There are enlargements in the story as retold above. Is this permissible? Will the people get confused if they hear the story being told in some other way than the Bible tells it? Generally not. Hyperbole is a good mode for making a story interesting as long as the hearer can distinguish the mode of the story as it is retold. Exaggeration intrigues as long as it is clear that the story is being exaggerated.

Hyperbole overdoes the truth with exaggeration in order that when the exaggeration is stripped away the truth is ever more clear than it was before. The late Erma Bombeck described the truth by overdoing the truth in almost every column she wrote. In one of her columns she alleged that she never skipped dessert. "Think of all the women on the Titanic who skipped dessert . . . and for what?" Were there women on the Titanic who skipped dessert? Maybe, maybe not. The point lies somewhere else. She said on another occasion that she knew women who were so skinny that when they finished their workout at the health club, vultures followed them to their cars. The simile is not literal, just a good oratorical device. Did Balaam really offer his donkey a sugar cube? The point lies elsewhere.

But once you pass beyond retelling the biblical story in another way, the work of story is only beginning. There are other parts to the passage that deserve accent and the parallel fascination that story can add to it. "Disobedience to God is a reckless path," says the sermon motif. Are there other instances in the Bible of saints or sinners who took that reckless path? Have you, the preacher, ever taken such a path? Did the poets? Wordsworth, Keats, Billy Collins, Sylvia Plath? On and on the opportunities begin to unfold as word studies become metaphors and metaphors suggest stories.[7]

Learning the Art of Clean Writing

In writing sermons—as in every area of storytelling—it is best to master the art of descriptive writing in the use of good nouns and verbs instead of modifiers. For instance, it is better to say:

His mood froze his face in furrows of grudge.

than to say,

His face was hard and cold.

The adjectives in the second sample are much weaker than the nouns in the first. Likewise, it is better to say:

He traipsed the flagstones in light.

than to say,

His felted feet flew silently over the solemn stones.

This kind of "substantive" thinking is a harder art to master than the use of modifiers which always lie nearer at hand. Adjectives and adverbs are tack-on and insert words and are generally much easier to tack on and insert than finding the words they modify. Great substantives need no modifiers, but they are harder to find and put in place. Notice the strength in the simplicity of Longfellow's comment on Paul Revere:

> One, if by land, and two, if by sea;
> And I on the opposite shore shall be,
> Ready to ride and spread the alarm
> To every Middlesex village and farm.

There exists in these thirty words only one modifying adjective and one adverb. The result is a kind of lucidity that would not be available had the poet insisted on filling his sentences with weaker modifiers.

The same is generally true of famous quips and quotes:

To be, or not to be: that is the question.

Consider the lilies of the field.

In the beginning God created the heavens and the earth.

There is a tide in the affairs of men / Which, taken at the flood, leads on to fortune; / Omitted, all the voyage of their life / Is bound in shallows and in misery.

Remember the Alamo!

For to me to live is Christ, and to die is gain.

None of these brilliant lines is marred by a single adjective.

Strong substantives are the slowly gathered, omnipotently simple words of the great wordsmiths. Adjectives and adverbs lengthen sentences and weaken them as they do. "Ye must be born again," is vintage Jesus. "Ye must have a redemptive and soteriological time of spiritual regeneration" is longer, not clearer, not memorable, not persuasive.

Learning the Art of Character Building

Stories consist of two parts. The first is plot, the second is character. Of the two, plot is the part that is far more instrumental in illustrating the sermon. But plot alone generally does not hold the interest one finds in good character development. As far as the teachings of Jesus go, his sermon stories are generally all about plot. I often cite this to those who ask, "Can just anyone tell a story?" As we said earlier, the answer is yes. But those who can successfully make a story live are those who can develop characters to the point that hearers are intrigued by the people in the story and not just their circumstances.

In Jesus' stories we have no idea about just what kind of people he told stories about. We know nothing of their temperament, their lifestyles, their moods, their goals, or their aspirations. We don't know what they looked like, nor generally what they believed about the world from which Jesus lifted their stories. But we want to develop characters that add a real sense of intrigue to the illustration we are using. There are four rules that make this happen.

First, describe a character in terms of someone that everyone knows. How is the character like Ebenezer, Shrek, Charlie Brown, Pollyanna, etc.? Simply to refer to any well-known literary symbol will push the image into the minds of your listeners. Does this person have a physique like a Greek god, a rock star, or the Pillsbury Doughboy? Does the woman at the center of your story have a demeanor like Eva Braun, Eva Perón, or Eva Gabor? Does she have arms like Rosie the Riveter or Arnold Schwarzenegger? Does a little girl seem as cute as Shirley Temple, as captivating as Annie, or as much to be feared as Lizzie Borden?

I have a sermon in which I describe the man who lived next door to us when I was growing up. The man seemed to me to be like Harper Lee's Boo Radley. While Boo, this odd and yet wonderful man in *To Kill a Mockingbird*, is the hero of the novel, he is aloof and appears sinister to all who know him. I describe a wheezing old man in another of my sermons as breathing like Darth Vader inside his black helmet. Be careful that your descriptions of anyone don't become unkind. To say his ears "stuck out like a taxi with both doors open" may be so unkind as to ruin you with your listeners. Watch malapropisms like "ditsy blondes" or "big palookas" or "scurvy little weasels." It's not that these phrases are altogether false, but they block the development of character by overdoing the descriptions. Also, they are politically unfriendly.

Second, liken the character to the most evident traits of those you describe. "Scrooge was a tight-fist at the grindstone." Yoda was all eyes and ears. Niobe, said Virgil, "was all tears." Judas was as tight as the purse he kept. Magdalene wasn't a woman, really—she was a cry for forgiveness. Paul's soul was a wound kept bloody by a thorn. Peter was all impulse and dare. David was a poet who traded praise for deceit and left his psalms for lust. Hosea was a man who couldn't quit loving and wouldn't keep weeping. Job tore his soul with question marks. John the Baptist was a trumpet. Jeremiah, a wailing cry in a time of war.

Learn to think of the characters you describe in terms of one good, short simile that overdraws the image. Take the bridegroom in the Song of Solomon, for instance. Is he

a stag in the springtime of love,

a warrior just back from the battles of life,

a lover made hungry for the pleasures of the desert, or

a gardener in love with the first new blossoms of marriage?

Applying these similes in a single line will give your sermons a sensory edge, and when any communiqué grows sensory, people feel the power of the biblical text.

Third, tell how you experienced the character you describe, especially in those illustrations where you are involved in meeting someone. How were you in contrast to the person whom you describe? Did he dwarf you? Was she so charming that in merely meeting her you felt like a bumpkin? When you shook his hand was it fishlike and limp?

Was his arm a mass of steel hard as tungsten underneath his shirt? Did she remind you of the librarian in your hometown, who was wizened and sharp-featured? Did the waitress have a row of gold studs running down her ear? Was there a steel brad in her lip? Did he have a tattoo that said "Mother" beneath the one that said "Harley Davidson"?

Fourth, how did the character speak? Did they drip mint julep? Were they honey-tongued? Did their hoarseness cause them to sound like Donald Duck? Did they rasp, sing off-key, or coo like a dove? Did they bellow, rattle, or whisper?

All of these things help an audience in positioning the character you are trying to describe. You don't actually have to drop into the kind of voice that they used, but you must present anything they said in such a manner that the audience is picking up on how the character talked. Very few storytellers do dialogue very well, but even those who don't can present a character in such a way that those who hear can supply the style and content of the person's speech.

The key is to work on it and write out the illustration magnifying the kind of character that is vital to your sermon illustration. Caring about character development is the first step to actually being able to produce it when you are up in front of the church.

The Moral: Applying the Story to the Text

It is obvious that the application of any story to the text will be much easier if the text has been given the almighty right to govern the sermon all the way along. If the text has been allowed to control the assembly and delivery of the sermon, then of course the application will be much easier to manage.

The moral was a typical feature of all storytelling in the earlier centuries. It was always easier to ferret out in the decades past.[8] In every novel, morals swim over us, as the following examples demonstrate.

> Scarlett O'Hara in *Gone with the Wind* makes this moral point: The selfish regard we have for ourselves in the good times is of little use in the tough times.
>
> In the novel that bears his name, *Silas Marner* offers us the tale of a miser who changed his value system.
>
> Darth Vader is proof in the *Star Wars* saga that evil never wins.
>
> Frodo Baggins stands out in the *Fellowship of the Ring* because he wears his Middle-Earth responsibility with unshirking allegiance and becomes in Tolkien's trilogy the very picture of the virtue of commitment.

But sermons go a step further in making a definite moral point. Sermons, far more than novels, exist to be changers of behavior and opinion. Sermons are heart cries to make some point that is crucial to God become crucial also to the believer. The following examples show this at work.

> A. J. Gossip's sermon "When Life Tumbles In, What Then?" was delivered by the noble preacher after the death of his wife to talk about the importance of God's love in times of tragedy.
>
> Martin Luther King Jr.'s "I Have a Dream" was a call to moral arms in a society that too long had condoned racial prejudice.
>
> R. G. Lee's sermon "Payday Someday" was a reminder that a willful path of sin will in time destroy those who think they can beat the system.

T. D. Jakes' sermon (later a book and then a movie) "Woman Thou Art Loosed" is a call to women to accept their God-given right to full citizenship in the world community.

Peter Marshall's sermon "Keeper of the Springs" is a call to mothers to stand up and continue dredging the pollution from American families in order to raise up a moral generation.

The difference between the idyllic novel and the sermon is that the sermon is called to be less elusive about the point it cries out to make. The sermon must call upon the listener to agree that God is the sponsor of the sermon's point, and thus to be in harmony with God is to adopt the sermon's agenda as the rule of life. This high view of the sermon reminds all listeners that God too has convictions, and these convictions are the reason for all preaching.

Once again we arrive at a point of dialectic with those who promote the "new homiletics" general approach to pulpit story-telling. Some would teach that the story has the burden to set the moral forth without specifically asking the listener to adopt it. The point of the story is the reason for telling the story and therefore when the simple truth is presented, the narrative alone is all that is needed to instruct the hearers as to the truth they are being asked to adopt.

But clarity is all important. The preacher must spell out the relationship of every sermon's story to the sermon's text, and the two must make the very same point. May they not ask for two different morals—if both are noble—to be accepted? No, they may not. The sermon has a single point to make and every part of the sermon must play its part in making that point. If any other point is to be made, it sidetracks the major point. If the sermon speaks with strength to establish any other argument, that argument must be set forth in some other sermon.

But spelling out the moral in an image-driven sermon is, to some degree, less imperative. The connection between what an individual story is trying to say is so firmly imbedded in the sermon's thesis and motif that the connection will be obvious.

The sermon story is simply going where the entire sermon is going and saying what the whole sermon is saying.

The Use of Your Own Pilgrimage as the Heart of the Story

How much should the story of your own pilgrimage hold its place among the various illustrations of the sermon? The answer gathers about the dividing line that separates narcissism from story force. Generally speaking, all of us like first person stories. Garrison Keillor never allows himself to become too separate from his Lake Wobegon roots. The fact that his stories are fictional is never allowed to pry him away from the force of those tales that have convinced us that these people, in one way or another, are his people. These stories, in one way or another, are his stories.

The preacher must go further than Keillor, however, in assuring his audience that all first person narratives are true. Still, in telling true stories his adage is also true: The story is the teller's art. That is to say that the pulpit raconteur must stake his integrity on what he says. The force of the sermon gathers from the audience assumption that everything I am hearing is the truth. But while truth is the absolute requirement for all that appears in a sermon, remember, truth can be very pedestrian. Yet it isn't just the preacher's personal stories that must be creative; the same goes for the preacher's handling of the truth. All of the book of Leviticus is truth, but not all of it makes for riveting reading in the minds of many postmodern churchgoers. So the creative mind must supply the interest in more plodding truth by the way we tell that truth.

Am I suggesting that we lie about the truth or even introduce fictional elements into the truth merely to make it more interesting? Certainly not. But I am suggesting that in relating a true story, care should be taken to tell the truth in the most riveting way. In the retelling of the narrative Scripture of our paradigm text about Balaam, we can easily isolate the elements of the retelling that correspond to those taken from Scripture.

Fictional Elements Added to the Biblical Account

The day was hot.
The flies were buzzing about his open collar.
Concerning his donkey, Balaam was hot under the collar.

Balaam was a good diviner who could read the fortunes of na-
tions in frog entrails.

The angel said concerning obedience that Balaam's donkey was
smarter than he was.

The repentant diviner offered his donkey an appeasing sugar
cube.

The donkey said, "Make it two, and I'll think about it."

Most all of these imaginary elements increase audience interest,
and yet do not violate the intent of the Word. If the preacher is
concerned that these enlargements might be confusing or mislead-
ing to the congregation, a qualification can be mentioned such as:
"It would be easy for me to see the plight of this pagan diviner in
this way." Then the preacher may proceed with the story and its
creative enhancements. But when the imagined story is told in
the straightforward manner as suggested, most people will have
no trouble separating the imaginary elements from the original
tale as it appears in Scripture, particularly when the text is read
at the beginning of the sermon.

The preacher's own ability to tell an interesting and true story
should lie in the way he approaches a tale. Here are the non-
negotiables that cannot be altered when telling a story in which
the preacher is involved.

Unalterable, Nonfictional Story Elements

The certainty that this recounting actually happened in the manner and at the time described and that the circumstances and
reactions surrounding the tale must surely be in place.

Date and time in the story, if used, must be true.

The outcome of the story must be exactly as it was in the event
being told.

If there are other players in the tale, they too must be reported
exactly as they took part in the tale. (Their names, even
genders, may need to be changed to protect both them and
you.)

The elements that can be and should be enlarged upon are as
follows.

Points for Creative Enhancement

Your reaction to the events.

Insights you gained.

Your feelings and hopes and fears.

Your changed life and altered values that resulted from the memoir.

How you relate this life-changing tale to the text.

But of all the rules which guide your storytelling, nothing is more important than your style. Your storytelling style can only be gained by a continual pulpit mystique whereby people come to know you and accept you as you are. Then the ease with which you slip in and out of a story and the impact you gain by being yourself while you tell your tale will in the telling be seen as a natural and effective part of your argument.

Literal Image, Literary Image, Paralleling

Let us turn our attention to consider a most powerful combination of narrative force with the power of the text set in an image-driven matrix. How do you combine the images and tone of your sermon with the best of literary insights from powerful classic texts that might illumine or add clout to the sermon text? This effect can be overdone but used in moderation such a combination can be powerful indeed. In this day when the classics have been all but neglected, their thoughtful introduction into a sermon will seem unique and perhaps welcome.

The task falls upon the preacher to consider what classic texts might be pulled alongside the biblical narrative to illustrate it. There have been several synopses and guides to the classics that are brief and tell the story that comprises a classic within a few paragraphs. Often these have been called one-minute classics or some such title. The one I keep at hand is called *The American Bathroom Book*. I keep the volume at hand when preparing a sermon, for it contains the two-paged synopses of around three hundred books. The characters, plots, or content of those books are clearly splayed to refresh the reader on what the whole unabridged volume contains. Within these three hundred books are thirty biographies (everyone from Euclid to Malcolm X), sixty-five fictional classics (from *The Scarlet Letter* to *Faust*), and a huge section on nonfictional contemporary classics on motivation, leadership, and business.

The key is to isolate the sermon's theme, thesis, and controlling text. Then consult such a guide to ask whether or not there is enough strong narrative or information (in the case of the nonfictional text) to enlarge the sermon with a strong truth.

How would sermon planning be done in such a way that the wisdom of these classics could serve as a parallel to add force to the biblical text? Consider the table listed below.

Text	Focus	Classic author or work
Exodus 18	The importance of delegation	Ken Blanchard
Deuteronomy 1	Leadership vision	Tom Peters
Joshua 1	Leadership in crisis	Winston Churchill
Joshua 24	Family life	Richard Steele
Ruth	Committed love	*Little Women*
John 4	On prejudice	*To Kill a Mockingbird*
Proverbs 31	The virtuous woman	*Our Town*
John 15:13	Self-sacrifice	*A Tale of Two Cities*

The payoff for the skillful use of this marriage of Scripture and the classics is well worth the effort required to do it well. I have a sermon in which I blend the plaintive lines of King Lear with those plaintive lines of David mourning the loss of Absalom. The dramatic tone of Lear is this:

> No, no, no life!
> Why should a dog, a horse, a rat, have life,
> And thou no breath at all? Thou'lt come no more,
> Never, never, never, never, never!
>
> "King Lear," act 5, scene 3, lines 308–10

David's grieving over Absalom goes like this:

> O my son Absalom! My son, my son Absalom! If only I had died instead of you—O Absalom, my son, my son!
>
> 2 Samuel 18:33

The tones of the passages are so similar it is both easy and dramatic to marry the passages in such a way that Shakespeare lends to David's anguish. As we have said before, when the passages are combined the drama should not be footnoted, lest the literary spell of the combined texts be lost.

One of my students preached on Mephibosheth from 2 Samuel 9. The plaintive case of the poor crippled son of Jonathan was noticeably close to that of Quasimodo in the *Hunchback of Notre Dame*. He quoted a passage from the novel describing the state of this pitiable creature whom grace set free on the bell ropes of the great cathedral, and there was Mephibosheth, or was it Quasimodo who flew? And we the audience flew with the cripple who trusted grace and dined at the king's table. The marriage of the Bible and Victor Hugo was powerful enough to cause us to adore the Christ whose grace sets every cripple free.

The same paralleling of Gabriel's appearance to Mary in Luke 1 can be easily coupled and smoothly added to Walt Wangerin's "Advent Monologue." The text "For to me to live is Christ" in Philippians 1 can be easily attached to the "Breastplate of St. Patrick." The passage in Acts 9 describing Paul's conversion can be coupled to John Bunyan's *Pilgrim's Progress*. Christian ran "till he came at a place somewhat ascending, and upon that place stood a Cross, and a little below it, in the bottom, a Sepulchre. So I saw in my Dream, that just as *Christian* came up to the *Cross*, his Burden loosed from off his shoulders, and fell from off his back, and began to tumble, and so continued to do, till it came to the mouth of the Sepulchre, where it fell in, and I saw it no more."

Other examples include Robert Heinlein's description of the second coming which could be easily attached to what Paul has to say about it in 1 and 2 Thessalonians. Or the book of Jonah could be coupled with Francis Thompson's great lines from "The Hound of Heaven":

> I fled Him, down the nights and down the days;
> I fled Him, down the arches of the years;
> I fled Him, down the labyrinthine ways
>   Of my own mind; and in the midst of tears
> I hid from Him, and under running laughter.

On and on the possibilities go of how the best of literature can be pulled—often done best in a few lines only—to strengthen the drama and impact of the sermon.

Keeping a Sense of "Apocalypse" as the Sermon's Finale

If any real comparison is to exist between preaching and telling the story, it must be that both of them must maintain the quality of apocalypse. The special ending is what makes a special story special. The same must be said for the sermon. As Shakespeare counseled us, all's well that ends well. And all is splendid which ends with a dominant sense of apocalypse. Remember that *apocalypse* comes from a Greek substantive that means to "reveal." It has the implication of "drawing the drapes." It is essentially a word that means to "draw out of hiding."

The best of apocalypse may be illustrated by the power of an unopened bag or box. What is hidden in the box or bag hides the force that lies at the center of the word *apocalypse*. But this undisclosed object is truth that keeps people listening. The apocalyptic finish to the sermon should not only keep the best parts of the sermon till the last, but use the "upper-level interest" communication device to produce an unforgettable conclusion. Movies and novels do not have to post the words "the end" to tell us they are over. This we know without being told. Both the story and the screenplay have led us compulsively to accede that our final interest is so great and so conclusive that we know the story is over.

So should it be for the sermon.

But to make this happen a great deal of craft is necessary. The danger in extemporary speaking is that the peacher's ad-lib style is prone to wander around the final post rather than make a beeline for it. This has been particularly true of evangelical preachers. The failure to see the sermon as a *narratio* with a definite beginning and end has been a weakness. The word *homily* itself may contribute to the indefinite ending since it means a "conversation," and conversations are generally informal and sometimes lingering. Further, in terms of the local pastor, community is the milieu, and living at the center of a community can keep sermons so relational and informal that crafting a specific end with a written form of any sort seems to war against the warm fabric of our togetherness.

Three dangers arise with an imprecise ending. The first danger of an indefinite conclusion is a loss of the sermon's significance. Unless some point is dramatically made the sermon will seem to have no point. This is one advantage of using a sermon motif as we discussed earlier. If the final crafting of the conclusion is strong and fits together with the sermon's strong motif, this can be one way to assure that the sermon will be memorable.

What's said last is what we carry longest, generally speaking. So the preacher must be sure to say last what is to be taken home and cherished or heeded by the congregation. If possible, this should be revelatory. The last moments of the sermon should "draw the drapes" on the brightest insights of all that's been said. The Scripture should come shining through here. If there is a story or poem that makes the sermon text unforgettable, it should stand at the end and dramatically demand the listener to package the truth and lock it up in the mind.

A second failure of an imprecise finale to the sermon is a loss of drama. There is virtually no Scripture well preached that wants for drama. But unless the preacher is willing to struggle with crafting the apocalypse, the greatest of texts will wander off the edge of the abyss, merely from the preacher's lack of respect for a well-planned ending. Drama is the result of two things: passion and craft. Passion sells and craft makes the purchase worthy and memorable. Without craft, passion degenerates into sound and fury; without passion, the art of even the best sermon preparation goes unremembered.

A third weakness of the noncrafted conclusion is anticlimax. For my part no novel, movie, or sermon succeeds which allows the best part of the craft to occupy a place too far forward in the performance. The strongest story, poem, or insight should reign over the ending. If the fire burns too early in a presentation, a kind of haunting absence may occupy the conclusion. People may have liked the earlier fireworks, but they ache because they cannot feel that same intensity at the end.

Consider Jesus, the master preacher: he put the story of the two homebuilders at the end of the Sermon on the Mount. All of the sermon is glorious, but the homebuilder's story is more riveting than the precepts which precede it. The same could be said for Amos' sermon where he spends a chapter preaching to Israel's enemies before he turns to denounce the sins of Israel. See Peter's sermon on Pentecost, or Paul's defense before Agrippa. Always the strongest part is last: there is no anticlimax.

So we who preach are the masters of apocalypse. We know how to "unveil" truth and wrap the endings of our unveilings in drama. We know how to draw the drapes and reveal the Word. We also know what to show just before we draw the drapes and conclude the sermon. We are artisans, dramatists, expositors. We care about the Bible and are committed to setting the Word free as a circus performer releases the lion from the cage. It is the lion that has power. It is the trainer who sets the drama, wide open and free so that people might fear and hear, wonder and celebrate the Word, not the artisan.

We who preach are in the mighty business of craft and study. Passion is not what we practice to achieve, it is the gut force we cannot escape. Craft, however, rises from our discipline. And here we make God appear as powerful as he is and the text just as almighty merely by caring about how we say things and about how our adoration of him keeps us from that lazy spirit that will not plan and cares too little about the kingdom.

As we conclude the issues of story and apocalypse let us return to five great questions that will enable us to craft and direct our narrative expositions.

SERMON PLANNING SHEET
PART 3

How can I "narrativize" this sermon?

What biblical genre is this?

What can I do within this presentation to make sure that the people understand, feel, and appreciate the genre?

_____

_____

_____

_____

What can I keep in hiding that will furnish the homily with an "aha" moment?

_____

_____

_____

_____

_____

What can I hide to be drawn into the light as the sermon concludes and thus lock the final part of my argument into the listener's soul?

_____

_____

_____

_____

_____

Part 3

Preaching
the Sermon

8

Style

Delivering the Sermon

Style. What is it exactly? Style is a way of being, a mode of self-expression. It is the outgoing definition of the personality expressing itself in artful ways. It may rise from the subliminal, but it is upfront with its exhibitionism. Style cannot hide itself. It is self-declaring. It is what we are when we are right out in front of the world. Style either endears us to the gawking globe or it condemns us. Except for the good Dr. Jekyll, and a few other bipolar souls, no person has two styles. Everybody has one, and when we meet anyone with two, we keep them at arm's length. I had a narcissistic roommate in a doctoral seminar on one occasion who was infatuated with the mirror as long as he was standing in front of it. Every looking glass for him was a wonderland of indulgence. He never walked anywhere; he strutted at all times. Even in the privacy of our room he wore blue silk pajamas which were monogrammed with his initials. Pajama monograms seem to be pointless since those who wear them generally don't wear them in public, though the monograms suggest that such people have an inner urge to do so. I have met few souls so dedicated to themselves as he was. I have no idea how he preached. I am sure he said nice things about God since preachers tend to do that. But I wondered if he changed his persona in the pulpit. I wondered if there in his pulpit robe the word *God* had two syllables. I know of nothing that is more of a turn-off than preachers whose pulpit audio misaligns with their day-to-day voices. I now believe that every basso pretense to a Sinai pulpit style springs from an ego-Shaddai syndrome. Such preachers may have a yen to wear monogrammed pajamas. The style that best engages a healthy congregation is born in the barbershop, the auto supply store, the do-it-yourself manual, coaching little league, and the school of hard knocks. Listeners prefer preachers who don't sound like one. Normal sounding preachers are easily heard for two reasons. First, when a plain speaking preacher says, "Thus saith the Lord," he makes it very clear that he's quoting God and not trying to be God. Second, a plain-talk preacher will not ask you to struggle with any agenda he has not daily set for himself. Such a man is undivided by pretense. He is Jekyll without Hyde. He wears no masks. He has never put a slug in a pay phone. He is afraid to call himself by any other name or lobby for his own viewpoint in the pulpit. He really believes Jesus might come again at eleven o'clock on Sunday, and the pulpit would be the very worst place to be caught masquerading as a saint.

Style—the inimitable trait is composed of chromosomes, DNA, and the ricochet of an honest soul off the environment around it. It all adds up to the most admirable of all preaching traits. Envy Swindoll, Spurgeon, and Peter Marshall if you will, but even they cannot exposit the Word as only you can. Do not envy them for their style. Their popularity is but a little edge that declares their style but does nothing to detract from your own. Being who you are is much easier than trying to be who they are, and it is so much more authentic and useful to your listeners. But more than authentic, it is properly persuasive. We never have more power to influence an audience than when we are busy about being ourselves and telling the world how we feel about God and his expectations for the church and the human race.

Being You in the Pulpit

Years ago I wrote a tribute to my own DNA and it has been quoted in various anthologies of children's poetry.

"I-Ness"

I'm me, and my "I-ness" is special to me.
Minus my "I-ness" I'd just be like you,
And you'd be like me and that's nothing new.
"You-ness" looks good, but only on you.
'Cause "you-ness" won't fit where "I-ness" should be.
My "I-ness" looks great, but only on me.

All of us shrink back from the notion that we are worthy to take the pulpit and become the chief expositor of truth. To employ a cliché, "It is a rotten job, but somebody's got to do it!" And those who do it best accept their calling and then live somewhat uneasily with it for the rest of their lives. But the attempt is always authenticated by style.

The key to style is not borrowing anybody else's style because you are so afraid of trusting your own. Yet Phillips Brooks's long-ago definition of preaching as "truth through personality" depends upon God's truth and your personality. This will generally mean that your style, when completely natural, will lead naturally to a unique way of preaching—unique because only you can do it in the way you feel it ought to be done. Why arrive at such an assumption? Because artificial yelling and "buzz saw" homiletics are never natural and cannot therefore result in a conversational style.

Developing a Natural Style

Every preacher—especially local pastors—must appear genuine and will only be heard in direct proportion to their integrated wholeness.[1] Two-faces may work for clever politicians, but preachers must wear a single face—promote and live out a single lifestyle.

None of us ever achieve the Socratic one-liner "Know thyself," for the ego has irregular edges, and the center of all we are rises in mists so dense we lose track of ourselves. Like everyone else, preachers embody many lifestyles: psychosexual, sociodependent, and low self-esteem. It has been years since Robert Schuller wrote *Self-Esteem: A New Reformation*, in which he points out that evangelicals are the group in America with the lowest self-esteem.

Preaching has been called the profession of those who arrive at their calling because of their need for approval. Sixty-plus percent of preachers—give or take a point or two—are professionals who were raised in a home where their mother was their only parent or their dominant parent. If dentists must accept higher than normal suicide rate, preachers must also accept their own needy emotional state.[2]

Preachers must also see this needy state as seeing their congregations as a part of a dumb-down culture.[3] Evangelicals are just plain dumbing down faster than the broader culture is as a whole. Os Guinness says that your chances of meeting a college educated person is better on the sidewalks of America than within the country's evangelical churches.

Passion

Whatever is meant by style, one caveat must be sounded: no style, however individualistic it may be, will sell unless it contains passion. Preachers simply must believe intensely in what they preach about. It does little good for preachers to insist they are simply conversational and warm and refuse to make an attempt at passion. They must believe and believe passionately. They must do this consistently, not just in an occasional sermon but in every sermon that is preached. Week by week no sermon text is to be selected about which the preacher does not have very strong feelings.[4]

Worthy sermons are the result of passion. There are no real sermons where there is no passion. Passion results from two things. Number one: a depth of feeling for truth, every truth that is to be preached on. If you have no real opinion about the virgin birth of Christ, pick another subject. If you do not believe in heaven, don't try to "whomp up" an emotional case for it. You simply should never preach on any subject—even if it is in the lectionary—about which you are not strongly prejudiced in favor of the truth it contains.

But passion also results from simplicity and the singularity of themes. The danger of three-point preaching is that it is not generally possible to be fervent about three things at once. And even if it is possible, this triple-dipping ardor gets tangled and confused in the minds of the auditors who usually cannot be led in too many important directions at the same time.[5] The fire in three different ideas quickly burns out when you try to put them together. So don't.

Sermons should say one thing. The reason that crying "Wolf!" works so well is that it addresses only one danger. Crying "Wolves and Tigers!" may say that some danger is real, but it is ambiguous and presents an alternative of devils, thereby clouding the issue of which demons are to be most feared. A lecture on cobras may fearfully frighten the listeners. But adding crocodiles and black mambas will only complicate the issue. Simple warnings are to be preferred over complex ones. One finds in all the Old Testament prophets singular warnings. They preached simply, warned simply, described the terrors they preached generally in simple images. Great sermons like all great speeches are not complex.[6] Churchill in a time of war didn't talk about all the civic issues that the English generally found important.

Preaching three-point sermons fits the text rather naturally on occasion. But generally the three points are artificially shoved into a single-point text for the preacher's benefit. The three-point approach on most occasions is a way to divvy things up to keep preparation time to a minimum. This gives the impression that the communicator has studied the text pretty extensively. The preacher seems to be seeing deeper subliminal implications than the listeners who have never had the privilege of seminary study. But in reality, making a text say three different things when it says only one is a nineteenth-century invention that brought a nuance into sermon preparation unknown in the centuries before it.

Great sermons are focused, content to say one thing well. Calvin Coolidge, upon returning home from church on a Sunday when Mrs. Coolidge didn't go with him, was asked by his wife, "What was the sermon about today?"

"Sin!" Coolidge replied.

"What did he say about it?" she persisted.

"He's agin it," said the president.

Apparently it was not a three-point sermon.

Avoid Imitating Other Pulpit Heroes

This is the carbon-copy age, whose hero is Xerox. Imitation is how copyist people authenticate themselves. Ernest Becker won the Pulitzer Prize for reasoning in *The Denial of Death* that in our age, people coped with their anonymity by deciding either to be a hero or to have one, and to make one of these two pursuits their passion.

Preachers have made themselves neurotic in the push to succeed. They are often trying to emulate some style they envy among someone more successful than themselves. The world of cable religion and the megachurch have coalesced in a common orbit of influence. This church or that church has offered programs that can be downloaded into those churches with lackluster commitment or unsuccessful methods. But the worst part of their influence has been to set the importance of a bogus pastoral image.

To comb one's hair like a prominent pastor in Chicago or Los Angeles is the least of the afflictions. But so many pastors try to sound like their heroes, preach their widely scattered CDs, and generally train their larynxes in the style of their prophetic heroes.

When I was in seminary, shortly after the earth's crust had cooled, Billy Graham was the role model for all who wanted to be a passionate preacher. It was said that some ate graham crackers in an attempt to get their diet just right. Many of those long-ago Grahamites combed their hair and sharpened their bugle-like tones to call the lost to Christ. They seemed oddly grandiose to their smaller, confused congregations. The mathematics were wrong: "The escalators are running. If you came on a bus, they'll wait for you. I want hundreds of you to get up from your seats right now and decide for Christ" didn't fit the county seat parish very well. Still the copycats were as ardent as they were ineffective.

What gets lost here is the notion that God wants every herald to be authentically who he made that herald to be. The Holy Spirit is not out to create identical preachers in pairs or colonies. It may be audacious to claim but I think God has never used a cookie cutter to mass-produce prophets. Nor will God ever clone a second orator because he has convinced himself that he did such a good job on a prior one. Trying to be anyone else is the sure sign that you're about to be ignored by the God of individuality, who is so fond of everyone's unique DNA that he never guarantees pulpit success to anyone who doesn't treasure individuality.

Preaching: Telling the Truth in Your Own Way

Truth only becomes riveting when it passes through the specific narratives of those who tell it. How a fireman describes a fire would be immensely different from how a nurse or a farmer might. None of the three would lie about it, but the story would be so highly individualized as to make it seem there were three different stories.

I love the Hindu tale of six blind gurus encountering an elephant. The first blind man bumping into a pachyderm leg said, "The elephant is very like a tree." The second, running into the tusk concluded, "The elephant is very like a spear." The third, running into the beast broadside said the elephant was very like a wall. The fourth, grasping its tail believed the elephant to be a rope, and so on. Truth was to each of them a matter of individualized integrity. Still each told the truth in a vastly different way. Story is made attractive and intriguing by the filter of personality. Great storytellers heighten the tale by the application of a hungering perception to add intrigue by how they see the truth they preach.[7]

There is no "wall" to the true storyteller. There is a "thick stone enclave of mossy defiance." There is no "shaggy dog" story to a real raconteur. There is, however, a "hairy St. Bernard, wooly as a mastodon." And to move the distance from a "caged bird" to a "trapped tanager" is an easy distance. Don't undersell a specific incident with a nondescript tale. Pay attention to the world. Let your descriptions of anything add force to your narrative.

Earlier we looked at the various sermonic forms that make the sermon work. But remember, style argues that all these sermonic forms—to be really effective—have to come at the audience through the lens of one powerful viewpoint: the eye and mind of the preacher. Consider how it looks graphically.

```
— Self — Self — Self — Self — Self — Self — Self — Self —
|                                                        |
Self            Self Is the Package                   Self
|         Text   Story   Proposition   Persuasion        |
|                                                        |
— Self — Self — Self — Self — Self — Self — Self — Self —
```

The truth expressed in this graphic is why I say consult the commentary last, well after the mind has had a chance to set the style of delivery within the individual framework of the preacher's highly personalized convictions. If that is not done, the graphic looks like this:

```
  —  Research  —  Research  —  Research  —  Research  —  Research  —
  |                                                                |
R |                                                                | R
e |              Research Is the Package                           | e
s |        Text    Story    Proposition    Persuasion              | s
e |                                                                | e
a |                                                                | a
r |                                                                | r
c |                                                                | c
h |                                                                | h
  —  Research  —  Research  —  Research  —  Research  —  Research  —
```

In such a bookish mode of sermon writing, the self drops out and self is the most powerful part of the sermon. Indeed, self is the most effective interpreter of Scripture. It is the bedrock of style. Without self, style never becomes usable and sermons remain weak and nonrelational. Remember, how we learn is relational. Relationship locks truth into the memory. When the all-powerful mystique of the preacher remains so imbedded in the argument that the sermon has no relational force, the sermon becomes only a repetition of the preacher's study notes. The preacher's words can never become human because the human that ought to be preaching considers humanity of little consequence.

People don't want to know the truth you read (they can read for themselves). They want to know how you personally feel about the truth you read. They want you to add to their worldview what your passion has added to your understanding of the truth.

Passion: Not Volume but Intensity of Feeling

Passion as a kind of rhetoric is false. Passion as an energy that fuels honest rhetoric is essential. Style is a way of life—a way of intersecting life, of feeling life. Evangelicalism in the nineteenth century arrived at a concept in homiletics which advocated urgency. After all, there was heaven and there was hell. People dared not die without being born again lest they perish instantly in hell. "Get saved!" was urgent and honest. Not only was their heaven and hell honest, but Jesus was honestly coming again. He might come at any moment, and since his arrival could be at 8:15 tonight—and it's now 8:14—everybody needs to get with it.

But urgency often has "volume" for its identical twin. It is hard to whisper the word *fire*. It is hard to say the word *hell* serenely. So urgency brought an upbeat passion to preaching.[8]

Unfortunately, the volume endured long after the urgency became less important. Heaven and hell are still very real but are less and less a part of sermons. I do not hear "ye must be born again" very often in church. Transcendent themes have been replaced by "how-to" and while "how-to" is a more reflective matter than "get saved," it is nonetheless set upon an audience with the fury of a bowling ball, sweeping down in fury on the dry-wood pins of the poor hearers. While eardrums take the abuse, many wonder if the ear-splitting noise level is really necessary in saying "God loves you." And some find it hard to pick some Monday insights out of Sunday's thunder.

I came late to live in Dixie, but I was unprepared for a style of urgency that often assaulted my ears with the thunder. I was amazed that even simple things like "love thy neighbor" were screamed at me so I could get the message. Loud seemed to be as important as truth. When I catch older people turning down their hearing aids after the song service, I always think, *Lucky them*.

Hamlet's advice to the players was this:

> Speak the speech, I pray you, as I pronounced it to
> you, trippingly on the tongue: but if you mouth it,
> as many of your players do, I had as lief the
> town-crier spoke my lines. Nor do not saw the air
> too much with your hand, thus, but use all gently;
> for in the very torrent, tempest, and, as I may say,
> the whirlwind of passion, you must acquire and beget
> a temperance that may give it smoothness. O, it
> offends me to the soul to hear a robustious
> periwig-pated fellow tear a passion to tatters, to
> very rags, to split the ears of the groundlings, who
> for the most part are capable of nothing but inexplicable
> dumbshows and noise: I would have such
> a fellow whipped for o'erdoing Termagant; it
> out-herods Herod. . . .
> Be not too tame neither, but let your own discretion
> be your tutor: suit the action to the word, the
> word to the action. . . .[9]

Suit the word to the subject is good advice. Conversely, passion may be measured in the silence set in the proper place as well. Good preaching should consider well the various uses of the voice as purveyors of passion.

The Six Purveyors of Passion

Since there are six purveyors of passion—silence, tears, urgency, volume, velocity, and poetry—ask yourself how they must be used in preaching to convince an audience that you feel strongly about your subject. Consider how these six elements of passion might be used to connote how you want your audience to feel the resurrection. Let us take the account in John 20:1–2, 11, 16–17.

Silence

"Early on the first day of the week, while it was still dark" (John 20:1a).

They said nothing as they walked.
Silence.
Aching silence.
Heavy, breaking, agonizing silence.
He was dead—dead—dead.

Tears

"Mary Magdalene went to the tomb and saw that the stone had been removed from the entrance" (John 20:1b)

Tears, hot, cutting, desperate.
He was not there.

"But Mary stood outside the tomb crying. As she wept, she bent over to look into the tomb" (John 20:11).

Urgency

"So she came running to Simon Peter and the other disciple, the one Jesus loved, and said, 'They have taken the Lord out of the tomb, and we don't know where they have put him!'" (John 20:2).

They have taken the Lord!

Volume

"Jesus said to her, 'Mary.' She turned toward him and cried out in Aramaic, 'Rabboni!' (which means Teacher)" (John 20:16).

Mary cried out at this point.
The volume must keep pace.

Velocity

"So she came running to Simon Peter and the other disciple, the one Jesus loved, and said, 'They have taken the Lord out of the tomb, and we don't know where they have put him!'" (John 20:2).

Mary came running (let the rhetoric pick up speed).

Poetry

> Christ the Lord is risen today, Alleluia!
> Sons of men and angels say, Alleluia!

This is but a tiny model of the aspects of passion but is valid in all the rhetorical aspects that compose passion. Use each aspect only when the text or your feeling about it connotes passion.

But anywhere you suspect that you're saying things louder than you feel them, then you need to rein in your rhetoric with conservative humanity and let the other aspects of passion show their stuff. But getting loud and staying loud is neither true humanity nor good homiletics.

Oral Interpretation Counts

When called to preach, most never consider themselves called to interpret anything. Regarding the sermon there are four principles

of interpretation that must be followed to be a great communicator, and all of them have to do with reading and interpretation.

Principle #1:   Don't merely read the Bible, interpret it. Find a
                    practical desire within yourself to set every word
                    of the text in its best motivational form.
Principle #2:   Those extrabiblical quotes to be used in the
                    sermon—if they are direct quotes—should be
                    read from the primary sources from which they
                    are obtained. You should not read from cards
                    which contain a quotation from a book. Books or
                    magazines are far more "intriguing" than quote
                    cards.
Principle #3:   Paraphrase quotes when you do not have the
                    primary source unless the word-by-word quote
                    is too important to miss.
Principle #4:   Memorize shorter quotes when possible.

Oral interpretation runs the risk of being melodramatic, and
any time you sense that your good intentions at interpretation are
spilling over into ostentation, beware. Do not overdo the dramat-
ics of a quote. You may need to get someone to help you who can
observe your presentation privately. This need not be a person
skilled in theater. Almost anyone can be your critic and can tell if
you have overdone a recitation. Ostentation is easy to spot. But for
the most part, the preacher is far more apt to *under*do the dynamics of a presentation than to overdo it. And for this reason, getting
a little help with good oral style is important. This is particularly
true if you have not been accustomed to public reading.

The Seven Axioms of Delivery

Axiom #1: "The speech before the speech" is step one in audience bonding.

The narrative exposition more than any other expository form
relies on bonding with the audience. This may be one of the very
few preaching texts you will read that will talk about this strategic
first step in pulpit communication. Bonding with an audience is

both verbal and nonverbal. The nonverbal elements of bonding have to do with deportment, propriety, and an open demeanor. During those first critical moments when the audience to be addressed first catches sight of a speaker, the would-be listeners are making up their minds as to whether or not they will be listening.[10] At this point they have their thumb on the remote control of their intent. Will they change channels once the speaker has begun or will they change channels even before the speaker begins?

This latter issue is totally nonverbal. Each of the persons to be addressed is sizing the preacher up with a series of questions:

Does the speaker look listenable?

Is the speaker sincere, amiable, and my kind of person?

Is the speaker dressed in a pleasing and nonostentatious style?

Is the speaker tattooed, dreadlocked, gushy, friendly, aloof, etc.?

First impressions pave or bar the way to being heard.[11] My ministry is largely itinerant these days, and so Sunday by Sunday I go from denomination to denomination and church to church. In a day of megachurch neuroses, I call the pastor to see how he dresses. Some megachurches are casual, and fiercely so. If you show up in a tie where the congregational détente is shorts and sandals, you will be suspected of being elitist and out of touch with the grass roots, who want to see the keynoter dressed in a disheveled and dowdy way. It may seem a small issue in light of eternity, but it will be a huge issue with those who believe the Holy Spirit only falls on the devoted disciples of Tommy Bahama. The opposite is also true: If the congregation is a "suit-and-tie" gathering, they will believe that the Spirit is looking for a good starched collar and a silk tie. To fail to pay attention to this is to violate the nonverbal code of acceptance and will make bonding more tenuous.

The most important issue of bonding has to do with the first words out of the preacher's mouth. These should not be the first words of the sermon's introduction. They precede the sermon's first formal thoughts. These words are the warm approaches to the audience. These words don't comment on the text. They don't drub the audience toward rapt attention for all that the preacher intends to say. They are the "Hi there" words that notice the world around them and reach to the crowd with enough humanity so that the divinity being stirred up may become instantly palatable. These words reference the little things of life: the weather, the Super Bowl, the choir which has just sung, the town in which the church is situated, the tragedy that has filled the newspaper for the week, the kindness the audience has extended, your admiration for the leadership of the constituency, or your warm opinion of the group who has come to listen to you.

The speech before the speech is not something you write down to say, anymore than you would write down your remarks for a reception line. You are there to acknowledge your openness and your joy in the circumstances of your togetherness. It is simple stuff, but essential. Without it, you will arrive too hurriedly at your private agenda. Without it, you say to your audience, "As I see it, what I am about to say is more important than our friendship." When done with sincerity, this axiom creates the bait for the important propositions with which you hope to snare their interest.

Axiom #2: Don't ask for people's attention, command it.

The violation of this axiom is often born in our insecurity. Every preacher I have ever known suffers from a common facet of low self-esteem: I am too dull—people will soon quit listening to me. I planted a church which in time grew to a couple of thousand listeners. When the church was small, I suffered from the notion that I would arrive to preach on Sunday and not a soul would be there. It never happened. Yet I believed it would. Even as the church became a large congregation, I would wake on Sunday morning wondering, *Will anybody come today?* Of course, they did. But all speakers suffer from the notion that even when listeners are present, are they *really* present? When they look like they're listening, are they? And when they don't look like they're listening, watch out, they probably aren't. One of the hedges against these fears is to say things like "Listen up!" or "Will you give me your attention?"

There are, of course, parts of a sermon that may need a special emphasis on attention. If you are working through the Levitical priesthood—an understanding of which is essential to your working through the book of Hebrews—you may want to ask them to carefully attend your words of explanation, because if they miss out on this part of the sermon, what is to follow later will be unintelligible to them.

But there is a difference between this kind of call to attention and the kind which continually—even habitually—asks people to listen. The continual saying of "Listen up!" grows from the preacher's insecurity that they may not be listening, perhaps because the sermon is poorly prepared and contains so little worth hearing, the preacher has to keep insisting that people listen.

The best remedy for asking for attention is to have something so vital to say and to say it so well that people listen because they are fascinated and need not be called to attention.[12] Such preaching is glorious. When the ear grows attached to the preacher's brain and larynx, there is no need to ask for attention. Any call for it is like bringing coal to Newcastle: the very call for it has been rendered pointless by the preacher's passionate and content-filled style.

Axiom #3: Move deliberately, don't meander.

The difference between a pond and a stream is mobility. Streams are ever more fascinating than ponds, and nearly everyone I know prefers white water to stagnant pools. This principle holds in the pulpit as well. Preachers who move are more interesting than those who don't. I realize that this principle of pedagogy is widely debated. More formal and liturgical congregations may want their preachers to stay "behind the pulpit," and in older church buildings, which have winebarrel pulpits, they actually prefer the preacher to climb in and out of "the barrel" for all godly pronouncements.

But the first time I ever heard Norman Vincent Peale preach (and indeed, every time I heard Norman Vincent Peale preach) he left the divided lectern and lit out for the center of a chancel and stood there, unseparated from his audience by any pulpit barrier. Only oxygen came between him and his congregation as he preached to us. I was a young pastor the first time I heard him, and I made a decision that if he could get by with that at Marble Collegiate Church, I could also get by with it in the church I was attempting to plant in Nebraska.

The best thing to be said of a pulpit is that (in spite of the fact it hides the speaker) it does locate the preacher to one place. Some preachers need that. Without the pulpit they become meandering messengers who pace back and forth like a caged lion while they shout out the words of their sermons. Pacing is bad, and it betrays the preacher's nerves, setting all insecurities right out in the open for all to see. But pulpits do not necessarily prevent the preacher from becoming a roaming reverend. In fact, many preachers have developed a peripatetic pedagogy just trying to abandon the pulpit. The trustees will not allow these preachers to take the pulpit out of the sanctuary, so they are forced to spend their years walking around it in an attempt to get away from having it come between them and their audiences.

This axiom champions the notion that while movement is commanding, pacing is not. So move deliberately. Take a few paces at planned intervals. Plant yourself in one position for a few minutes of your sermon before you move easily to the next point from which you deliver more of the message.

Above all, remember this: a chancel is to church what a stage is to the theater. In the theater movement from upstage center to downstage center is the most powerful kind of movement in terms of making the playwright's words come alive. The same is true in the chancel. Walking toward an audience when you are making a point has far more effect than walking away from them toward the rear of the chancel. In either the theater or the church, the weakest kind of communication movement comes in moving pointlessly from one side of the stage to the other.

But either actors or preachers should not wander about the stage. Actors work at "blocking" or planning their movements. They realize their position on the stage is part of their interpretation of the role they play. I have never seen either King Lear or Hamlet do their soliloquies from anywhere other than center stage. There is a reason for that. The best of preachers know what the reason is and behave accordingly during the delivery of their sermons.

Axiom #4: Identify as much as you can with your audience in dress and politic.

We have already spoken of the importance of audience identity. But the issue of "like" is powerful. People want the preacher to believe what they believe in just about everything. They like their heroes—cultural or subcultural—to behave, dress, and think as they do.

I remember when George W. Bush went to the Yankee Stadium to throw out the first pitch of the game, shortly after 9/11. I was so impressed with the fact that he wore a brown sweatshirt and slacks, I caught myself dressing in brown the next day. I never realized I was doing it until my wife remarked that I looked "presidential" that day. I suddenly realized that most people are anxious to imitate or at least to celebrate people they admire. I had never really isolated the feeling before. But Bush had earned my copycat esteem. I could see that in his world where any one of a hundred thousand people might have taken a potshot at him, it really was an openly courageous thing he did especially at that intense time of national paranoia.

To a much lesser degree, most people don't just like their pastor, they have a strong admiration. One shouldn't make a god of this adoration lest we leave off speaking the Word of God in favor of what would make us popular. But to care about this as much as we might brings a camaraderie into communication, which would not be there were we to act in ways that might intentionally "jangle" them.

This is so important to me that I call every church where I am to preach on any given Sunday. I call to see what the détente is in terms of style, worship, and politics. In evangelical churches, Democrats are increasingly in short supply. *If* the preacher is honestly a Democrat, it is not necessary to become a pseudo-Republican just to "butter up the audience," but it would be wise not to antagonize them for unimportant reasons. In a nation as deeply divided as ours is it is just smart to avoid saying anything deeply partisan with passion. As the cliché runs, pick carefully the "hill you want to die on."

Axiom #5: Light the pulpit: people won't hear what they can't see.

Obviously, this concern about good lighting is *not* a "hill to die on" for itinerants like me. I simply accept having to preach in dark, old, poorly illumined sanctuaries, many of which were built before electrification had become sophisticated. But for local pastors, it may be that they will want to explore what might be done to get light on the pulpit.

I have twice preached in a dimly lit church where the people were looking back at me with that "squinty eyed" stare that one sees in theaters as the lights are being dimmed. The worst thing about such poorly lit sermons is that people need to be able to see the passion, the body language, and the drama of what they attend. Great words spoken in darkness quickly become invisible as well as inaudible.

Axiom #6: Never let the audio system work against your delivery.

I was on a program with Robert Schuller once. He never knew I was there. He had top billing. He was, after all, one of the most prominent preachers in America. I was, after all, not prominent anywhere. One of the greatest differences between our sermons—other than the size of the honorarium we each received—was the microphones we were given. He was, of course, given a great state-of-the-art lapel microphone, while I was given one that looked like a 1945 Army surplus walkie-talkie. His was a "positive thinkers, be-happy-attitude" FM tuner. Mine was a whistling feed-backer that shrieked into splitting eardrums, virtually defying the Holy Spirit to get involved in what I was saying.

But I did learn something that baleful night. If you must follow a national celebrity, ask the sound technicians to give you the big man's mike as soon as he is through with it. This has been my policy ever since. Most technicians will know you are not the big deal and will struggle with your insistence on the matter. What works here—other than a full nelson and a body slam—is being tough. If you are not, you will find yourself wearing the '45 walkie-talkie and thereby serve to make the pundit look wiser than you are by feed-backing your squawky rhetoric into the ears of people who will agree with the sound crew that you are clearly not of any great importance or you would have gotten better equipment.

Tell the sound crew to keep your sound level midrange and not to play with the knobs while you are preaching. It is better to be a bit loud or a tad soft than to be up and down throughout the sermon. Many of them will smile piteously at any suggestion that you make, since most sound crews are Calvinist, even in Arminian churches, and feel they are predestined to do what they want to. But try anyway because there have been a few isolated cases of sound crews actually behaving in a Christian manner. When they do, it is a wonderful gift to those who listen and those who preach.

The only other observation is to watch out for floor cords. They can trip you up literally. If you have the good fortune to preach after the Olivet Octet, there will usually be a full eight mikes and cords for you to negotiate as you try to remember what you want to say, keeping your eye contact with the audience while you avoid the zigzagging wires that coil like anorexic anacondas about your feet. One false move and you could stumble into a seven-ton amplifier and electrocute yourself.

Axiom #7: Work to eliminate all affectations of manner and voice in delivery.

Of all the axioms this one is the very hardest to eliminate for it requires dividing your brain into two parts, one of which is delivering your sermon and the other of which is monitoring the delivery. Almost every preacher (at the beginning of ministry) has some affectation in delivery that prevents the sermon from arriving in a crisp, intelligent, and forceful manner. The affectation may be as simple as a vocalized pause or a nervous pacing during the delivery that keeps the sermon from being understood, or at least bars the preacher from ease of comprehension.

I've seen student preachers (in years of homiletics classes) run their hands distractedly into their pockets twenty times during a ten-minute sermon. There is a Presbyterian pastor-author whose writing I admire much more than his preaching. His preaching comes punctuated by a nervous clearing of his throat. He is a kind of tubercular Demosthenes. His written oration is potentially as pretty as his manuscripts are riveting. Alas, his affectation is so bad that most of us at first want to lend him an inhaler and at last want to hear someone else speak. There is no physical reason for his affectation, and yet one of this intensity is very hard to clear up.

As a young man I was affected by what Edwin Newman (in *Strictly Speaking*) calls the "y'know" syndrome. During a twenty-minute sermon I would say "you know" at least fifty times. I finally managed to subdue the bad habit, but it required the utmost in discipline until I achieved it.

All affectation requires the dividing of the brain into two specific lobes, one of which runs the sermon through the larynx and the other which sits like a school master pointing out when the affectation is inserting itself into your speech. Naturally, it is maddening work, but it must be performed over and over again until the horrible little interrupting demons have all been exorcised.

In my case it required a year of effort to get the "you know" grit out of my speech. I have worked with students on the "uhs" and "ers" of vocalized pauses. I usually count them during a presentation so they will know how pervasive these little interrupters are. I can't keep them from continuing down the trail of affected sermonizing, but I can point out to them that it is their responsibility to take care of their problem or else spend all their preaching careers locked up in poor communication.

Correcting the problem is complicated by passion. If we really want to say what possesses our souls, it is difficult to care about what may at first appear to be trivial. This kind of problem is like a stutterer making a 9-1-1 call. The passionate need of the moment seems more important than being understood. But it is not. In preaching, clear speech and an unaffected delivery is essential to strong persuasion and riveting interest.

Issues of Focus

Outlines vs. Manuscripts in Delivery

How much support do you take into the pulpit with you? There has long been a contest between how much of the sermon should be written and how much of what is written should be read or closely followed during the preaching of the sermon. Traditionally, sermons were written and read, and only after the awakening of the nineteenth century did the passion that came to accompany evangelical preaching render read sermons as both wooden and lacking in interest. At the gradual passing of the sermon manuscript there arose a briefer guide for the preacher: the outline. Outlines became so famous in time that books of outlines came to dominate in some preachers' libraries. Outlines let the sermon appear far more spontaneous and interesting.

If there ever was an age for read sermons, ours isn't it.[13] And those preachers who do read must do it so smoothly that they appear virtually extempore. Does this mean that sermons should never be written out word for word? I myself have arrived at a hybrid argument on the subject. I continue to write sermon manuscripts, but never carry them into the pulpit with me. The reason I do this is that I am not convinced that sermons can acquire a literary quality without first existing in a written form.

But is it absolutely necessary that sermons have a literary quality? No. It is more important that they succeed as relational and riveting. But by "literary" I mean that in terms of oral style, a preacher must learn to handle words and apply them with enchantment and conviction and passion. I am convinced that most preachers cannot arrive at a professional use of rhetoric without developing a love of words. And the power of oratory must be given the kind of advantage that only comes with writing—at least portions of the sermon. Two portions that should always be written are the introduction and the conclusion. The introduction because it the sermon's liftoff, the conclusion because it is the sermon's final call.

But taking very little of the sermon into the pulpit—no more than might be scribbled on a sticky-note pad and tucked alongside the text—keeps the homily both focused and honestly relational. Preachers needs to appear that they are preaching what they believe and not just what they had written down to say. Spontaneity and passion are powerful motivators of interest and decision whatever the sermon would like to urge the hearers to decide.

Many of the best homileticians would urge the preacher to take no notes at all into the pulpit. I like the idea, I confess. But I also believe that memorizing complete outlines to preach week after week to the same congregation may over-challenge the preacher. For me it was too great an effort, and thus I came at last to the system I now use and have here described. A good thing about the minimal notes outline is that to the audience it appears no notes are being used at all, which suggests that all the preacher is saying is born of the moment from his convictions. Of course when the sermon has content week after week, everybody realizes that the appearance of the form cannot deny the obvious: the pastor is a scholar whose apparent passion always comes from an informed soul and that as the pastor grows, so grows the flock.

Eye Contact and Gestures

We have already talked about eye contact and gesturing. Just remember that "eye contact" means exactly what it says: the eye of the speaker meets the eye of the listeners. Looking over their heads in an attempt to fake the phenomenon fools no one. And certainly, closing the eyes, either out of an attempt to look prayerful or dramatic, usually betrays the preacher's insecurity. If you feel insecure looking into people's eyes, get over it! They will not hear anything you say while you elude meeting their eyes.

As for gestures, they can be practiced with some success, but practiced gestures are not the most natural way of letting the body add energy and movement to the sermon. There will be times when you may want to practice certain movements to accentuate the verbiage. But on the whole, the most natural gestures occur without practice when the passion in your sermon becomes so intense the arms and the body jump in on their own. The dead rhetoricians, who rarely gesture, don't gesture for the same reason they aren't interesting: they believe too little in what they are saying. When they believe it more, their body will perform what Cicero called the *sermo corporis*, the speech of the body. It is often said of Italians, "Tie their arms down to their side, and you put a gag in their mouth." The same is true of a credible herald. Their gestures but serve their passions.

Image and Altar

Make the sermon a picture of what you're going to ask them to do. We have used the word *image* so far in terms of a sermonic icon. But in this final use of the concept of image, I would like to use the word to define how your auditors are coming to see themselves in terms of what you are encouraging them to believe.

If there is any doubt about how pictures furnish the world with a guiding icon, you only have to consult men's and women's ads in magazines, or indeed the cover of the scores of magazines that are out to furnish a mental poster to the clients who buy their products. This ad-conscious world has seen to it that we are an image-driven culture, and the whole on-demand sales scenario of our culture is witness to the fact.

But while it is easy to sell photos of the ultramacho male and the sensual female, how do we accomplish the same sort of thing in terms of preaching the spiritual ideals of Scripture so as to make these virtues desirable? In such preaching we must form images of what ought to be imitated for our listeners to want to become like Christ.

Altars are the places where self-image is dealt with and perhaps changed. Most people want a healthy self-image, and when the sermon provides an altar, those who feel the need to change may actually do it. But how do they go about it? They pick the image they want to have over the one they are ready to discard.

Altar-driven images come in three sizes: the hero, the lover, and the insecure dependent. Any one of the three, or all three in combination, can be drawn to furnish the altar with what the world ought to be. Then the world will desire this when the proper image is held up for emulation. The first two categories might be applied to Jesus as the arch-model of how everyone ought to aim their lives. But the third will provide a contrast with Christ, since he was not insecure in the least. Yet most of us like to hear of those who are afraid of some overwhelming dread or life goal. And all of us have sympathy (maybe even empathy) for those who struggle and fall short of all they have struggled for. But is it right to hold up any human being as worthy of consideration when the church ought to be holding up Christ?

Healing images need to be presented in an indicative and not in the imperative mood. It is best to hold up the picture of what they ought to become and let them arrive at the truth that they actually desire to become the picture of. Tell the story of William Carey, or Jim Elliot, or Mother Teresa, but tell it in a straightforward way that leads them to reason inwardly on the kind of life they ought to be living. It is less effective to say, "Be like Carey" or "Live like Mother Teresa" than it is merely to describe their heroism, their values, or their sacrifice. Then let the sermon's own inductive soul create a sense of personal altar and need within the hearers' lives.

Altars—whether actual or inward—become the places where the pictures you ask your audience to identify with get framed and hung in the galleries of their minds. But these places of decision are always consensual. Altars are places where both auditors and the God being presented agree to be in oneness and serve in union. Altars bring the agenda of God and the submission of the deciders into a single arena and confer a kind of dignity on the sermon that will not occur unless this happens.

Altars are the business of the kingdom, and the kingdom is the business of the sermon. Preachers keep the altar by laying out the ethics, morals, callings, and demands of the King. They do not make any requirements that hearers must regard them with any special esteem. God is to be served by all. Altars are to be frequented by all. Sermons are to be heard by all. All in all preaching is glorious work.

In the planning sheet that follows, I have incorporated many of the facts of sermon planning so far discussed. Work a text and title through the entire questionnaire.

ENTIRE SERMON PLANNING SHEET

Text _____

Sermon Title _____

Sermon Theme

_____
_____
_____

Sermon Motif

_____
_____
_____

Focal Text: What is the part of the sermon text on which the sermon's argument is based?

_____
_____
_____

What are the strongest word or words in text that relate to the sermon's motif?

_____
_____
_____

Correlating Texts

_____
_____
_____
_____

What are the two best insights on the text gotten from study resources?

_____
_____
_____
_____

Write a brief paragraph recounting your life experience with the text.

_____
_____
_____
_____
_____
_____
_____
_____
_____

What is the strongest precept in the text (is this the strongest point of my sermon)?

_____
_____
_____
_____

How can I gild the precepts in the text with a memorable form of narrative or metaphor?

_____
_____
_____
_____
_____
_____

How can I "narrativize" this sermon?

_____

_____

_____

_____

_____

_____

_____

_____

_____

What biblical genre is this?

_____

_____

_____

_____

_____

What can I do in this presentation to make sure that the people understand, feel, and appreciate the genre?

_____

_____

_____

_____

_____

What is the image-changing information they need to arrive at a better self-understanding?

_____

_____

_____

_____

_____

9

The Sermon Journey

Text and Altar

In choosing to attend a sermon, people don't come to sit and listen. Not really! They come for the trek and they are eager for the journey. They come to travel from point A to point B. Point A is Sinai, point B is the Promised Land. The exodus is the metaphor for moving from struggle to serenity. The preacher stands like Moses on the mount and reads from the ancient Word and says, "The wilderness is hard, the struggle is intense, but I have seen the green fields of Zion. Follow me!" Then he invites the crowd to open the atlas, and he tells them the page. He reads the text, and points out the route. The hazards are great, but the dangers are manageable. Behind them, the lifeless Egyptian army floats face down on the waters. The Egyptians are those who tried to complicate the journey. This glorious herald asks them, "Have you ever passed a day without seeing the cloud of smoke? Have you ever spent a night when you could not see a pillar of fire? See the ark moving silently along the turnpikes of hope. Lift up your feet! We are not dawdling aimlessly without a destination. We are marching to Zion." If there is any shortcoming in our philology, it is that we have forgotten that two-thirds of the word *God* is *Go*! Sermons, therefore, should not be come-and-let's-sit events, but let's-get-moving events. *Go* is the word of cultural excitement. The word is shouted at football games, horse races, and political conventions. We say things like, "Get going," "You do go on," "Going-going-gone," and "Go get 'em." We have a go-go prefix we add to stolid nouns that are too sedentary on their own. We go shopping, go to church, go to pieces, go on to glory, and go far in life. In sermons we are going to heaven, going to hell, going into all the world, and going to become better people. So sermons exist to get people going. But where do sermons get them to go? To get them to a place of encounter with God, who can guide them in the going? Sermons end as naturally at altars as homecomings (or goings) end naturally at home. I realize the word *altar* when used by a Baptist homiletician scares Episcopalians to within an inch of their Edwardian confession. Still altars are places where God and his children get together. They are in essence the starting places of sermon journeys. So whether we get people there by singing "Just As I Am" or whether we get them to a more symbolic altar of the heart, there the journey begins. Like in all journeys it is there that we take our leave of old affections, crippling philosophies, and the dry manna of Sinai. There we say God is in the somewhere out ahead, and the sermon is both a call to the trek and bread for the journey.

Making the Sermon Journey

Every sermon is a trip—a movement from where we are to where we ought to be.[1] Preaching always assumes that the world is not quite right as it is, that where we are would be better served if we were somewhere else and the sermon has in mind how to get us to that place. In a highly individualistic world, not all of us want to go to the same place and many are more comfortable with where they are than they believe they would be with where the sermon wants to take them.

During the first thirty-five years of my vocational life, I was a pastor and served what I sometimes felt was a God-sized calling of planting a church and then moving it ever further in the direction that God wanted it to go. During the last fourteen years of my life, I have been a professor and layman going to church to serve some other pastor's vision, which I no longer have a part in casting. Now, at last I can see that all of our lives in the church are tangled in the various neuroses of where people don't want to go and the sermon journeys they do not want to take.

The sermon is a voice set forth in the tangled individual taste of all the members. It is a voice that lobbies for the sincerity of the pastor's preaching vision, but it is not a sovereign voice.[2] The journey is not one that everyone agrees to take. And the call of the sermon gets drowned out by a myriad of postmodern appetites within liberated thinkers who generally agree that God should be served by all the people but feel that their own view of how to get it done should be the dominant voice in the church.

Nevertheless, preachers must guide the sermon journey in the nearest way. Preachers—even great ones—do not take their flocks on a perfect journey. I have had years to repent of my youthful enthusiasm as a sermon guide for a serpentine journey that sometimes doubled back over itself when I—the pulpit voice—thought I knew some nearer way to Christian maturity. But then who, at twenty-nine years of age (the age I was when I began the founding of the church that became my final pastorate lasting for more than two decades), doesn't think he knows more than he does?

I must confess that my ongoing tenure in a single pulpit did take them on a long journey. The journey was circuitous and much longer than it needed to be at times. I read books that lobbied for me to try programs or publish dreams that diverted my preaching. Along the way, I had an unworthy role model or two, but by the time I discovered their faults, I had led the church down a blind alley so far that we had to retreat to the original point where I had begun to mislead them. Then of course I had to "reload" and "repreach" them out of some cul-de-sac I originally thought was the right direction.

I sometimes think young pastors should be defrocked for a week or two for joyously creating mayhem along the way. And many a church has ended up in a dead-end, dreamless world, led there by an overjoyous pulpit that loved the journey but never had a fondness for maps.

But most of the laity were kind to me and tended to listen to my sermons as though they thought I was right. And when I wasn't right, they patiently waited till I got it right, and thus by their good grace I preached for nearly twenty-six years in the same pulpit where I seemed to preach right more than I preached wrong. But allow me to get a bit philosophical as we wrap up this study and suggest some ways to make the sermon journey the nearest way to Christian maturity for everyone.

Five Guides for the Sermon Journey

Guide #1: Keep the audience together as you travel.

How is the body of sermon attenders to be kept together? No other public communicator has the frightening task given to the pulpiteer. There are old and young present, Democrats and Republicans, mature believers and new converts, left-brainers and right-brainers. Into this muddy swim comes a single voice of pulpit clarity. What a daunting task. However is it to be done?

The preacher must serve as a docent serves an art gallery. A docent leads a gallery tour aware that some in the group like Matisse, some prefer Monet. Some just philosophically prefer football, never having met a painting they considered as important as their subscription to *Sports Illustrated*. The preacher knows the subject and is determined to move the whole crowd through an "exhibit" of the sermon text. Together, they journey ever further into the text. A good docent is aware of stragglers who don't "get art" and are pulling away from the consensus of those who do. But the good preacher wants to take everyone along and leave none of them behind. So often the stragglers fall into one of two categories: the first grouping is the right- and left-brainers who attend the sermon, and the second is the mature believers versus the immature believers.[3]

HELPING THE RIGHT- AND LEFT-BRAINERS KEEP UP WITH THE JOURNEY

I have long seen this first grouping as the hardest hurdle for the sermon. Throughout my life, both as a preacher and later as a professor, I have been lobbying for creative sermons. By creative I generally mean image-driven, inductive, metaphor-saturated, and what I generally consider to be "interesting" sermonizing. The problem with this is that while the creative part of the congregation really enjoys this, the more left-brained would like preaching done in simple verbs and nouns that put up some rigid mental scaffolding and build heavy outlines and structures. Theologically, these groups may tend to line up along Calvinist and less-Calvinist lines. But always they line up along lines: the less artistic only like art when you can tell what it's a painting of, and the more artistic want to think about it, ruminate over color and form, and suffer inwardly with all the angst that gets in the way of just "hanging purdy pitchers."

But these gallery arguments are not new.

As I earlier said, when Jesus told the story of the soils in Mark 4:3–20, he seemed to tell the story twice. He tells it first for the inductive right-brainers (who glory in the imagery and allegory) and then works through the tale a second time, labeling the various parts of the metaphor for the left-brainers. If this is any part of Jesus's methodology in preaching, he seems to make the point for keeping the entire congregation together as he preaches.

The sermon is for all. And while it may be challenging to keep everyone together, it is a must. To do it well will require a resourceful approach. It was a Republican Administration in the 2000 national election that contrived the educational motto, "No child left behind!" That ought to be the motto for every sermon. A given truth may be difficult or ornate, straightforward or baroque, but every preacher should say, "No person will be left behind when I preach."[4]

Helping the Mature and Immature Stay Together on the Journey.

In the healthy church there are always a great many new Christians and a great many who are new to the particular denomination in which the sermon is being preached. It is better to remember Luther's word on the subject. When asked how he preached consistently to the brilliant Melancthon and the other scholars who attended his sermons, Luther wisely answered that although he knew there were scholars present, most of the time he just "preached to Hansy and Betsy."

Who were Hansy and Betsy? German housemaids, perhaps. But Luther realized that the sermon was for all of God's children, and to favor the intellects and the scholars was not only unwise, it was in a sense un-Christian. But it is equally poor preaching to preach only to Hansy and Betsy and ignore Melancthon. Showing the new Christians the beginning of the road must not fail to help the more mature to "get on down the road." How we go about keeping the sermon accessible to all is the point of the next guide.

Guide #2: Read the feedback.

INFORMING THE SERMON IN PROGRESS

Reading the feedback while the sermon is in progress is a guide reminding us that the sermon is not a monologue. People talk back in many ways. Their faces beam saying, "I agree with you, and aren't you brilliant." Or their faces scowl saying, "I don't agree with you. I can't believe I'm listening to this." Other times their brows wrinkle into question marks, saying, "What are you trying to say?" Their bodies grow rigid, indicating they're thinking about a public stoning for you. They look away, letting you know they've slipped the noose of your fascination. They help the children sort their Crayolas to color on the worship bulletin, as if to say there should at least be a little color in some part of the world.

Once the feedback starts, you adjust the message. If they're scowling, think about what you could do in the sermon to get them to stop it. If they're coloring with their children, what could you say short of "Fire!" to get them to put the Crayolas away?

None of these desired adjustments can likely be done while sticking to the sermon you wrote and can only be attempted when you agree that the sermon is an amendable dialogue that takes part of its shape as it's delivered. But doesn't it take years of practice to pull off these "in progress" changes? Of course experience helps. But the real key is to keep the sermon in a "dialogue" or "relational" mode as you deliver it.

Remember, the sermon's best definition is "homily" or "conversation." If you are treating it as an impassioned oration, it is harder to amend. The urgency of your rhetoric will preclude your adopting a more casual tone just to be human. G. K. Chesterton said that the reason angels can fly is that they take themselves so lightly.[5] Further, the more impassioned you become, the more you will be blinded to even seeing the audience let alone read their feedback.

The worst blinding that occurs, occurs when a preacher has developed a "preacher's tone." This is a constant habit among evangelicals who often want to sound "urgent" at the expense of being human. Why they do this is to appear sure of themselves when they often are not. Clyde Fant years ago wrote sardonically, "When in doubt, when in doubt, run in circles, scream and shout."[6] Too bad, too. Human beings listen better than urgent rhetoricians do. The healing can only come by listening to the silent yet screaming body language of the listeners.[7]

THE CHANCEL AS THEATER

We have briefly introduced this idea before, but chancels and pulpits have long been seen as places of boredom. A part of the reason for this is that speakers have not considered the issues of voice variation, body language, and movement. Let's look at these issues one by one.

VOICE VARIATION

Throughout any given span of our lives we do not talk in the same level. We shout, we whisper, we intone, or we grow forceful. We hit all these variations as a function of life as usual. Monotone would never occur to us. When our children misbehave, a shout seems appropriate. But if our spouses call to say they love us, we coo softly into our cell phones amour. Sermons should use all the same variations. The Psalms require a different attitude, posture, and sound than do Amos or Jude. Further, an illustration when taken from life should run the same gamut of variation as the part of life from which it is drawn.

Life is not mono-anything, it is multi-everything. Preachers should record their sermons and listen critically until they have learned the art of vocal variation—until all the "mono" has been replaced with "multi."[8] In severely entrenched cases of a boring voice style, the preacher may need to get help from a spouse or a friend; in severe cases perhaps a therapist or drama coach.

BODY LANGUAGE

The evangelist Billy Sunday preached with a very exaggerated body language. Similar styles can be seen on TV in cable religion today. However, athletic homiletics is not the best style for communicating a serious gospel. But neither is a stolid, pulpit-nailed rigidity.

When Cicero spoke of the *sermo corporis*, he was not advocating that we become pulpit acrobats for Cirque du Soleil. But he was reminding us that the body has a speech of its own, and when allowed to speak along with the larynx, an element of passion is produced that is welcome and persuasive.

No one can tell you exactly what the borders of propriety are in this matter. As I said earlier, "Excess within control" is my rule.

"Let yourself go" in a natural and conversational style. But when any sort of physical frenzy begins to intercept effectiveness, it should be stopped.

MOVEMENT

The same rules that apply to body language apply to all movement while delivery of the sermon is going on. We earlier spoke of the chancel as theater, and I continue here with the same argument. As actors "block" their speeches (see axiom #3 in previous chapter) so preachers must learn to "block" their delivery, which keeps all movement from degenerating to a nervous pacing. Hypermovement is no more to be praised than stolid presentations. But paced (maybe even practiced) movements can add greatly to the pastor's style and effectiveness.

LIVING GENTLY WITH THE UNEXPECTED

There can be little doubt that all the hard work of sermon preparation can be easily wrecked by the thoughtless interruption of a single church member. In a thoroughgoing individualistic society it is as likely to happen as not. The same child cries every week, the same elderly gentleman talks out loud. The same young person acts up. It isn't just the study and writing preparation that goes down the drain. Also lost is the spiritual cathexis the preacher creates when delivering the sermon. This rapport can be cancelled by people's insensitivity and bad manners. It is generally the case that preachers who attempt to address such disturbances while preaching tend to stir up more animosity than can be quelled by a preacherly rebuke. Therefore it is my conviction that such interferences should be left alone. To deal with an interruption midstream is generally to lose the audience altogether.

The rule is this: live gently with the unexpected. If the same interruption becomes chronic, the other auditors will likely take the matter in hand and deal with it at times other than the service time. If it becomes impossible to speak over the barrage, close the sermon early and see what can be done about it "offstage" before the next service.

LET YOUR HUMANITY TEMPER YOUR PASSION

The best discussion of propriety belongs under the earlier mentioned rule of "excess within control."[9] However heated you feel your sermon should be, commit yourself to being human. Say exactly how you feel and no more. If you find yourself talking louder and holier than you usually do, let go of your death grip on the pulpit, smile, and start the last point over in the fond hope that the deaf section will turn their hearing aids back on.[10]

Every sermon should reserve the right to be passionate, but remember that passion should punctuate, not define, the sermon. Let your humanity define rather than punctuate the sermon. All congregants prefer a preacher who is always a human being in search of passion, rather than a passion-driven screamer in search of humanity.

Guide #3: Learn to pace the delivery.

Pacing the sermon is incredibly important. Every semester I invariably have a preaching student who has an explosive, rapid delivery. This fault is one of the very hardest to correct. One of the most difficult transitions I had to make in the 1990s was my transition from the pulpit to the lectern. I discovered that thirty-five years of twenty-five minute sermons in no way prepared me for a life of fifty-minute class lectures. The lectures had to come at a much slower pace and depend a great deal more on ad lib and conversational style than did the sermon. But overall making this transition has been good for me in that it taught me a slower pace in the pulpit.

Pacing is a conscious attempt to keep the verbiage flow coming at a rate that can be apprehended by all. This pace allows us to set the most difficult subject matter before people without asking them to drink from the fire hose of a high-pressure gush.

But ever more important than listeners' comprehension is the issue of the preacher's conversational style. A pace which rams information at them should be replaced by a relational pace that allows them to keep up. The sermon should be an Emmaus Road conversation with the Savior. It should be a trek, not a sprint.

I had a friend who did a four-day Holy Land tour. There were some good things about it, but he said the pacing was all wrong. He said he had rewritten the old hymn "I Walked Today Where Jesus Walked." He now called it "I Ran Today Where Jesus Walked."

I've heard sermons like that. I have actually preached sermons like that, but I'm trying to quit.

Guide #4: Live with the ups and downs of week-to-week preaching.

There exists a universal myth that every sermon preached has to be better than the last. The end product of this myth is a terrible neurosis that ends somewhere beyond an early-death syndrome and a nervous collapse. We who preach are more important and—what's more—more enduring than our words. Every preacher will somewhere have that golden moment that seems at the time of delivery to rival Pentecost. The sermon lives, it flies, it exults, and the lost cry out, "What must I do to be saved?"

But every preacher also preaches a "dawg" or two. The lost do not cry out and most of the saved would rather be at a rock concert, and they don't much care for rock concerts. The key to happiness in the pulpit is to surf the waves of oratory. When you are tempted to play "Russian roulette" after a bad sermon, summon up your defects, gird up your homiletical loins, and say loudly, "It's Monday, but Sunday's comin'! Next Sunday. O yes, thank you Jesus for next Sunday! I promise I'll do better!"

We evangelicals suffer from alternate Jekyll and Hyde syndromes. Jekyll is a kindly, committed soldier of God who (secretly) wants God to have the credit for his pulpit successes but longs to agree with all those who tell him at the back door that he was like Whitefield, like Spurgeon, like Elijah. Of course, he ducks his head at their applause, saying, "I owe it all to Jesus." He feels great! He secretly wonders if he will be nominated as homiletician of the year. But when he fails, he is prone to say, "God, where were you!?" It is hard not to celebrate our successes while we give God the credit for our failures.

Do we ever reach the stage when we preach entirely for the glory of God with no investment of our own need to be celebrated? I haven't and I'm all but seventy years old. I would give anything if I didn't care a fig for human applause, but doggone it, I want to be loved! And knowing that it won't happen every week, I still want people to like my sermons.

"I am a sometime artist." This is my demure way of saying, "I am a terrific artist." I usually say the first phrase outwardly and the second phrase inwardly. What I have desired is that artists—myself included—paint to exhibit. When somebody criticizes my painting, I can tell they are not schooled in good judgment. When they praise or purchase, it is easy for me to see how well schooled they are in art criticism. I feel pretty much the same way about my sermons. I wish I didn't, but I do.

But I have learned this above all: whether a sermon is good or bad, I mustn't put all my chips on one presentation. This is particularly true of a pastor. Weeks give way to years and years to lifetimes. Any single message, no matter how glorious or dull, should not be allowed to define the quality of all preaching.

I truly believe we are not really free of these periodic, idiotic mood swings.The preacher must become the message. Or as the media critic Marshall McLuhan observed—in quite another artist—"the medium is the message."

We have grown so accustomed to *writing* sermons, it is hard for us to think about actually *being* sermons. Only twice in my life did I get to hear Martin Luther King Jr. speak. In neither case did he appear to have a manuscript or even have written one on his subject. I doubt if he rated the sermons he preached, and for sure none of the rest of us went to hear him in order to examine his homiletic theory. By the time in my life that I heard him he no longer wrote sermons, he had become one.

I have known older pastors whose lifelong mix-up with pastoral care had made them, at the end of their lives, what they had faithfully taught in early life. Becoming the message is the end of all good pastors, who conceive the sermon's main task not as something merely to be interesting or inspirational but as the divine lever sent to pry the world away from its godless orbit and back into the center of the gravity where God originally located it.

Thus I remembered this view for years and commend it to all preachers. First of all, liberate your need to be complimented by remembering that your sermon is a workhorse and not a show pony. The sermon has a job to do and it is a job too important to give preachers time to pursue good public opinion.

Second, remember you are only a kind of religious showman when you preach for any kind of applause. But if you burn with intention, your sermons will soon become you, and you will know you have conquered ego and taken up the most worthy of all crosses—the preaching of the kingdom. Let this be the cause out of which your sermon grows. The cause of Christ will be the sail that drives your sermon and the sunlight that draws it upwards. Then you will not have to be better next week than you were last week. Your life will be too large to be measured in weeks.

Guide #5: Preach over the long haul to create community.

The pastor and the sermon are to stand at the center of community.[11] It is a great place to stand, for the ongoing sermon at the center of the community will in time create the community. For most of my life I was involved in church planting. My messages were constantly missional. I was an evangelist, and I wanted my evangel to create a community. In twenty-five years I baptized twenty-eight hundred people, most of whom were adults. After two and a half decades we had over three thousand members, all created by sermons (not always excellently preached) that defined the community as a caring, loving, redeeming community.

I mean no comparison here, but when I visited Calcutta many years ago, I could tell that Mother Teresa had created a community around her devoted life. I've read so many of her books; I can only suppose her preachment came from her books or maybe her preachment was the very stuff of her books. But when lives are sermons and sermons are lives, vital communities are born.

Does Familiarity Breed Insight or Contempt?

It's a question, I suppose. If familiarity does not breed contempt, it at least breeds ho-hum! All the laws of group dynamics say we are more prone to be impacted by someone new than someone we have known for a long time. Yet the work of creating a community is more a function of tenure than newness.[12]

There is a real sense that the sermon is less heard the longer we know the preacher. But it is also true that it will function more powerfully as a community center the longer that it stays in place. The sermon becomes more of an "oracle" than a "pep rally." Here the hungry come for sustenance. The sermon is bread they have eaten before, but when it is not in place, the flock goes hungry.

The pulpit must be a road map to community. Sermons are most effective when they are least obvious.

Conclusion

"There was something of God in the past hour" is the one remark that clues the pastor in that there was a sermon. It is fun to hear, "Nice sermon, pastor!" but it is only ego fodder, and while self-esteem building can almost always use a boost from the few congregational members who indulge in the art, it is a vacuous comment that really doesn't prize biblical exposition as much as it is something to be said at the back door.

Postsermon comments both intrigue and belittle. They are less significant than the infrequent soul who says, "But how can I ever do what you were asking this morning?" This is saying in effect, "I listened to you preach and wrangled with who I was and struggled over God's direction in my life." One thing is for sure: we who preach shall drive ourselves crazy if we take ourselves so seriously that we believe every week will be a new existential encounter with lofty absolutes. To care supremely about the important lessons of the exodus on Super Bowl Sunday will leave a zealot at least deflated and maybe devastated.

It is probably not possible to care too much, but it is possible to lose touch with normal workaday people who can't help wondering where the old pastor was who went to the evangelism conference a real human being and came back a harsh neurotic, breathing rarefied air and talking in a falsetto urgency, like he'd been sniffing helium from a gospel balloon. Pacing is important. It is even godly. Rest every ten steps or so on your marathon world-redemption sprint. Read the Bible and believe it, then preach for change, no turning back, no compromise. Sit still and watch a DVD movie once in a while and eat a little popcorn. "Thus saith the Lord" is a heavy responsibility for any mortal. It is better to stay on good speaking terms with God than to feel like the universe rides on every sentence of your sermon. Never feel that you will somehow be untrue to the martyrs if you tell a joke in a sermon. Life is a bit of this and that, bric-a-brac, and meandering. The sermon is there to inform the sojourners that they are on the way to union with Christ, but the sermon itself is not the way. Preach the Word with fire when fire is demanded. But find a cool place to lie down at night where you agree that God can take care of it all while you get a little sleep.

The sermon journey is a lifetime calling yet four out of five ministers do not survive their first decade as a preacher. One of the basic reasons parishioners fire or abandon shepherds has to do with how poorly preachers preach and how long it is between great sermons. For the preacher it is a thankless job. If a preacher has been in the pulpit for a number of years, even the best sermon may not be complimented. The laity may like it, but they rarely say so. But if that same preacher has a bad sermon, the report will get back in one way or another. If the pastor consistently preaches what the laity refers to as bad sermons, the pastor will likely not survive the ministry.

But if in the process—and it is a process—the community becomes formed around a purpose, and that purpose is the central theme of the sermon, the preacher will have given the parish a great gift. The church knows who it is and why God has set it down in the middle of a needy world.

Afterword

Narrative Preaching: The Discipline and the Art

There are very few geniuses in any realm of endeavor. Preaching is rarely a work growing out of a sterling gene pool. Good story-telling and good preaching are the work of those committed to doing the hard work that in the passing of years comes to appear as an art form.

Our contemporary world is infatuated with the word *entrepreneurial*, which is the way the corporate, industrial world pronounces the word *creative*. *Creative* is the way some of the world says *artistic*. But preachers are artists and artists are interpreters. Using mere sermons, preachers take the customary world and make us see it in ways we never have before. Most of us can readily spot and label pulpit entrepreneurs and see that they are quite talented. Seeing them, we often lament our own lack of talent. Further, most of us are superstitious in our view of talent. Talent, we believe, is magic. It's part DNA, part luck. It is usually referred to as "it." He's got "it!" She's got "it." If you got "it," you got "it." And if you've got "it," flaunt "it."

But in preaching, as in any artful endeavor, talent has always been the wrong place to begin looking for creativity. *Talented people simply do not exist.* Only people who consider themselves untalented think talented people exist. Those who are talented rarely consider themselves talented and usually protest every notion that they are. Suffering from low self-esteem, talented people deplore every claim to special giftedness. Most talented people die feeling untalented. Who knows how many potential Spurgeons, McLarens, and Swindolls have been bought off by their own self-imposed feelings of mediocrity? How and why do these nonstrugglers surrender to such low self-esteem? Their limited success came to be because they yielded to the great pulpit lie: Creative sermons are superstar stuff, and I am incapable of producing them.

This low self-esteem sometimes grows out of the adulation we give to pulpit superstars. The resulting self-doubt is not a healthy humility nor is it spiritually admirable. It is rather a hobbling mind-set that keeps us from risking ourselves in the painful struggle to discipline our gifts. We often try to copy other people's talent rather than develop our own, so we go on listening to preachers of great reputation and doubt that any of their megaglory can take root in our microworld. Our denials of talent can become the ladder rungs we furnish our heroes, who climb past our dull homilies to glisten in their own sunny pulpits. Thus, we lock ourselves into the odd ritual of buying their cassettes or CDs when we might be selling our own. Further, the local parish is not a good place to gather the positive feedback we need to think well of our sermons. *And unfortunately we have no way of assessing the level of our talent except by their feedback.* There is not much hope of success without some positive feedback. Vincent van Gogh sold only one painting during his life, and it was only the appraisal he received from Theo van Gogh (his uncelebrated brother) that kept him at his work.

In one of my previous books, *Spirit, Word, and Story*, I said that not everyone can preach well, but everyone can preach better. So at the outset, let us say that not everyone can be a top talent, but everyone can be *more* creative. Five steps are required in developing a more creative sermon style. For those who wish to step up to the challenge, I would like to phrase these steps in terms of nurture rather than achievement. Therefore, as we examine these five steps let us admit that talent is never a state; it's a pilgrimage. It is a hungering after excellence, and therefore always remains an elusive pursuit.

Step 1: The Creative Risk

While we should never accept ourselves as talented, we must accept ourselves as unique. This is the first and hardest battle of our creative pilgrimage. We throw up every possible barricade to keep from accepting our special status. We are not worthy. We are the nothing-nothings who serve behind the sacred desk. Calvin's theology of wormhood has "wormed us away" from all homiletical pride. It thus condemns us, not to humility but to weakness. We cannot see our potential glory because, frankly, we have not even seen our present glory. Preachers should be humble; everyone knows this! For the grace of God to shine through us brightly, we must try to be contemptible in our own eyes. Right? Wrong! *Grace* means "gift" in Scripture. It is by his gift of grace that we were transformed and called in the first place. That same grace ought to release in us feelings of giftedness and special status. As any good parent, God constantly encourages us to see that we are unique and that our lives contain some once-in-a-universe gifts that must be given to the world or the world will be poorer.

I recently passed a sharply dressed lad of seven years in the hallway of the church where I served as interim pastor. I lowered my six-foot frame to one knee, coming to his height. He smiled warmly at me. "I like your sermons," he grinned.

"Really?" I probed. "Whatever for?"

"Because you're funny . . . you're a good preacher."

There was no hint of flattery in his young, bright eyes.

I felt truly affirmed. Yet we all bask in and are healed by the compliments of children. Thinking of how seminary enrollments are thinning and fearful of what they might become in the future, I encouraged him, "Maybe you'll preach when you grow up."

"Not me," he beamed, "I'm an actor!"

"You're going to be an actor?"

"Nope . . . already am! I do television commercials and speaking parts in community theater."

I enthusiastically hugged him. I was glad he hugged back, because I felt audacious hugging a real actor who knew it; it was like hugging a Redford or a Hopkins in process—our insecurity always needs permission to hug these who are very sure of themselves. What glorious parents this boy must have to give him such self-certainty.

There are three ways we gain such self-certainty, and they all have to do with living out our role in our faith community. First, we must have faith in our community. Our community will from time to time affirm our talent by compliment. Let us trust our community's appraisal at such moments. Let's use their compliment as a springboard to take that leap of faith into stronger self-image.

The second and harder mode of affirming our uniqueness will be found in overcoming the negatives of our feedback community. Every church offers a terrible double bind to its leadership. In seasons of celebration and joy, churches make preachers feel unique. In seasons of criticism and pain, they make preachers feel rejected and worthless. Still, negative feedback offers us the best possibility of defining ourselves. Criticism is the physician of our art. We should bless its diagnosis and proceed with the sermonic surgery it prescribes.

As to real pulpit creativity, only one fearful trial can tell us the level of our talent: Risk! The third component of nurturing our creative spirit has to do with our willingness to take chances with our ego in full view of our community. To discover if our suspected talent really exists, we have to put it on display! But behaving creatively in front of those we love paralyzes us with fear. Peer-fear is a pulpit demon. This demon is a leering exhibitionist. His fiendish laughter mocks us into sameness. We are finally so afraid of him, we champion a killing Sunday. Normally, we bury our great ideas in three points and a poem: it seems to go better with the anthem.

How does peer-fear get started? It begins in the third-grade pageant where we spoke too quietly to be heard and twisted our shirttails in our fists. We looked at the floor and turned sideways to the audience. Now its strongest manifestation is passionless preaching. But make no mistake, it's the same grade school fear of embarrassing ourselves in front of our community. It guts the force we need to sell our oratory.

The risk of creative exposure is frightening. It spawns those "going public" stomach knots and Pepto-Bismol neuroses. Closing our sermon by singing a song may or may not work. Monologuing Hosea instead of preaching—it may or may not work. Oral interpretation of a Vachel Lindsay piece; playing the piano as a part of the sermon; introducing a combo in which you have a part; inviting a fellow staffer in to help you preach a sermon or two—none of these things may work. But the risk of new agenda is precedent to all discovery . . . *all*! The risk may tell us we have no talent or it may open a glorious new way of seeing ourselves. Risk is fearful. But it is one perilous step toward self-definition.

To keep at bay the fear of being embarrassed in a big way, it is sometimes good to try any new pulpit form first in another congregation. This is exactly a Broadway producer's reason for opening a play off Broadway. The reviews come out a comfortable distance from the risky place he really wants to make the performance work.

Barbara, my wife, and I often do pulpit readings together. We did not try this at our home church first. Some years ago we were going to Toronto to lead a couple's conference, and I suggested that some of the dramatic pieces I was reading would work very well with two readers. "Look," I said, "why don't we try this in Canada. We're a whole nation away from where we really have to succeed. If it works there, we'll take our act back to our local pulpit. If it bombs, we'll return to our church unscathed by the bad reviews of critical Canadians." It worked beautifully, and we took it back with us.

But most times the discovery of any new suspected area of creativity will have to be tried at home. Confidence will come only as we take the risk and measure the feedback. It is really the whole process in reverse. Because it worked at home, we can export it to other gatherings. These distant audiences then can serve as invaluable reviewers of the new form. Those furthest from the parish will give us a more frank, honest-to-goodness, body-language appraisal.

Step 2: Observation and Imitation

Let's leave the creative spirit for a moment and turn to creative application, which involves observation and imitation. The creative spirit says, "I want to be . . . no, I'm starved to be more creative in my preaching." But creative application is the result of a leap of faith that stops brooding "I wish I were" and cries "Geronimo!"

Only two basic dynamics determine pulpit creativity. The first is the *sensate dynamic*. Noncreative preaching (indeed, noncreative anything) relies almost entirely on our thinking faculty ("left-braining" your way to pulpit acceptance). But creative preaching depends upon the feeling or sensual faculty. We who must continually give out the substance of our souls must be continually gathering something into our souls as well. The problem is that preachers are so bound by the logical hunger (How is this Scripture to be explained?) that they give little time to the sensual world (How is this Scripture to be *felt*?). The latter poses the primary question for the creative person.

The sensate must inhabit the rational. The best communicators are indeed those who impregnate their communiqué with sensations that must be picked up by the nervous system as well as the gray matter. No wonder the beloved Georgian Flannery O'Connor wrote:

> The beginning of human knowledge is through the senses . . . where human perception begins. . . . [Y]ou cannot appeal to the senses with abstractions. . . . The first and most obvious characteristic of fiction is that it deals with reality through what can be seen, heard, smelt, tasted, and touched.[1]

Until we communicate emotionally, we will, for most, have only a ponderous and boring speech. C. S. Lewis long ago said that it was a mistake to think that our experiences are concrete and can be communicated as "concrete experiences" with precise and literal language. Emotion spoils that concreteness, but this is the glory of emotion.[2] It opens us up to a level of rapport that only emotion can establish.

Basically, emotion is the stuff of religion. In his novel *Job: A Comedy of Justice*, Robert A. Heinlein said that religion was the most powerful drive in the human spirit, and when it was present you could "smell" it. It is pointless to say that great preaching is mainly teaching the Scripture. Great preaching is making the audience feel the Scripture: it is a sensate immersion in such things as the fall, the flood, the cross.

But more than speaking the emotion of the soul, the sermon awakens the emotion of hunger. This is a fourth-dimensional hunger—a terrible craving for the world of the spirit. This is a liminal hunger (remember, the word *liminal* comes from the Latin *limen* for "threshold") for the unseen world of spiritual reality. This unseen world begins a sensate encounter. It must be touched, felt, and seen.

Biblical scholar Bruce Lockerbie elicits the German idea of *Sehnsucht* as that elusive drive at the heart of the church's communication. In a sense, our best word for it is *homesickness*, that longing for union with Christ that thrills us with future hope. It is time to cut up your acetate slides and academic word studies. We need to touch this glorious *Sehnsucht*. Throw away your crutches when you talk to us of heaven. Make us see the city. Let us feel the high clear air of his transcendence. C. S. Lewis referred to this homesickness as "our inconsolable secret . . . our lifelong nostalgia, our longing to be reunited with something in the universe from which we now feel cut-off."[3]

The rational now must bow to the liminal, and the language of feeling must have the day. America's beloved Newberry medalist Madeleine L'Engle wrote long ago of Christmas:

> This is the irrational season
> When love blooms bright and wild
> Had Mary been filled with reason
> There'd have been no room for the child.[4]

The sensate must invade the rational.

The sensate may be encountered in four areas. First, we must apprehend it and try to appreciate it. It is the hunger of great writers and thus the substance of great books to sense true reality. This reach to feel inhabits the world of reading as a whole. I recommend an indulgence in fiction—good fiction (classics are best)—to study how good writers make us emote. I do not argue for fiction alone; I have found myself weeping during the reading of Harrison Salisbury's *900 Days in Leningrad* or Dee Brown's *Bury My Heart at Wounded Knee*. I found myself enraged when I read Malcolm Muggeridge's *Sentenced to Life*, awed when I read Barbara Tuchman's *A Distant Mirror*, and laughing out loud when I read James Herriot's *All Things Bright and Beautiful*. But plays too are contrived to make whole theaters emote. Their creativity is marvelously transcendent. We move through several fields of emotion in many works. I laughed, I cried, I became enraged, and I was awed at my first reading of *Cyrano de Bergerac* and *The Merchant of Venice*. In *Beck Is Back*, John Updike's account of a

Holy Land tour caused me to laugh so hard that my wife had to restrain me. Reading is a primary way to garner a sensate pulpit mystique.

Hearing is a second way to develop this sensate pulpit dynamic. Many great books and plays are recorded on audio cassette or CD. These audio books so abound in bookstores that even the busiest of pastors are furnished little excuse for failing to encounter the sensate side of creativity. Novels, sermons, and great philosophies are as accessible as the grasping slot or tray of your tape or CD player. Make something of your drive time, especially during longer commutes. For those who are prone to gorge their minds only on pop gospel tapes, for shame! Get out of the easy listening mode and into a critical listening mode.

Third, watching is the "hot" medium. "Videoing" your way into the best of cinema is here. But beware: watching is addictive and can make you a videoholic, couch-lounging, pulpit potato. So determine that your watching will be measured.

Fourth, you can make your watching live by joining a community playhouse or any theater series where there is live drama. Actors before the curtain and preachers before the sermon have many things in common—the cold death sweat in the palms of the hands and the agonizing fear that an incipient episode of Alzheimer's will storm through our souls midsermon and leave our minds vacant. Actors and preachers also are alike in that both depend upon the audience for performance feedback. But in one way, preaching remains quite different from a play. Preaching is a performance done once; it comes live and cannot be edited or retracted, even in part. What you see is what you get. Talk about the sensate dynamic! While we try to speak of Christ or the glory of the cross, we suddenly must switch to track two of our minds. Preaching must deal with feedback midperformance. Is our message overdone (hammy), underdone (cool), or unseasoned (bland)? But our suffering knows an intermittent glory! On every seventh Sunday, things click. The babies don't cry. The children watch. The hardened golfers are rained out. The old people turn their hearing aids up and lean forward in their pews. The angels sing. And we bring the greatest exposition of all time. Our gestures are seismic, our text crackles with fire, and our psyche congratulates us in the splendor of our calling. "Great Scott! We're preachers!"

Step 3: Feeling as Suffering

One further question demands examination: "Can preachers authentically preach with emotion of things that have not stirred or shaken their own existence?" How important is bleeding to those who want to speak to the bloody? Does not suffering fill a mighty sermon with a sensitivity unavailable to the little talks of those preachers whose lives have known only minor pain?

There does seem to be more than a casual connection between Toulouse-Lautrec's art and his deformity. Demosthenes stuttered his painful way to enthralling oratory. Byron hobbled through his fleet verse on a club foot. Besides the physical challenges that sensualize art, there are countless examples of those who climb psychological barriers to sensate enthrallment. Bach was considered heretical for using his thumb on the keyboard. Shakespeare's popularity caused many to say his work was trivial![5] Pain itself does not make us preach well, but it builds a sensitivity that does make our particular emotional experience speak to that of the whole. Only weathered wood makes singing violins.

As potential creators, we ought to say: "What is there in my dark times that might fill my homilies with light? How can I employ this pain or use that hurt?" If nothing else the pain will tenderize the preacher and the preaching like water flowing from a fountain gathers sunlight in the process of fall and splash.

Step 4: The Imitation Dynamic

The imitation dynamic asks only two questions: "Am I impressed by this, and can I do it too?" The first question is again a critical question, and the second is a question of risk. It is this "Can I do that?" question to which we must turn. But we first need to ask, "Is imitation fair or is it plagiaristic?" We all learn by imitating. Children learn almost everything this way—all sensate aspects of our appreciation are learned by imitation. Further, they are learned in community: as we gather together to hear and watch each other, we instruct each other. Artists watch each other paint; writers read each other's writing; and preachers (lamentably ofttimes) preach each other's sermons. But before we imitate, let us add to what we see and hear with the uniqueness of our own form. Then the imitation of others is right, but only when it becomes a synergism made authentic by the addition of our *own* style and substance to someone else's form. There is much truth in the old cliché: Copy from a single source and you're a plagiarist; copy from two or more and you're a creative speaker.

Remember, Shakespeare did not invent *Romeo and Juliet*, he only deleted and accreted his own rendering of an Italian source (this is true for most of his plays). Neither did Leonard Bernstein totally invent *West Side Story*; he merely deleted and accreted *Romeo and Juliet*. The key thing is that each person in his imitative turn was highly creative and a genius at synergism.

The key question is: "Can I do this?" One of my favorite songs from *A Chorus Line* is "I Can Do That"! The song is the testimony of a young person who, in seeing another entertainer get rich while he dawdled along, said to himself and to his own credit, "I can do that." Nurturing the creative spirit means that along the dawdling course of our uncreative lives we say out loud—loud enough for God and the entire world to hear it—"I can do that!"

Before we can honestly say, "I can do that," we must ask who the preacher's best role model is. The obvious answer is Jesus. In studying how Jesus preached (for all but the totally impious), the statement "I can do that" will come slowly. Watching Jesus will lead us to the conclusion that it is not only the "what" of preaching that is important but the "how." Aristotle laid down the importance of crafting the sermon when he said, "It is not enough to know *what we ought to say*: we must also *say it as we ought*!"[6] Bruce Lockerbie reminds us that Jesus' sermons came with simplicity and directness of style. They had originality and integrity. His parables are sensate and most pictorial and yet never overwritten or extravagant. He never stumbled over clichés or resorted to melodrama.[7]

Watching Christ, we gain the sensation of sermon as thrift. One wonders how Christ's marvelous sermonic economy could ever spawn the verbose and redundant pulpiteers of our times. A closer imitation of Christ's economic style might shorten the sermon into listenability!

Once we decide to run the creative risk of trying some new form, the danger arrives. Sometimes we find that we really *could not do it*. But we have not failed! We have only better defined ourselves by locating one creative form that is not to be ours. Still, in the attempt, we nurture our creative spirit. Learning the limits of our creativity is also important. The money on the game is that our listeners also see and learn our creative limits. But from time to time they also see our joyous successes. Actors are never remembered for the shows that close off Broadway. They are enshrined only for those standing-room-only nights when roses smashed against them in the floral stonings. We too will also be best remembered for the times we did it well.

Step 5: Drama and Humor

Drama and humor taken together label us as creative. Their absence labels us as BORRRING! "Dramatic" is that tenuous sermon quality that falls between those two deadly prefixes of *melo-* and *un-*. Evangelists have had a long-standing reputation for sermon illustrations that stay too close to these poles. Finding an authentic way to illustrate a sermon that finds a comfortable middle ground for drama is most important. Here are three important considerations for those who find this medium cool enough to handle.

First, let your drama build from the simple issues of life. Jesus's parables thrived with the power of simple dramas. Annie Dillard won a Pulitzer Prize by describing such things as a mockingbird swooping downward from a roof gutter. Her description is powerful and dramatic. Barbara Tuchman won a Pulitzer Prize for describing such things as the lusty singing of a confident German army. Both are beautiful in context. But in the pulpit it is better to side with Annie Dillard than Barbara Tuchmann. To build contagious attention to our simple drama is better than to risk yourself with Cecil B. DeMille illustrations that so easily snuggle us into the "melo" and "un" of drama.

Second, remember that specific details give illustrations reality. Powerful illustrators harness the emotional storms with the cables of time, date, and place. History and theology abound with powerful tales that can bring most of an audience to tears, but such dramas are powerful precisely because they come furnished with specific information. A lack of specific handling allows truth to float away in the direction of clouded fiction.

Third, don't forget that an especially powerful illustration tends to be a showstopper and should therefore be placed at the end of the sermon where the show can come to a logical end. At the sermon's end there is nothing left over that can be considered either "melo" or "un" dramatic or even anticlimactic. Does this dramatic illustration end the sermon in a way that leaves people wanting to serve the call of the sermon?

To make this clear, here's what not to do: I well remember an evangelist who told a heartrending story about a little boy at a church prayer meeting who requested prayer for his abusive father to be "saved." According to this raconteur-evangelist, the boy's father learned that his son had requested prayer for him publicly. "If you ever ask that church to pray for me again, I'll beat you to death," said the unrepentant father. The boy, ignoring the father's threat, did request prayer once again for his father. True to his word, his abusive father, livid with rage, took a tire iron (or maybe a pipe wrench, I can't recall) and beat his small son senseless. The illustration closed the sermon as violently as Rambo had once dispatched the Vietcong. As we, the benumbed, stood to sing the invitation, the children were in tears. Many of them came forward ostensibly to confess Christ but really they were only feeling sorry about the poor little boy who "died lying face down in a pool of blood" at the sermon's end. My own four-year-old daughter said to me on the way home from church, "Dad, it sure was too bad about that little boy lying face down in a pool of blood, wasn't it?" I was horrified that her little mind had been traumatized by a drama that was abusive and destructive. Drama should serve, not sever, the human spirit.

Jokes, per se, are best avoided. They can serve our creative reputation, but even when they are done well, they lend a note of contradiction to the overall seriousness of what a sermon should be about. Using stories that deal lightly with light interest is another matter, however. Life has its funny moments, and to preach life means that by necessity the sermon will, from time to time, be funny. If such welcome and wholly acceptable humor finds its way into preaching, the clever use of adjectives may be the way it is done. Description more than event usually supplies the humor.

One further observation: Leisure and lightness keep the same company. Humor works best where the sermon is unhurried in its delivery. If its speed is hyped with a heavy sermonic agenda (like evangelism or fund-raising), the pace can cancel the lightness. The vocal pause and the planned pace invite laughter. Not that laughter is good for the sermon, but please let it be remembered that laughing and crying (emoting in general) bring congregational separateness into unity. When people emote together they come together.

Conclusion: Crafting Life Feedback

The creative spirit is always an evaluative spirit; it appraises all incoming data, especially sermon response. As people give us feedback, we interpret. As we interpret, we edit. The creative process is always one of editing. Once we become critical thinkers, we will find ourselves asking in the middle of novels, plays, movies, concerts: "How could these bad spots have been eliminated and the good spots elongated?" The surest evidence that our creative spirit is maturing is this critical spirit. All artists are artists because they have this spirit. Naïveté is the only other option. Those who cannot edit the creative feedback will prematurely celebrate poor art. A mature spirit comes only with wide taste and experience. It is only those who have listened critically to a great number of sermons who begin to judge rightly the quality of all sermons.

The creative spirit is nurtured by time and evaluation. Evaluation of any art form, including sermonic art, is enhanced in its clout as time passes. Long-term preparation is the best guarantee of the best scrutiny. Putting a sermon away for a rest and taking it out after long periods of time will allow the most mature judgment to be made about its real quality. Those special sermons that bear great importance in the life of a church should be given this refining edge of long-term preparation.

But whatever our mode of editing, we must remember that without it, creativity never grows. The creative spirit is nurtured by those who care about excellence, and excellence is never merely a matter of informing the audience. Rather, it is a matter of working through our suspected artistry into a more certain glory. When all of this is in place we will understand how inspiration must reckon with our best judgment. *Art* will then become a real word for us, and our hopeful suspicions that we have talent will find a mature acceptance in our never-ending struggle to please him who gave us our job.

Appendix

Mentoring from the Contemporary Masters

The sermon is not a sermon until it is preached, just as football is not a game until it is played. Coaches may plan and rehearse plays, scheme strategies, and goad the players onward with the rhetoric of victory, but football occurs only after the players align themselves on the AstroTurf and the whistle blows. Sermons likewise may be planned, outlined, researched, and manuscripted, but they become sermons only on "game day." The "kickoff" comes as the last strains of organ and anthem fade. Then at last the sermon rises from the coach's playbook and struggles to effect change in the lives of its hearers. But sermons are different from football games in that they actually have two starts.

The first start is an indirect, congenial beginning that may be slightly or largely unrelated to the text. In this slanted start a bridge is built between speaker and communicants. A bridge is also built between the praise and adoration of worship and the instruction and challenge of the sermon. We have already established that the mode of the narrative sermon is casual. This congenial start has the "nice 'n' easy" feel of casual. It's a touch of the human spirit that paves the way for the divine. This easy glide into the sermon's formal start may consist of complimenting the choir, thanking the drama team, or speaking in a relational way of the worship theme for the day.

This congenial beginning does its best work for preachers who are delivering sermons out of their usual home congregational context. These important away-from-home sermons delivered to institutional or denominational gatherings also profit from such easy beginnings. Where more formality is in order, preachers will usually comment on and extend greetings to old colleagues, reminisce a bit, and, in general, try a casual and conversational shift into the academic or formal subject matter assigned to their sermons.

I call this casual start "the speech before the speech." Some will object to this informal start because its congeniality breaks the "God feeling" one gets in worship, as solos and anthems settle down upon us to create a receptive mood for the sermon. Some see it as undignified and antiliturgical—in short, as disruptive. There is a sense in which each of these criticisms is true. But within the congregation this kind of beginning more often translates as human and warm. For all that it may contribute that is disruptive, it will more than compensate by creating a sense of family and conversation, the latter of which, after all, is the meaning of the word *homiletics.*

The second start for the sermon is the more formal approach— the offering of the first lines of the written but unread introduction. Upon hearing these first formal words the audience will say within themselves, "Aha, now . . . down to business!" Still, the casual beginning has played its part in making the business of the sermon welcome.

Moving into this second start will be all the more welcome if the preacher has not confused the casual start with an overdose of homiletical "horsing around." The formal approach will capitalize on the first line and a developed attention-grabber. As we begin the formal sermon, the shift from casual to formal should be obvious. The audience should track with the move. If any single word describes the narrative sermon, it is the word *casual.* Still, at least the thickening of content and the obvious use of illustrations, precepts, statistics, and textual analysis ought to say, "The main argument of the day is now officially underway."

Once the sermon is underway, there are ten indispensable elements of form and style that will identify and define what the sermon is. These elements have been set forth by a great many writers and preachers but I would like to offer the works of ten different scholars, whose work cannot be overlooked without impoverishing the preacher's overall sermonic styles. I have arranged these values in a way that should characterize within the sermon those logic-driven values that we can control, then moving to those more creative things that gild and build intrigue and inspiration into the sermon.

For instance, take developing a basic, steady worldview as defined by who we are. This is something everyone must do. However, issues like interest, artistry, movement or pace, spiritual power, and altar response are items that not all preachers possess in the same amounts. In other words, every preacher should be able to study and present a content-filled and insightful sermon. The real electricity and passion of our communication belong both to our own spiritual formation (more simply our love for Christ) and the desire for pulpit artistry.

In the case of each of these ten elements, I will be referencing each point to pulpit scholars who have had more to say about this particular issue than all others. I hesitate in many ways to do this because I am more than confident I shall miss some insights from those scholars whose work I have yet to discover. However, a book like this, and certainly an appendix like this, presumes many limitations. In forming my own philosophy of preaching, I have borrowed so much from these men and women that I want to commend their contributions to your own sermonic form and style as well. Should any of you from whom I have borrowed feel unfairly represented, please inform me and forgive my misunderstanding.

Meat and Potatoes (The Expository Base of the Sermon): Haddon W. Robinson

In his preface to the second edition of *Biblical Preaching*, Haddon Robinson confesses that biblical preaching is not just a gift to men in ministry but has passed the gender bias and has become the province of all who are called to preach. He freely confesses the need for expository preaching in a growing secular world which sometimes sees it as a quaint or irrelevant art. His definition of that art has endured across the past three decades until no serious expositor would pass it by:

> Expository preaching is the communication of a biblical concept, derived from and transmitted through a historical, grammatical, and literary study of a passage in its context, which the Holy Spirit first applies to the personality and experience of the preacher, then through the preacher, applies to the hearers.[1]

This means that for every expositor the sermon text must govern the sermon's content. It must always remain the sermon's force. The center of textual force is what Robinson calls the "big idea," and he shows how the expositor is to develop that idea through "subject" and "compliment."

In chapter 3 he discusses how to use the tools of exegesis (commentaries, word studies, dictionaries, etc.). In chapter 4 he discusses how to move from text to application. But it is chapters 5 and 6 that glisten with practicality. The sermon always works between selecting the passage and the formulation of the outline. But the steps of preparation always progress in a clear way that enables the hearer to understand and apply. Yet this is all clearly outlined at the beginning of each chapter, so the expositor is never left without enough rails to reach the exposition goal of changing the world in ways consistent with God's Word.

Still every procedural step needs chapter 10 of the book to move the sermon from form to interest. Here in chapter 10 lies the big question: "Can expository preaching carry its heavy biblical payload and yet be done with interest and relevance?" Preaching in an interesting way is mandatory. Being heard, no matter how important our exposition may be, requires us to pay attention to how we speak, as much as to what is said. But Robinson does not leave us bewildered as to the issues of how we hold attention in an entertainment culture. All in all, this book is the meat and potatoes of the art to which all pulpiteers are called. Small wonder it is a beginning point of all that needs to be our modus operandi in a culture that needs our basic word to be foundational.

The Mind of the Sermon: Ian Pitt-Watson

The Second Helvetic Confession says, *"Praedicatio verbi dei est verbum dei."*[2] For discussing form and style, I want to take the character of the preacher as a given and also say, "The preaching of the Word of God is the Word of God." This is why Ian Pitt-Watson in his *A Primer for Preachers*, for me, pins down the fundamental issue of form and style. Older books on preaching have always rooted the sermon's validity in the character of the preacher. If one's character is invalid, all the rest of homiletics can't matter much. The sermon is only as strong as the preacher's unwavering commitment to truth. That continual commitment should not change from sermon to sermon.

Sermonizing from week to week will gain a hearing in a congregation only when that congregation believes that the preacher believes something, and they *all* know what it is. In other words, those who listen must be able to locate the preacher's worldview. This means, of course, that the preacher too must know what that worldview is. I strongly suggest that all preachers write down the various points of their worldviews and, if possible, put next to them a scriptural text or two that supports what they believe. I realize that scripturally documenting all the elements in our worldview may not be universally appealing, but I am convinced most Christians want a preacher who is certain about every issue of faith.

Pitt-Watson reminds us that it is never possible to know who we are until we know who God is and what he has done.[3] In a sermonic sense, our worldview is inseparably linked to God and our view of him and his involvement in our lives. Who humanity is—our origin and destiny and meaning—are also involved in our worldview. Pitt-Watson declares that the theologically consistent heart of the sermon is the sine qua non of biblical preaching. The heart of the sermon should issue week to week from a single, unwavering view of God and humanity. Small wonder then that Pitt-Watson declares that the "what" of our preaching is more important than the "how."[4] The "what" is the content of our worldview. This issue of interpretation comes before all others. It comes way before the use of commentaries and word study sources. The sermon is about God before it is about us.[5] Therefore, it is imperative that the preacher's worldview remain moored to the text of Scripture. "Theology empowers the ethic," says Pitt-Watson.[6]

A real danger of the narrative sermon arises at this point. So many of the megachurch pastors have begun seeker services to attract seekers. Theology has been seen as a kind of "white" demon that destroys the secular draw. In tiptoeing around people's worldviews, an impression might be left that the preacher's real worldview is too offensive to speak about openly. A caution must be sounded. Worldviews are so essential that preachers must not try to give seekers any reinforcement that their own worldview is okay as it is. Nor, God forbid, should preachers imply that their worldview is identical to those who hear their sermons. This soft approach has in every earlier generation fostered unholy syncretisms. Such glitzy appeal distracts the heart with trifles while the deepest issues of conversion and discipleship go unmet.

Remember that conversion has always been the work of the Holy Spirit. To foster the opinion that conversion is anything *less* than a changing of worldviews is at its heart unethical. It behooves us all to carry into the pulpit a clear understanding of what we believe about God and our world. It should be so powerful that it cannot help but show through.

The Subject of the Sermon: Bryan Chapell

Bryan Chapell's magnum opus, *Christ-Centered Preaching*, is a work inviting the struggle of soul for all preachers. It is a vast treatise with a multitude of worthwhile junctures to the sides of his central issue—every side trip does not go too far afield and all of them are worth the trip. But the center of his argument is a hunger for the ideal center of Scripture—Jesus Christ. There is something rich in the touch that Chapell keeps with the book of Acts and the apostolic mission to tell the world about Christ.

It is this vital heart of preaching that makes Chapell's book so worthwhile. He argues for the vitality of application that devolves from a clear understanding of the "Fallen Condition Focus." What was lost in Genesis 3 is the whole of all that is essential to a great relationship with God. The rest of the Bible—following Genesis 3—is a focus on Christ and how to regain the glory of our lost estate. The world does not primarily need sermons, only

Jesus. Yet sermons are to present Jesus as God's final answer to the tragedy of Eden. Preaching the Bible is not shallow, but it may not be redemptive. Preaching Christ as he lives at the center of Scripture *is* redemptive, and to understand all that Jesus is enables us to apply the sermon to human need.

There is, after all, no sermon when there is no application. Chapell gives us the application key in the following account:

> A former student recently telephones me for assistance because his congregation seemed to be growing less and less responsive to his preaching. "Last Sunday during the sermon," he said, "they just looked at me like they were lumps on a log. I got no feedback whatsoever. What am I doing wrong?"
>
> I asked him to describe his sermon to me. He responded by giving me the main points of his outline:
>
> Noah was wise.
> Noah was fearless.
> Noah was faithful.
>
> "I understand," I said. "Now, why did you tell them that?"
>
> There was a long pause on the other end of the phone line. Then he groaned. "Oh yeah. I forgot!"[7]

Like Robinson before him, Chapell takes seriously the matter of study and structuring the sermon. But no one can preach or apply in the best way without an open admission that illustration and story are fundamental to the communication of the Word of God.

> Christ actually followed a long-established pattern. First there was the pre-Christian rabbinic tradition in the form of Haggadah (the way of story, as opposed to Halakah, the way of reasoned reflection on the law). In addition, the Scriptures themselves are replete with symbols, images, and narratives that are the regular instruments of the communication of religious truths. Alister McGrath summarizes this point emphatically: *"Narrative is the main literary type found in Scripture."* "Remove the narrative content from Scripture and only fragments remain," says Ralph Lewis. Henry Grady Davis states that this does not mean that propositional truths are not presented but that their proportion is diminutive compared to the experiential descriptions and narratives in the rest of the canon.

The Spirit that inspires Scripture reinforces the conclusion that people tend to seize images more readily than they do propositions, and if they take hold of enough images, they can grasp apt principles.[8]

But story like precept must always speak of Jesus and thus requires from the sermon's auditors what Jesus would require.

Christ-Centered Preaching is a huge, all-important book. I never teach my way through it without realizing how much it has to say and how little of it I get across to my students. But then my thirty-five years as an evangelistic pastor has deepened my awareness that Christ must be the subject of every sermon and the ruler of every life—both preacher and "preachee." Chapell's book is too vast to master, but to miss considering it is like willfully ignoring the Pacific while claiming to be an oceanographer.

The Soul of the Sermon: Barbara Brown Taylor

Barbara Brown Taylor is one of the foremost preachers and homileticians of our day. She is one of those rare scholars who has a pastoral bent to all she says about preaching. While she has written widely on the subject of preaching, nothing glistens more than her 1997 Lyman Beecher Lectures published under the title *When God Is Silent*. While her book is reminiscent of Helmut Thielicke's *Silence of God*, the subject matter has to do with all that is literary and profound about the soul of the preacher and preaching. I have tried not to practice any idolatry toward those I admire, but it is hard not to extol the virtue of this woman of God, who has brought all the streams of good homiletics together and forced them to flow beneath the white light of contemporary need and the "listenability" of sermons.

Her work shines for three distinct reasons. (And believe me, I am reluctant to imply that her whole counsel can be wrapped up in the three little packages of my contriving. Still, to set my particular case for narrative preaching, the points are three.)

First, she understands the narrative context of all modern sermons. She says:

The best stories and images are those which have the most recognizable life in them, which means that they are rarely simple or neat. I worry so much that what people hear in church is a cartoon version of real life—sermons populated with one-dimensional characters who work out their problems without ever using language that might threaten their ratings. Meanwhile, many of our listeners are the same people who pay good money to see movies such as *Slingblade* or *The Company of Men*, which—for all their rawness—have provoked more moral discourse among people than any sermon I can think of at the moment.[9]

Barbara Brown Taylor isn't suggesting that improprieties which turn people off are brilliant forms of preaching. She is saying that churches nourished on moralistic or puritanical clichés will rarely develop a congregation of people who understand real life enough to cope with it.

As an evangelical I understand the huge gap that exists from my own Baptist protectionism. Unfortunately, sermons that cannot measure and transcend that difference have little chance of "reaching people for Christ," for they have painted the picture of a Christ who separates himself so far from the streets that the only place he may be brought up is inside the church. Such a milquetoast messiah reigns over people who, if they think at all, think like their sheltered Christ—sidestepping the values of a bent world that desperately needs a real word from people who are committed to truth with its ultimate and hard definitions. Narrative preaching will only be truly redemptive when the narratives that drive them are truly redemptive.

Second, good sermon preparation is comprised of a great deal of silence. These are not times when we run to commentaries or Bible dictionaries. They are times when we manage the art of silence. Sitting in our own silence we encounter the silence of God and his silence invites our participation in the arena of human need. "Who," she asks,

will volunteer to conduct lightning from heaven to earth? Who will offer a guided tour through the beating heart of God? People who are more faithful than we have gotten killed doing things like that, and yet plenty of us climb into pulpits Sunday after Sunday with no more sense of danger than if we were climbing into our cars to go fetch a quart of milk. We do not even put our seat belts on. Why? Because we do not expect anything serious to happen, any more than congregations do. . . . "Every religion that does not affirm that God is hidden," wrote Pascal, "is not true."[10]

All of this goes without saying that the silence of God is the business of the preacher. And Brown Taylor says that it is a problem we are hired to solve. She quotes from a thirteenth-century Persian poet, Jelaluddin Rumi, who said it for all of us:

> I've said before that every craftsman
> searches for what's not there
> to practice his craft.
>
> A builder looks for the rotten hole
> where the roof caved in. A water-carrier
> picks the empty pot. A carpenter
> stops at the house with no door.
>
> Workers rush toward some hint
> of emptiness, which they then
> start to fill. Their hope, though,
> is for emptiness, so don't think
> you must avoid it. It contains
> what you need![11]

Brown Taylor is not down on scholarship when she encourages a meeting of the silences to form the vital sermon. She is just big on that reality that can't be learned from all the homiletics exercises in the world.

Third, she wraps her argument for biblical preaching around Amos's metaphor of famine (Amos 8:11–12). She suggest that the "meat" of the word is often overwhelmed by the "potatoes" in preaching. It is hard to find enough spiritual protein to survive in a world where Christians are malnourished by pulpits which have ceased to care about soul hunger. From a friend of hers, she received this advice: "I have this recurrent nightmare. . . . In the dream, I die and find myself standing before the house of God. When I knock the door blows open and it is clear that no one has lived there for a very long time."[12]

She cites as evidence of the Word-famine the entire chatty religious culture. "Our problem is not too few rations, but too many. The proof that we are in the midst of a famine of the Word are the suffocating piles of our own dead words that rise up around us on every side. It is because they do not nourish us that we require so many of them. It takes thousands of words coming at us every moment, to distract us from the terrible silence within."[13] She concludes the matter by saying: "Our language is broken. There is a famine in the land. God's true name can never be spoken. What's a preacher to do? 'In dispersion, the text is the homeland,' says George Steiner."[14] Indeed, the text is where God lives, and preachers who fail to preach the Word force the society to live in exile. The Word-famine then produces a wasteland, a desert where nothing of value lives, for the rains never come, and T. S. Eliot's words are ever true: "This is the way the world ends . . . not with a bang but a whimper."

I have yet to find any book more crucial to understanding the task of the preacher than this book by Brown Taylor. I really believe that to miss this book is to live an impoverished life and thus to face the shame of coming breadless to the hungry.

The Witness of Preaching: Thomas Long

Congregationally specific sermonizing has for its greatest sin the loss of mission. To continually speak to those inside the church as though they were the only ones to be considered important in the hearing of the sermon really only compounds the problem. If Jesus, for instance, is to be considered the model preacher, one must remember that while his sermons speak to those who listen, they are really for the world as a whole. Where local-specific preaching is the diet of the people, there is a bondage to interiorization. There develops an egoistic ecclesiology whose number one question is, "What am I getting out of church?" Where there is real preaching, the sermon is always reminding the flock that the church doesn't just get together to be told how to live more morally but to remind itself that the church is on a mission.

Thomas G. Long has taken preaching a long way back toward the subject matter of Christ's sermons. His book *The Witness of Preaching* doesn't really arrive at a strong sense of evangelism in preaching, but at least it does declare that the church gathers to bear witness that it lives in defense and testimony of all that Christ and the Scriptures call the church to be.

The witness of preaching is most valid when the pastor picks for himself or herself the herald image, says Long.[15] For those who preach, the most important question for the preacher is not "What shall I say in this sermon?" but "What do I want to happen?" This herald image is borne out in the guiding mark of excellence: "Is this sermon good news for me, for us, for them?"[16] And the good news reaches a summation in Christ and in the truth that God is in Christ reconciling the world to himself (2 Cor. 5:19).

There is something otherworldly about biblical preaching. It is this motif that so often wins it a bad reputation among homileticians. We have made such a god of relevance in preaching that we are prone to forget that in doing this we have actually widened the gap between biblical teaching and current living. The old cliché that "we are so heavenly minded that we are no earthly good" has too much influenced our sermon preparation and delivery. The Bible is in every sense an otherworldly book, but then the message of the kingdom is that, to be relevant, preaching must be future-oriented and touch only on those lasting values of spirituality, meaning, and destiny. Relevance usually does deal with meaning, but so often it does so only in the short run of things. Real meaning lies in mystery, and mystery and relevance are made to appear at variance in much of modern sermonizing.

The church exists to make preaching a call to eternal relevance and to equip its members to make real the gospel of Christ to all who live. This mission will not seem irrelevant when properly preached. On the other hand, the church will have a dynamic reason to be, and the services—once made little by little issues—will grow incendiary and global when the church preaches within its sanctuaries its globally redemptive themes. Such preaching will give the church an eye that will pierce its poor sanctuary walls and make it rich with vision.

The Philosophy of Preaching the Sermon: John Stott

John R. W. Stott quotes P. T. Forsythe as saying: "It is into the Bible world of eternal redemption that the preacher must bring his people."[17] The preacher is inevitably a person who knows that to please God and keep people listening at the same time, the sermon must plunge fearlessly into both worlds—ancient and modern, the biblical and the contemporary—and listen to both.[18] John Chrysostom was praised as a man of the world and a man in the world.[19] While no one likes to be called worldly, the relevance of preaching must come from one who knows both the world and God.

But let us not speak too quickly of knowing God and the world as though they are both to be known in the same way. A preacher is to know the world empirically and know God personally. We are to know the world in terms of understanding and to know God in terms of commitment. We should know the world in terms of study and know God in terms of spiritual intimacy.

To know the world in terms of where it is morally and rationally will keep us from appearing naïve in the pulpit. But to know it experimentally will mire us in a lifestyle that will allow us no power. Stott quotes Karl Barth and gives us Barth's insights on how he went about solving this heavy dilemma of bringing the world to the Word and being sure that the meeting is warm with profit for both. Speaking of his dozen or so years in the pulpit, Barth said,

> I sought to find my way between the problem of human life on the one hand and the content of the Bible on the other. As I wanted to speak to the people in the infinite contradiction of their life, but to speak the no less infinite message of the Bible, which was as much a riddle of life.[20]

Barth went on to describe the dilemma of preaching as a man in the pulpit who lives life in this agony: "Before him lies the Bible full of mystery, and before him are seated his hearers, also full of mystery."[21]

To live and preach in these two worlds will involve both a sense of the adequacy of God and the need of the people. But the people neither know of their need nor the adequacy of God. Since they are so schooled in the things of this world, their whole concept of relevance in the sermon will be not how close it has lived to the world of God but how close it has lived to the media. When Karl Barth was asked years later how he prepared his Sunday sermons, he said it was with the newspaper in one hand and the

Bible in the other.[22] Spurgeon also answered this question in a title of one of his *Little Shilling Book* sermons: "The Bible and the Newspaper"![23]

Years ago I heard Martin Marty say in a conference: "Always read the people section of *Time* magazine first, it's the only subject God's interested in." Whether or not this seems narrow to the effective pulpiteer, the truth still remains: Preach only on God and we shall lose both the attendance of God and people, but preach on humanity and everyone will listen.

Nonetheless, this little cliché must not be allowed to dupe us into believing that the Bible is irrelevant. There exists no other burden quite so heavy as that of pulling the biblical Word and the contemporary world together. Every preacher who wants to please Christ while wanting to have people listen knows the heaviness of this weekly burden.

Making the ancient world contemporary, however, does not lie, as we might suppose, in addressing everything the national network anchorpersons address. No, rather, the issues of contemporaneity group themselves around six questions:

1. What is the purpose of my life?
2. What am I doing here?
3. How did I come to be?
4. Where will I end up?
5. How can I be happy, or happier at least?
6. What does it mean to be human?

Such questions as these inevitably occupy the attention of every generation.[24]

But how do these questions square with knowing about our world: the world of arts and entertainment, for instance? It is easily answered. These questions are the big questions at the center of novels and sculpture as well. These questions lie behind almost every story on the evening news and in the columns of the events that compose every newsmagazine. Preach to these themes, and people will listen. Preach to these themes out of the fullness of Scripture, and your congregation will not only listen, they will have answers that are often not found in the arts and entertainment.

The Narrative Base: Eugene Lowry

There is scarcely a preaching book written that does not take seriously the idea of story. Narrative preaching has become a strong claimant for the title of the best sermon style. No preacher has been more vocal or has more to say than Eugene Lowry on this matter. The issue of so many stories in preaching and using a single story as the basis of narrative preaching (and this, by definition, is narrative preaching) has become the model operation of many pulpits in the interest of holding interest.

Nothing quite holds people's attention like stories. The reason for this has to do with compelling intrigue of character and plot. Plot above all locks people in and builds into the sermon a magnetic sense of intrigue. Eugene Lowry defines plot as "the moving suspense of a story from disequilibrium to resolution."[25] Resolution kills interest. It is the opening of the sermon package that keeps people listening, not the laying open of the contents of that package.

Whatever else it may be, plot is mystery concealed. But it is not mystery only, it is the promise of mystery revealed that draws and maintains attention until the mystery is entirely exposed. Obviously, to keep people listening, we must not expose the mystery entirely. The thing is to unravel the exposé artistically, gradually, and with compelling use of adjectives.

We are, after all, "doing time" in the pulpit, and the time that we "do" is all important. Time is the medium of life, wrote Thomas Mann.[26] It is within the frame of time that the sermon must serve. If the sermon refuses to take this stewardship of time seriously, then the whole idea of story intrigue is spoiled. None of us likes overlong stories. A story must neither hurry nor dawdle. It must work with time, and if it sins against time with brevity or longevity, it loses the power of interest.

One thing is sure: throughout our lives we pay attention to movement rather than still life.[27] Streams are more interesting than ponds. Stories are generally more interesting than precepts. The key thing is that the telling of a pulpit story or the preaching of an entire narrative sermon should be careful to create the same kind of tension that the original writer or teller of the story felt as he or she created the story in the first place. And what is this tension? This is the tension of remembrance: All great stories do not spring spontaneously from their creators. They grow and develop even as they are told.

Neil Simon once wrote that the "writing of a play is like walking through a dark woods; you are never sure what you are going to meet next."[28] Since stories tell themselves to the novelists and playwrights who write them, they must appear to have the ensnaring interest to the preachers who tell them. When they totally ensnare an audience, they are a force. But to the preacher, the story has appeared with a power of its own and is telling itself. The powerful spell of narration wraps the gospel up in marvelous intrigue even as it unfolds its spellbinding plot.

The Movement of the Sermon: David Buttrick

David Buttrick's *Homiletic* was subtitled *Moves and Structures*. At first, this subtitle seemed like an oxymoron to me. It appeared contradictory. If it moved, it could not be structured; if it is very structured, it will scarcely move. His contribution, however, is well worth considering. The pacing of a sermon has to do with movement and with linking blocks of content together as a freight train would link cars to keep all the issues of the sermon in motion.

Sermons are to involve a kind of sequential talking.[29] This is especially true if the sermon moves according to the classic definition of preaching as conversation. Buttrick includes the following illustration to demonstrate his conversational moves:

> "Are you going to Chicago?"
> "No, I'm going to Traverse City, Michigan."
> "There's a cherry festival there every summer, isn't there?"
> "I don't know, I'm going to a music camp."
> "You're a musician?"
> "Maybe someday—I play the French horn!"
> "Oh, that's supposed to be difficult."
> "I guess so, I'm struggling."
> "Well, take some time to go fishing, there's salmon now in Lake Michigan."[30]

Buttrick deals severely with preaching when it becomes so conversational it can change subjects at this pace. Still, his example does illustrate that incredible speed at which conversations move from subject to subject. As odd as it may sound, it is the casual style that can be used to move the sermon along at an exciting pace. Although Buttrick would deplore using the casual style just to pick up sermonic velocity, the ideas do relate. Hurrying the sermon along may still not supply enough intensity to keep people listening.[31] Neither will merely stepping up the pace of the sermon supply it with power.

Three things pick up the pace but do not hurry the sermon past excellence. First of all, the sermon should have no long illustrations (at least inordinately long).[32] Long illustrations tend to intrigue listeners while they chop the shorter, more effective illustrations from the message. Thus longer stories are often the most discontinuous.

Second, pacing will become ineffective if more than one illustration is used per move.[33] Piling story upon story usually builds deadness, and there is a point at which an overillustrated sermon will not be able to count on the stories to hold attention any longer. It will be like going to a seven-movie marathon at a drive-in theater. There comes a point when the mind will lose interest in the continual stream of narrative.

But third and most important, Buttrick claims that every sermon should move in harmony with a double hermeneutic. Not the Bible/newspaper hermeneutic so often attributed to Barth, but the knowledge of God/knowledge of ourselves hermeneutic.[34] This is the most instructive and substantially paced hermeneutic of all. The key is not only to make a sermon move but to make a sermon move with communication and content.

In the Buttrick concept of moves and structures, the most acceptable mode of outlining is the one-point sermon. Three-point sermons and oral exegesis models will teach more, but they do not cohere as sermons, and they lose the oratory in favor of pedagogy. This is to say they begin to succeed at catechism and lose the function of worship and exhortation.

The Spirit and the Life of the Sermon: Donald Coggan

Donald Coggan makes it clear in his short but glistening work on preaching, *Preaching: The Sacrament of the Word*, that to keep our sermons from going dead, there are three integers, all of which must be taken seriously: the preacher, the person in the pew, and the Holy Spirit.[35] Coggan also reminds us that there is no sermon without the Holy Spirit.[36] In the act of preaching, the total church goes into action, since the cast of worship does indeed include these three primary actors.[37] It is deadly for the sermon to call itself a fait accompli with only one or two of these integers in place.

The ministry of the Holy Spirit joins with all of the senses in making real worship possible. I would like to recall what I have said in another place: The eye picks up the architecture and worship ornament that are put in place for the preaching service. The senses become the apprehenders of the Spirit. They garner into the matrix of our hearing and feeling the total impact of the spoken word. These senses gather the motives of the Spirit for all that he wants to use in terms of sermon impact in our lives.[38]

The Holy Spirit also animates and impassions the sermon.[39] This idea accentuates the fact that passion is not a matter of voice level or the preacher's cathexis with the subject. The power of the sermon, its "anima" or life, is a direct result of God's participation in the preaching event.

The Sermon and the Altar: Calvin Miller

I hate to conclude this list of luminaries by adding an emphasis from my own books, and I would not presume to do so except I find the emphasis—for some odd reason—missing from other important works on homiletics. For this reason alone I must add my own word on the sermon and the altar. My conversion and subsequent life in Christ all occurred—and still does—within that wide stream of evangelicalism that focuses worship and preaching on the altar. Therefore I have long believed that the sermon is not a showpiece of homiletic art. The sermon is there to facilitate God's work of change in the lives of people. All of us who believe in Christ are undergoing sanctification. This is to say that God is never finished with his maturing work in our lives. I cannot deny that this tenth element of form comes from my own years of preaching. The altar call has permanently marked my view of what God is about in the world. Therefore, I will likely always miss seeing it in place at the end of every sermon that is worthy of bearing the name *sermon*! Evangelicals have always had the feeling that God wants to do something special in the sanctifying and finishing of each and every one of us. Further, they have assumed that spiritual growth is achieved in a series of leaps of faith that are crystallized leap by leap in specific decisions. These decisions are often made at church and made formally at public altars.

The prominence of altar theology among all evangelicals presumes four things about the sermon. First of all, the sermon is not a speech. The altar, in effect, has every preacher saying, "My words contain his words, and his words are not to be taken lightly. In fact, when his words are through flying at you, you will be given the opportunity to respond to God. This sermon is not all that important, but your response to God is. Think about his words, and focus on your needs. The altar time at the end of this service will give you a chance to bring these two together."

Second, this altar presupposes the issue of time. Time, like every sermon attender, belongs to God. The issue of a given sermon is not how long or short it is; the issue of this sermon is that each of us have unfinished transactions with God. The altar will allow each listener the chance to complete this transaction. How long will all this take? The question is pointless. Will the roast burn if you tarry too long beyond noon? How superficial a question! In the meeting of a King and the receiving of his commission, such questions pale into insignificance. Just focus on your need and his sovereignty. The clock is set to measure many things, but not this.

Third, the altar is a forum for application and not a place of education. The sermon should and does teach, but teaching is not the issue of the altar. The issue is encounter. Experiencing the reality and presence of God is what altars are all about. So let the preacher not grieve that the sermon lacked Greek roots or dogma. The sermon sets up the communication channel that brings heaven and earth into oneness so this necessary and formidable union of heaven and earth may apply to the listener and require a longing of the empty hearer to be filled.

Fourth, the altar is a place of mystery. The sermon should contain the issue of mystery, and house its compelling intrigue. The altar should continue this intrigue as it brings the demands of the sermon to glorious completion. Here, classically, in evangelical worship services, mourners mourned and overcomers celebrated.

And in these days when ecclesiology has shifted ever further from seeing the altar as necessary, it is difficult for those of us who have known its counsel to see it abandoned. The altar remains imperative, whether or not it physically exists in the liturgy or whether it is implied. The altar must inhabit and haunt the sermon, as it calls people to a rendezvous with God and encourages them to touch the face of God—to decide and be changed.

Notes

Introduction

1. Fred Craddock, *Preaching* (Nashville: Abingdon, 1985). This text, although twenty years old, remains for me incisive and scholarly, precisely because it does come with the academic authority of the scholar who produced it. Craddock himself became the filter for decades of scholarship, without the tedium of lots of internal quotes.

2. John R. W. Stott, *Between Two Worlds* (Grand Rapids: Eerdmans, 1982), 292. Stott confesses that it is not the length of a sermon that makes a sermon seem long but the preacher's lack of interest in the subject being preached.

3. Keith Willhite, *Preaching with Relevance* (Grand Rapids: Kregel, 2001), 131. Willhite, like most sensitive scholars, agrees that there is no substitute for the power of the Holy Spirit in preaching. Great preaching rises from the numinous as much as from the communicator's library.

4. Bryan Chapell, *Christ-Centered Preaching*, 2nd ed. (Grand Rapids: Baker, 1994; repr. Grand Rapids: Baker, 2005). For a further discussion of this subject, see Chapell's book, page 48ff. Citations are to the 2005 edition.

5. Craig A. Loscalzo, *Apologetic Preaching* (Downers Grove, IL: InterVarsity, 2000), 28. Incidentally, Craig Loscalzo corrects Josh McDowell by reminding us that apologetic preaching does not create faith, only a climate friendly for the birth of faith.

6. "The State of the Church, 2000," The Barna Group, March 21, 2000, http://www.barna.org/FlexPage.aspx?Page=BarnaUpdate&Barna UpdateID=49.

7. "Religious Activity Increasing in the West," The Barna Group, March 1, 2004, http://www.barna.org/FlexPage.aspx?Page=BarnaUpdate &BarnaUpdateID=159.

8. Philip Jenkins, *The Next Christendom* (Oxford: Oxford University Press, 2001).

9. James Shaddix, *The Passion-Driven Sermon* (Nashville: Broadman & Holman, 2003). Shaddix has a wonderful discussion of the true nature of passion and its imperative force in great preaching.

10. Joseph Seaborn Jr., *Celebration of Ministry* (Grand Rapids: Baker, 1990), 31. Seaborn quotes Spurgeon as saying that without passion the world drifts asleep: "To stand and drone out a sermon in a kind of articulate snoring to people who are somewhere between awake and asleep must be wretched work."

11. Warren Wiersbe, *The Dynamics of Preaching* (Grand Rapids: Baker, 1999), 76. Wiersbe says that great preaching is only possible through the mutual ministry of preacher and listener. Dialogue is at the heart of healthy homilies.

12. Malcolm Muggeridge, "The Fourth Temptation of Christ," *Christ in the Media* (Grand Rapids: Eerdmans, 1977).

13. Chapell, *Christ-Centered Preaching*, 2nd ed., 178–80. Let me differentiate between what Chapell calls "illustrating the sermon" and what I mean by story. Chapell calls illustrations a slice out of life; story is more a medium of interpretation and relating the Scripture and contemporary need. The longer I teach homiletics the more I don't like the word *illustration*, for it is too weak a word to serve its huge purpose in communication. Nowadays it comes across, as its Latin based meaning suggests, "to light up" the propositions of the sermon. Stories do not serve any single proposition: they are bigger, more important than that. They outdo the proposition—they become the interpretation that lies at the heart of the sermon. They are more than little moments of "once upon a time"; stories come to out-endure the propositions preachers often employ them to "illustrate."

Chapter 1 Who's Talking?

1. Edward Markquart, *The Quest for Better Preaching* (Minneapolis: Augsburg, 1988), 58. Markquart observes: "People want their preachers to be authentic human beings . . . who experience all the same feelings and struggles as the laity, who do not hide behind the role of 'Reverend So and So.'" Being human is the first qualification of being an authentic communicator.

2. Ralph Waldo Emerson, *Letters and Serial Aims*, vol. 8, *Complete Works of Ralph Waldo Emerson* (Boston: Houghton Mifflin, 1917), 96.

3. J. Philip Wogaman, *Speaking the Truth in Love* (Louisville: Westminster John Knox, 1998), 82. "Prophetic preaching," writes Wogaman, "deals not only with evils to be overcome; it offers hope that they can be overcome. . . . No matter how wretched the situation may be, no matter how powerful the forces of evil that confront us, no matter how futile all aspirations may seem—still nevertheless it is God's world, so there is always hope." By implication Wogaman also says that the despair around us is real, a scenario that megachurch theology has overlooked. Nothing seems desperate, and when nothing seems desperate love is less important and hope doesn't matter. Preaching never comes to be in such a rosy, unreal world.

4. Willhite, *Preaching with Relevance*, 17. Many preachers today are torn between what seems relevant and what seems biblical preaching. Willhite admits, "I hesitated because I feared that a focus on relevance would lead to what I think masquerades for appropriate Biblical preaching. We hear sermons that are no more than pop psychology (Ten Timely Tips to Tame your Teenager, or . . . How to Hold Up in a Fold Up World). . . ." Willhite admits that these thinly veiled biblical sermons lose touch with Scripture in an attempt to achieve relevance.

5. Donald Coggan, *Preaching: The Sacrament of the Word* (New York: Crossroad, 1988), 32. Coggan admits the only valid place to begin thinking about the sermon is to begin thinking about God.

6. Calvin Miller, *Spirit, Word, and Story* (Dallas: Word, 1989; repr. Grand Rapids: Baker, 1996), 49. This citation is to the 1989 edition. All other citations are to the 1996 edition. Back in 1989 I wrote, "Rhetoric alone will not convince our listeners that the spiritual world is an enduring one. Mystery is not an oral argument: mystery is an aura. It is sermonic light, seen, not heard, so that those who attend the sermon know that there is more to the indwelling Spirit than the senses can measure." Once again this mystery, filtered through a soul who is no stranger to mystery, is all that really qualifies as preaching.

7. James Crenshaw, *Trembling at the Threshold of a Biblical Text* (Grand Rapids: Eerdmans, 1994), 12. Crenshaw believes that the greatest wonder of the sermon and of worship is that these two realms, heaven and earth, can actually touch each other, and there the preacher really does become a purveyor of wonder, a channel of miracle, a medium through whom God touches the world of the needy listeners who have come to listen.

8. Leander E. Keck, *The Bible in the Pulpit* (Nashville: Abingdon, 1980), 32–33. Leander Keck admits that the church needs the Bible in the preacher, the Bible in the pulpit, and the Bible in the people. When it is missing in the preacher, it has little hope in being found in the latter two.

9. Robert Chisholm, "שַׁד [shad]." Willem A. VanGemeren, ed., *The New International Dictionary of Old Testament Theology and Exegesis* (Grand Rapids: Zondervan, 1997), 4:47.

10. Kenton C. Anderson, *Preaching with Conviction* (Grand Rapids: Kregel, 2001), 89. Anderson reminds us that one of Fred Craddock's central adages was that the common ground between the elitist purity of the text and the common need of those who hear a sermon is the preacher's humanity. It would do us well to remember that being human is the only real hope of bringing our hearers into the presence of God.

Chapter 2 Who's Out There?

1. George Bernanos, *The Diary of a Country Priest* (New York: Macmillan, 1937), 30. The country priest understood that you can only talk at people till you know who's before you and then you can talk to them: "If only God would open my eyes and unseal my ears so that I might behold the face of my parish." Until we understand who's listening, we are powerless to really speak.

2. John R. Claypool, *The Preaching Event* (Waco, TX: Word Books, 1980), 89. John Claypool says that the best way to preach truth that may save others from the whips and scorns of life is to preach the truths that have already saved ourselves.

3. Thomas L. Oden, *After Modernity . . . What?* (Grand Rapids: Zondervan, 1989), 168–69. Thomas Oden, in describing our last-ditch attempt to relate to the know-nothing opinionated, pictures the way we have tried to strip down what we preach in this way: "We have learned in modernity to keep fashionably silent about the incarnation, atonement, and resurrection and to develop positions less controversial and more agreeable with the assumptions of modernity. . . . We have cheated our young people out of the hard but necessary Christian word about human sin and divine redemption."

4. Ronald J. Allen, *Interpreting the Gospel* (St. Louis: Chalice, 1998), 99. This self-centeredness in congregations and our attempt to tell them something of what they want to hear leads pastors into mass confusion as to what they ought to preach about. One young pastor lamented: "For me, the hardest part of preaching is knowing what I want to preach about."

5. John MacArthur, as quoted in Michael Duduit, *Communicate with Power: Insights from America's Top Ten Communicators* (Grand Rapids: Baker, 1996), 129–30. MacArthur says, "I must measure my own life before God. I must first of all be a man of God. What I say is the overflow of who I am. I will never be powerful in the pulpit if I am not speaking out of the vortex of a dynamic relationship with the living God. . . . Nothing

is more precious to God than his word, and every time I interpret a passage, I exercise a sacred trust."

6. Coggan, *Preaching: The Sacrament of the Word*, 21–22. When a newly ordained American Episcopal priest receives his ordination Bible, it comes accompanied by these words: "Receive this book; here are the words of eternal life. Take them for your life and declare them to the world."

7. Rick Ezell, *Hitting a Moving Target* (Grand Rapids: Kregel, 1999), 87. "When the Barna Research group asked unchurched people what might bring them to a church, the number one response (given by nearly one out of five) was better messages. I suspect that what they meant by better messages was sermons that spoke to them where they lived and addressed their pressing needs. People want Christian public speakers to know them personally, to empathize with their hurts and to revel in their joys. Such messages are practical, for they teach people their similarities each to the other."

8. David P. Mulder, *Narrative Preaching* (St. Louis: Concordia, 1996), 11. "I have a high respect for seminary education. Pastors need the preparatory work it provides. Far too often, however, in the academic atmosphere the student writes sermons to please the professor, who is usually a scholar. Many seminary students also personally identify with their professors. They hear the professor lecture day after day. It should come as no surprise when a new preacher sounds much like a professor, during his first years of ministry."

9. Marva Dawn and Eugene Peterson, *The Unnecessary Pastor* (Grand Rapids: Eerdmans, 2000), 218. Marva Dawn makes this point with these words: "Everybody is looking for love, for loyalty, for sure solutions to lonely yearning expressed in the questions, 'To whom do I belong,' and 'Whom can I trust?'"

10. Henri Nouwen, as quoted in Dawn and Peterson, *The Unnecessary Pastor*, 190. Henri Nouwen writes: "I am deeply convinced that the Christian Leader of the future is called to stand in this world with nothing to offer but his own vulnerable self. That is the way that Jesus came to reveal God's love. The great message we have to carry as ministers of God's Word and followers of Jesus, is that God loves us not because of what we do or accomplish but because God has created and redeemed us in love and has chosen us to proclaim that love as the true source of all human life."

11. Miller, *Spirit, Word, and Story* (1996), 93. Preaching a cold Bible may come from a scholarly soul who has never admitted that the love of study is more important than the love of people. Commentaries and all other tools of preparation are good, but to love them more than to love the congregation is never wise. "Commentaries can subvert relevant

preaching in two ways. First, the commentary can provide the preacher with a ready-made outline that fits neither the needs of the congregation nor the sermon's intended goal. Second the commentary may give the preacher ready made ideas that keep him from digging out the material himself." Probably worse than either of these two weaknesses is that the love of commentaries may cause the preacher to become a bookworm and cease to cherish shepherding the sheep, whence comes the ultimate love of his life.

12. Frank G. Honeycutt, *Preaching to Skeptics and Seekers* (Nashville: Abingdon, 2001), 111. Honeycutt describes a recent installment of "Kudzu" in the Sunday comics, the Pulitzer Prize–winning cartoonist Doug Marlette depicts Will B. Dunn addressing his congregation from the opening panel. He looks out over the top of his glasses and says to his flock, "Okay, Gang! Pop Quiz!" The Reverend Will B. Dunn is obviously pleased with himself and says to his flock, "Brothers and sisters, today I want to give you a test—a spiritual maturity test. This test will measure your depth of spiritual development as a congregation. Okay, ready? First question—Complete the sentence: 'Whosoever will smite you on the right cheek . . .'" and without hesitation the congregation thunders back. "Waste 'em! Sue his Carcass! String him up!" The last panel shows a depressed Reverend thinking these words to himself, "I may be forced to grade on the curve."

13. Chapell, *Christ-Centered Preaching*, 2nd ed., 283. We have to remember that preaching the second coming gives us the certainty that Christ is ultimately winning." The entire Apocalypse is about this drama and it is easy to see how it brought a sense of confidence to those who sweltered under Roman persecution. This kind of preaching is dramatic stuff and it calls the church to recall the ultimate victory that is theirs. This kind of preaching will spawn an ongoing sense of joy in worship and preaching.

14. Os Guinness, *The Call* (Nashville: Word, 1998; repr., Nashville: W. Publishing Group, 2003), 4. Citation is to the 1998 edition. The answer to this question of purpose is hidden in these words of Os Guinness: "Answering the call of our Creator is the ultimate 'why for living.'"

Chapter 3 Whadda Ya Hear Me Sayin'?

1. Barbara Brown Taylor, *When God Is Silent* (Cambridge, MA: Cowley, 1998), 22. When our lives are not captive to the presence of Christ, we become ensnared in our own pulpit foolishness. "I listened to an Easter sermon once in which the preacher stood up in front of a church full of people hungry for good news and told us Easter bunny jokes, one after another. He never met our eyes. He looked up at the light fixtures as he delivered his punch lines, never noticing how we laughed less each time.

Finally he said something about how Easter was God's joke on death and we should all laugh more. Then he said *amen* and sat down. I have never in my life wished so badly for pulpit police. I wanted someone with a badge to go up and arrest that guy, slap some handcuffs on him and lead him away." The sermon can degenerate into all kinds of slapstick when the preacher has no committed love for Christ.

2. Keith F. Nickle, *Preaching the Gospel of Luke* (Louisville: Westminster John Knox , 2000), 48. Altars do point to critical moments, commitments, and callings. Keith Nickle says, "Sometimes an overemphasis to the community of faith eclipses awareness that the community's worship and study are not just to praise God but to equip the community to go forth with Jesus beyond the confines of its own self-identity to engage in service on behalf of God to God's world."

3. Hugh Litchfield, *Visualizing the Sermon* (Sioux Falls, SD: self-published, 1996), 37. But when the speaker and the hearer are both right-brained, story has its maximum impact. "The easiest material to picture are the historical stories, narrative material and the gospels. They usually have a well-defined plot, good stories, colorful characters. Much of the Bible is couched in this kind of literary genre. As we work with such texts let them take flesh and blood and come alive in our imaginations. Let us step into the scenes and see and hear and feel them happening."

4. James W. Thompson, *Preaching Like Paul* (Louisville: Westminster John Knox, 2001), 13. Narrative preaching, says James W. Thompson, is reluctant to speak with authority and make concrete demands. He admits that Paul's precept-driven style of writing (and likely preaching) may not have contained the narrative elements so important to today's listeners, but he also points out that sometimes the narrative sermon rolls over us with its fuzzy, unclear requirements.

5. E. K. Bailey and Warren Wiersbe, *Preaching in Black and White* (Grand Rapids: Zondervan, 2003), 57. But a warning must be sounded here. The key is to make story a natural part of our lives: a really interesting subject cannot be exaggerated into vitality. And propositonal preachers who try to fake a narrative style will usually be found out. When we try forms unnatural to us we can become dry as dust. E. K. Bailey referred to this as getting in the flesh, and this always results in a dry and boring pulpit style.

6. Barbara Brown Taylor, *The Preaching Life* (Cambridge, MA: Cowley, 1993), 79. The temptation when the sermon is falling on doubtful ears is to make it some kind of show-and-tell time. But Barbara Brown Taylor cautions us to remember that "[w]e speak as members of the body and not for ourselves alone, which means we may not dominate the sermon anymore than we may be absent from it."

7. Craig A. Loscalzo, *Evangelistic Preaching That Connects* (Downers Grove, IL: InterVarsity, 1995), 109. Craig Loscalzo causes us to remember that the world is looking for what we've got and are really anxious in many ways to get tuned in. "The good news insists that a new world view is on the scene, a new order of thinking, a new way of making meaning, a new way of treating people, a new way of glimpsing who we are in the sight of God."

8. Eugene L. Lowry, *The Homiletical Plot* (Louisville: Westminster John Knox, 2001), 25. Eugene Lowry points to what people are really interested in: "The homiletical plot must catch people in the depths of the awful discrepancies of their world—social and personal. It is to these very real discrepancies that the gospel of Christ is addressed."

9. Barbara Brown Taylor, *The Luminous Web* (Cambridge, MA: Cowley, 2000), 1. Whatever else is to be said the sermon must seem real and relational because the preacher is real and relational. Abraham Heschel, quoted by Barbara Brown Taylor, says that compassion (which is always the stuff of relational preaching) is more important than authority. "Religion declined not because it was refuted, but because it became irrelevant, dull, oppressive, insipid. When faith is completely replaced by creed, worship by discipline, love by habit; when the crisis of today is ignored because of the splendor of the past; when faith becomes an heirloom rather than a living fountain; when religion speaks only in the name of authority rather than with the voice of compassion, its message becomes meaningless."

10. Eugene L. Lowry, *The Sermon: Dancing the Edges of Mystery* (Nashville: Abingdon, 1997), 33. According to Lowry, Harry Emerson Fosdick agrees with the argument I am making here: "The preacher's business is not merely to repent. . . . Nor merely to talk about the available power of God to bring victory over trouble and temptation, but to send people out of their worship on Sunday with victory in their possession. A preacher's task is to create in his congregation the thing he is talking about."

11. John Killinger, *Preaching the New Millennium* (Nashville: Abingdon, 1999), 43. "I may be wrong, but it seems to me that the amazing surge of spirituality (or at least the hunger for it) in the last couple of decades has something to do with our disappointments in the old millennium and our unconscious feelings of hope as a new one approaches."

Chapter 4 So What's to Be Done Now?

1. Mark Galli and Craig Brian Larson, *Preaching That Connects* (Grand Rapids: Zondervan, 1994), 22. "The question is not whether our communication is manipulative. Of course it is manipulative—in the good sense. We want to influence, shape, alter, change how people think and

behave—but not for personal gain. We do not want to be deceptive. We do not want people to become so emotionally charged they'll do anything we say. We do not want to overpower people's free wills. But we do want to influence people."

2. Ian Pitt-Watson, *A Primer for Preachers* (Grand Rapids: Baker, 1986), 21. "What is preaching? Is it proclamation, not just moralizing? It is Good News, not just good advice; it is gospel not just law. Supremely, it is about God and what he has done, not just about us and about what we ought to do. Logically and theologically (though by no means always chronologically) preaching is about God before it is about us; it is about what God has done before it is about what we ought to do."

3. F. Dean Lueking, *Preaching: The Art of Connecting God and People* (Waco, TX: Word, 1984), 24. "Love provides the only right motive for the act of preaching itself. It is the power which moves the one who preaches out among the people with care for the uniqueness of every human. It quickly shows the manner as well as the content of preaching. The difference between preaching *at* people and preaching *for* people is the difference that love makes."

4. Charles L. Bartow, *The Preaching Moment* (Nashville: Abingdon, 1980), 13. "Some preachers . . . convince themselves that their 'much speaking' has accomplished something. In preaching, however, as in any form of communication, you will discover that talk is never all. The talk is only half and it is the least important half. The other half, and the most important half, is listening."

5. Martin Luther, *Luther's Works*, vol. 36 (Philadelphia: Fortress, 1959), 116.

6. Stanley Hauerwas and William H. Willimon, *Resident Aliens* (Nashville: Abingdon, 1989), 103. "Our lives begin to take on a form and a pattern, and we come to see our ethical quandaries, not as isolated situations that require us to say yes or say no, but as a continuing story of God with God's people."

7. Thomas G. Long, *The Witness of Preaching* (Louisville: Westminster John Knox, 1989), 100. It is inevitably metaphor and story that make abstractions concrete. Thomas Long admits: "Homileticians like Craddock and Lowry have gone a long way toward restoring creativity and excitement in sermon form because they overcome many of the problems of the static outline and provide the means for enabling hearers to be active and responsible participants in the preaching event."

8. David Buttrick, *Homiletic* (Philadelphia: Fortress, 1987), 11. How does preaching connect the ancient text with the now? It does by seeing the biblical world as part of the past/present continuum. "Preaching constructs in consciousness a 'faith world' related to God. Preaching transforms identity by adding a new beginning to our stories." This new

beginning of ours is a textual beginning. But the remainder of the stories includes us, indeed it is our story.

9. Elizabeth Achtemeier, *Preaching as Theology and Art* (Nashville: Abingdon, 1984), 129. From a sermon preached during Pentecost, Elizabeth Achtemeier says: "So it is similarly with the yoke of Christ. If we would have the good life, if we would find rest and release from the burdens and problems of our life, then we must take on an additional load, the responsibility of doing Christ's will, in the world—of following his commands."

10. Ralph Lewis with Gregg Lewis, *Inductive Preaching: Helping People Listen* (Westchester, IL: Crossway, 1983), 163. Ralph Lewis and Gregg Lewis quote John Stott as he defines what true expository preaching is. Such preaching is not defending a view of Scripture (such as inerrant or expository). It is bringing out "of the text what is there and exposing it to view. But the text in question could be a verse or a sentence or a single word. It could be a paragraph, a chapter or a whole book. Whether it is long or short, our responsibilities as expositors [are] to open it up in such a way that it speaks its message clearly, plainly, relevantly, without addition, subtraction or falsification."

11. Thomas H. Troeger, *Imaging a Sermon* (Nashville: Abingdon, 1990), 15. "When we are attentive to what is, we do not gum up our consciousness with preconceptions that remove us from the truth of our experience. We trust, as did the biblical writers, that common things may be the source of Revelation."

Chapter 5 Dealing with the Text

1. David L. Larsen, *Telling the Old, Old Story* (Wheaton: Crossway, 1995), 16. Larsen locates the preacher's artistic drive by quoting G. Stanley Hall: "Let me tell the stories, I care not who writes the textbooks."

2. Naming a sermon receives very little attention in homiletic texts. The neglect of the subject is baffling to me. This makes me think of the books of names we studied before our children were born. We understood that this was the way our progeny would be denoted throughout their lives and even after that. It would have been unthinkable to have been haphazard in the matter. Nothing really begins to have identity that endures until it is assigned a name.

3. David Buttrick, *A Captive Voice* (Louisville: Westminster John Knox, 1994), 76. A Broadway play opened in 1964 called *Beyond the Fringe*. The play was built around a spoof on an Anglican sermon and grew out of a single verse in Genesis: "But my brother Esau is an hairy man, but I am a smooth man." Whatever may be said of the key line, it is memorable and it stands at the front of the play. Titles in the same way perform the same purpose.

4. Markquart, *Quest for Better Preaching*, 101. "Martin Luther insisted on finding the *sinnmitte*, the heart of the text. That heart or *kern* is to save the preacher from getting lost in details. . . . The main point of the sermon is to be so clear in the preacher's mind that it controls everything that is said."

5. Allen, *Interpreting the Gospel*, 10. Nearly every homiletic text has some definition of the purpose for preaching. One reply to the issue exists in the very title of Ronald Allen's book *Interpreting the Gospel*. But Allen goes on to say it very well: "Preaching is a mode of witness to the gospel. The distinctive vocation of preaching is help the congregation name and interpret the divine presence and purpose."

6. William H. Willimon and Stanley Hauerwas, *Preaching to Strangers* (Louisville: Westminster John Knox, 1992), 37. Stanley Hauerwas wrote Will Willimon a letter commenting on a sermon and by coincidence touched on the very thing that makes sermons memorable. "I thought your opening sermon for the school year was challenging and truthful. One of the reasons that I thought the sermon was so good is that I heard a bit of myself in it. I loved the part about making up their own minds because that's a theme I've been developing lately." The sermon was good apparently because it struck the listener in the middle of his own working through of some of life's issues. Preaching that manages this kind of intersection is always memorable.

7. The old answer to the thesis-less sermon lies in this old adage: "What did the preacher preach about? I don't know, he never said."

8. Honeycutt, *Preaching to Skeptics and Seekers*, 11. "One of my problems with so-called seeker services and seeker-sensitive churches is that, in my pastoral experience, whatever most people are seeking it isn't Jesus." The word *contemporary*, which really means at the same time as the rest of culture, has come to stand for a style of preaching and worship which in most cases has abandoned its basic roots in theology.

9. All of the quotations below are taken from Markquart, *Quest for Better Preaching*, 101–2. This motif can be related to or even identical with the thesis, as I outline it in this book, or what many homileticians call the "theme statement." Helmut Thielicke had called this one-sentence statement his "textual thematic" guide to the sermon. He said this one, correlating "textual-thematic" would do four things: First, it would make sure the sermon remained rooted in the text. Second, it would enable the preacher to better achieve order and clarity. Third, it would enable the hearer to better retain what the sermon was about. Fourth, it would help those who were new in church or the Christian faith to have a little help in understanding and retaining the expository sermon.

"I try to express the thrust of the present sermon in one clear sentence," said Allen and Herin.

"Because the preacher can state his point in one simple sentence, he knows the destination of the trip that will be his sermon," said Fred Craddock.

"The first step in preparing a sermon is to state in one sentence the content of the sermon," said Richard Halverson.

"I do not think that any sermon ought to be preached or even written until that sentence has emerged, clear and lucid as a cloudless moon," said John Henry Jowett.

10. Mulder, *Narrative Preaching*, 87. David Mulder cites a sermon on Philippians 3 called "Press On! Press On!" The title itself suggests a motif that might be used within the sermon to focus and channel the delivery. Once again it would be impossible to speak of just how much the two short words should be repeated. I once heard a preacher preach a sermon called "Go On!" It was actually a spoof on the hyperdrama that too much repetition can inspire. The sermon went: "Go on! Go on! GO on! GO on! Go on! Go on! GO ONNN! GO ONNN! Go on, go on, GO ON! GO ON! GO ON! GO ONNNNNNN!" etc. He intended it to be humorous and it was; when a motif is not humorous is when the preacher has no ear for artistry and wallows in some boring redundancy, whose drudgery he doesn't suspect.

11. Richard L. Eslinger, *Pitfalls in Preaching* (Grand Rapids: Eerdmans, 1996), 71. One of the pitfalls of preaching that definitely affects pacing is the preacher's refusal to close off one part of his sermon before he proceeds to the next. This usually results from a hurriedness of delivery that may originate in the preacher's feelings of insecurity. The more insecure we feel, the more we are likely to hurry (out of a secret fear that we might bore our audience in some way). Eslinger says, "A notable pitfall relates to a lack of attention to closure systems both within the 'three points' approach and within more recent homiletic methods. . . . Even rather clear signals that a new meaning is being developed may not serve to close off the previous location's meaning." A sermon that clips off ideas mid-formation is moving at too fast a pace to be meaningful and may even be unintelligible.

12. Mark Barger Elliott, *Creative Styles of Preaching* (Louisville: Westminster John Knox, 2000), 21. "While Henry Mitchell has encouraged celebration and the importance of details in the text, Samuel Proctor spent his life prodding preachers to cultivate an instinct for sermon design. He believed the crafting of a sermon should always follow 'an orderly, productive, tested procedure.' . . . 'A serious preacher,' writes Proctor, 'will be concerned about the anatomy of each sermon . . . because the sermon's structure will determine largely how the message it bears

will be conveyed.'" The more crafting and structure that are employed the more the sermon will tend to an automatic pacing which will leave it not only more organized but more intelligible.

13. Taylor, *The Luminous Web*, 100. A word of clarification: drama is not loudness. Drama is truth, and if it is an exciting truth it ought to be said excitedly. Barbara Brown Taylor moves me deeply with her sermons. I find her writing equally engaging. She would never use sheer volume to get attention, but neither would she set forth exciting truths in dull ways. In her book *The Luminous Web* she quotes Einstein and allows him to make the point so well: "The most beautiful emotion we can experience is the mystical. It is the source of all true art and science. He to whom this emotion is a stranger, who can no longer wonder and stand rapt in awe, is as good as dead. Teilhard de Chardin, the Jesuit Paleontologist, said, 'Less and less do I see any difference between research and adoration.'" Such a truth would be no more dramatic if screamed while thumping a pulpit. It is strong enough as it is. Preachers I know who feel they must scream everything have not moved on from a naïve understanding of preaching to real pulpit communication. Hellfire-and-brimstone is okay as a style, when one is speaking of hellfire-and-brimstone. But as an ongoing style for saying everything it is most shoddy.

14. Long, *The Witness of Preaching*, 61. "Sometimes the preacher and others who plan for worship create, in effect, a local church lectionary. The seasons of the Christian year, the denominational program of special days and emphases, and the congregational calendar of events are all combined to produce a schedule to which biblical texts are matched. As long as a wide spectrum of Biblical texts is included, the advantages of this plan are the same as those of a regular lectionary, minus ecumenical support and resources."

15. Ibid., 76. We should not reach for a commentary "until we have done our own homework on the text."

Chapter 6 Digging for Treasure

1. Duduit, *Communicate with Power*, 222–24. Michael Duduit quotes the way Warren Wiersbe comments on this idea: "I think sermons are getting shorter. Bob Cook used to tell us in Youth for Christ that a sermon does not have to be eternal to be immortal. Sermons are getting shorter, preaching is getting more personal, and the preacher has to be more open and transparent. The day is over when people simply accept the authority of the text; they also need to be assured of the authority of the preacher."

2. Klaus Issler, *Wasting Time with God* (Downers Grove, IL: InterVarsity, 2001), 26. "Biblically minded people generally adhere to a standard, three-fold test of truth, of which the first test is foremost to the other

two: (1) Biblical test: Is the claim in agreement with the data of Scripture (e.g. Acts 17:11)? (2) Intellectual test: Is the claim reasonable, logically consistent: does it make sense (e.g. Luke 24:11)? (3) Experiential test: Is the claim realistic, fitting within our life experience as human beings created in God's image? Does it work in life?" It is this last place where the expositor makes the Scripture reasonable by reason of his or her own relationship with it.

3. Stott, *Between Two Worlds*, 144. "We should be praying that God will raise up a new generation of Christian communicators who are determined to bridge the chasm; to struggle to relate God's unchanging Word to our ever changing world; who refuse to sacrifice truth to relevance or relevance to truth; but who resolve instead in equal measure to be faithful to Scripture and pertinent to today."

4. Markquart, *Quest for Better Preaching*, 58.

5. Calvin Miller, *The Empowered Communicator* (Nashville: Broadman & Holman, 1994), 55.

6. Ezell, *Hitting a Moving Target*, 85. "Like a good teacher, Jesus started with the interests of his students and moved them toward the lessons he wanted to cover. Like a good salesperson, Christ started with the needs of the customers and not the product to be sold. Like a wise manager, Jesus began with the concern of his employees and not his own agenda. He knew the exact location of his target audience, where they needed to go and what he had to do to help them get there.

"One can learn immensely from the methodology of Jesus. All Christian public speakers are wise to communicate spiritual truth by first discovering the needs of their target audience and then using this information as the starting point in their presentation." In a sense this was Jesus's "how-to," designed to meet the needs of his listeners and in a sense to tell them "how to" build the kingdom of God on earth.

7. Alister McGrath, *A Passion for the Truth* (Downers Grove, IL: InterVarsity, 1996), 55. "When Holy Scripture speaks of God, it does not permit us to let our attention wander at random. . . . When Holy Scripture speaks of God, it concentrates our attention and thoughts upon one single point. . . . If we ask further concerning the one point upon which, according to Scripture, our attention and thoughts should and must be concentrated, then from first to last the Bible directs us to Jesus Christ."

8. F. Scott Fitzgerald, from "Notebook N" in *The Crack Up*, ed. Edmund Wilson (New York: J. Laughlin, 1945), quoted in John Bartlett, *Familiar Quotations* (Boston: Little Brown, 1968), 1037.

9. John Reid and Reg Grant, *The Power Sermon* (Grand Rapids: Baker, 1993), 121. "F. Scott Fitzgerald was right; a good story invites us to the edge of a precipice. There we may be enshrouded in a dense cloud of

fear with Anne Frank or breathe deeply the autumn-crisp air of freedom with Harriett Tubman or splash in the crackling cold joy with Helen Keller. On the edge of the story precipice we can celebrate a wonderful party with a girl named Alice, or fire the last shot from 'Ol' Betsy' at the Alamo. A good story never bores. Balancing on the edge of a precipice brands the memory so that the story is often the only part of the sermon people will recall and try to recount to a friend."

10. James McClendon, *Biography as Theology* (Nashville: Abingdon, 1974), 37. McClendon reminds us that propositions alone make neither theology nor sermons. "Christian beliefs alone are not so many 'propositions' to be catalogued or juggled like truth functions in a computer, but are living convictions which give shape to the possibility that the only relevant, critical examination of Christian beliefs may be one which begins by attending to lived lives. When we find ways of reforming our own theologies, making them more true, more faithful to our ancient vision, more adequate to the age now being born, then we will be justified in that arduous inquiry. Biography at its best will be theology."

11. John Killinger, *Fundamentals of Preaching* (Philadelphia: Fortress, 1957), 47. "Now we arrive at the real test of the preacher's dedication to the task of preaching—whether he or she is willing to pay for the actual shaping of the sermon. It is one thing to entertain glorious dreams of what one could do. But it is quite another to be willing to work at it, to carry it in one's thoughts day and night, to tinker with outlines or sermon plans until they are just right, to sweat over the wording till it is at once vivid and precise, and finally to get it all inside one's head for preaching, the way one gets a firm hold on any important word to be said to people who really matter."

12. Gustav Wingren, ed., *Luther on Vocation* (Philadelphia: Fortress, 1957), 72. Luther understood that the world which gathered around the preacher and his flock was full of things to see, and this became the best way to give the sermon light and memory and pictures to hang in the mind of his parishioners. "Only look at your tools, your needles, your thimble, your beer barrel, your articles of trade, your scales, your measures, and you will find this saying written on them. You will not be able to look anywhere, where it does not strike your eyes. None of the things with which you deal daily are too trifling to tell you this incessantly, if you are but willing to hear it; and there is not lack of such preaching, for you have as many preachers as there are transactions, commodities, tools and other implements in your house and estate and they shout this to your face: 'My dear, use me toward your neighbor, as you would want him to act toward you with that which is his.'"

13. John Hines, as quoted in Gordon S. Jackson, ed., *Journey Wisdom for the Way* (Colorado Springs: NavPress, 2000), 131.

14. Calvin Miller, *The Sermon Maker* (Grand Rapids: Zondervan, 2002), 70. "Many preachers see exposition as a matter of verse-by-verse illumination. Let me assure the preacher who preaches this way that I am not against this method. What I am against is boredom. So often preachers who preach this way are not very interesting, but for the few who are I say, 'Bravo!' Besides being boring, verse-by-verse often fails to correlate the widely separate parts of the Bible, so the listeners are focused so intently on a single word or phrase that they ignore the rest of the truth in Scripture."

15. Coggan, *Preaching: The Sacrament of the Word*, 75.

16. Miller, *The Sermon Maker*, 76. But what of those who cannot or choose not to speak to genre because it means they must come to a new way of seeing? To see the Bible and preach the Bible as it is may mean breaking some old prosaic habit to really preach the genres of Scripture. "Old habits are hard to break. Nothing is harder than seeing a sermonic weakness and setting out to change it. The preacher must ever confront this weakness, contemplating a new role on stage. Actors spend hours of rehearsal just to capture a mannerism, an accent, used in the role they have been assigned to portray. Preachers too must ever be rehearsing, taking up new roles, and doing daring new things before their audience. Such continual newness will require a flexibility of homiletic style that grabs for audience interest." This is certainly true to portray or exposit true literary genre as found in the Scripture.

Chapter 7 Imaging the Argument

1. Austin B. Tucker, *A Primer for Pastors* (Grand Rapids: Kregel, 2004), 56. "A sermon needs illustrations. Unless the text itself is a story, the sermon will need a narrative quality. Jesus told parables and other stories. They made his message both plain and portable. Children love stories and so do the rest of us." Austin is not only right about this, it must be said that stories are as expositional as precepts and it is time we acknowledge this openly. To relegate storytelling to second-class status in preaching is not only unwise, it is wrong.

2. Miller, *Spirit, Word, and Story* (1996), 187. "Our urgency is so great that many would argue it is pointless to tell our little pulpit stories when so many are lost. . . . That being so, why is the salvation story so often reduced to an exercise in boredom?"

3. Ibid., 154. "I have yet to be convinced that story obliterates precept. In the Scriptures, story and precept come bound together. Take the Decalogue, ten marvelous precepts, but they come packaged in narration—splitting seas, bloody Passovers, Miriam's tambourine celebra-

tions, Aaron's calf and manna showers. Which is more important, story or precept? Well, they are inseparable. Likewise, the New Testament precepts come packaged in the parables and narratives of Christ." Since the Bible mixes story and precept so inseparably together, the Bible itself becomes the best guide on how to build a sermon.

4. Calvin Miller, *Marketplace Preaching* (Grand Rapids: Baker, 1995), 87. "The second word that characterizes our day is the word *video*. Perhaps more than any other generation, ours has been the generation of the eye." People will not hear what their minds have not seen. So getting them to listen is the imperative matter of speaking visually. Image must outshine verbiage if we expect people to listen to our sermons.

5. Miller, *Spirit, Word, and Story* (1996), 125. "Preachers like authors must choose their words so that others can't second-guess them. Whatever our first words are, we must avoid the predictable." The quickest way around lazy verbiage is to begin with a word study. These words are the detonator on a powder barrel. They explode with light and power.

6. Ibid., 125. Consider the refreshing beginning to *Huckleberry Finn*. "You don't know much about me, without you read a book by the name of 'The Adventures of Tom Sawyer,' but that ain't no matter. The book was made by Mr. Mark Twain, and he told the truth mainly. There was things he stretched, but mainly he told the truth." What Huck implies is that the story belongs to Mr. Mark Twain and he can tell it any way he wishes. To every storyteller there is a special "rite of passage," and the story is his or hers to speak in the way the storyteller wishes. The preacher has an obligation to tell true stories, but even true stories get more true when they pass the larynx of the raconteur who owns them.

7. Warren Wiersbe, *Preaching and Teaching with Imagination* (Wheaton: Victor, 1994), 43. "It is by using metaphorical ideas that you change people's ears into eyes."

8. Ibid., 52. "Parables start off like pictures, then become mirrors, and then become windows. First there's sight, as we see a slice of life in the picture; then there's insight as we see ourselves in the mirror; then there's vision as we look through the windows of revelation and see the Lord." Parables make morals visible, and visible images imprint the truth on the hearer's mind.

Chapter 8 Style

1. Thomas G. Long, *Whispering the Lyrics* (Lima, OH: CSS Publishing, 1995), 15. To be genuinely oneself is a hard task indeed. Who can tell exactly when we are our true selves? Searching for self-authenticity is an arduous quest. Thomas Long writes: "We are all pretenders, hypocrites. None of us is so worthy as to merit God's favor; our religion is a mask we hide behind. But God is gracious and redemptive in spite of

our pretense. Perhaps, then, Jesus reprimands the hypocrites because only a sharply pointed rebuke can poke a hole in the hypocrite's façade, allowing just enough light of the gospel to stream through with the news that every human being longs to hear: but when the applause of the admiring crowd dies out and the theater stands dark and empty and the pretender in all of us removes the mask and stands there . . . all alone, there is still God—the God who knows our conduct grades and is well aware that we have primped around the classroom showing off for others, the God who nevertheless sees in secret, the God who looks behind the mask to find the child yearning to come home, and the God who beckons us to come just as we are."

2. John R. Cionca, *Before You Move* (Grand Rapids; Kregel, 2004), 21. "Never open your mail on Mondays! That's the advice one pastor gives to those who are at the end of their parish rope. Questions of self-worth and ministry effectiveness can easily surface after an exhausting Sunday, especially in a situation where appreciation is rarely given." The reason that he says "never open your mail on Mondays" is that if there is a letter of employment opportunity from a new church, it might lure you to take the easy way out. Pastoral low self-esteem is a killer of pastoral tenures and ultimately a killer of much pastoral ministry. But its most immediate effect is to kill the sermon by deflating its enthusiasm and vitality. A broken and needy minister seldom preaches a strong gospel.

3. Parker Palmer, *The Courage to Teach* (San Francisco: Jossey-Bass, 1998), 17. There are two observations that must be made about the dumb-down culture. First, people of the dumb-down culture are rarely of any real emotional support. Parker Palmer observes that "we lose heart because teaching is a daily exercise in vulnerability." What he says of teaching of course applies to preaching. Preachers—nervous systems exposed—stick out where anyone may take a whack at them or their views. The other thing Parker observes is "[u]nlike many professions, teaching is always done at the dangerous intersection of personal and public life." No wonder preachers are needy and in the middle of self-involved culture; they find support always too scant to prop them up.

4. John A. Broadus, *On the Preparation and Delivery of Sermons* (New York: Harper and Brothers, 1876), 260. "One who speaks under the influence of strong feelings is very apt sometimes to use broken constructions. He will be so absorbed sometimes so as not to notice the syntax. . . . The most impassioned speakers and writers naturally employ such expressions. . . . They are very common in the writings of the apostle Paul. Whenever actually prompted by real feelings, broken constructions are admissible and forceful." These words were first written in 1876 and carry the import of saying that it is better to split an infinitive than to bore people with better English and less passion.

5. James Daane, *Preaching with Confidence* (Grand Rapids: Eerdmans, 1980), 58. "Every sermon must say one thing and one thing only; and this one thing must be capable of statement in a single sentence."

6. Ibid. "The reason for the contemporary loss of faith in the proclamation of the Word from the pulpit lies in the widespread depreciation of words today. Sermons are said to be ineffective simply because they involve twenty or thirty minutes of preacher-talk." James Daane goes on to say in the very same context that ineffective words are "puffs of air, mere sounds that die on the wind, lacking inherent power. Like broken arrows they never pierce reality."

7. Reg Grant and John Reed, *Telling Stories to Touch the Heart* (Wheaton: Victor, 1990), 9. "A good story doesn't permit casual observation. It wraps you up in truth and recognition and won't let you go. You are there, in the story; your imagination is kindled; you are involved; you interact with truth on a deep and personal level because you are in the story and the story is in you."

8. James Forbes, *The Holy Spirit and Preaching* (Nashville: Abingdon, 1989), 51. "Those who testify to the anointing of the Holy Spirit will go forth in ministry fully convinced that their efforts will make a difference." No wonder Spirit-driven preaching is passionate.

9. William Shakespeare, *Hamlet*, Arden edition, ed. Harold Jenkins (London: Methuen, 1982), act 3, sc. 2, lines 1–18.

10. Homer K. Buerlein, *How to Preach More Powerful Sermons* (Philadelphia: Westminster, 1984), 13. Buerlein quotes Robert Kirkpatrick's *The Creative Delivery of Sermons* as saying: "Teachers of homiletics have correctly assumed that the content of a sermon can have no adequate substitute in the voice and manner of its delivery. But the vehicle of expression is as important to a sermon as transports are to troops in war. The power of a sermon is measured at the point of its contact with the pew."

11. For a fuller discussion of these ideas, see Calvin Miller, *The Empowered Communicator* (Nashville: Broadman & Holman, 1994).

12. Ronald J. Allen, *Preaching for Growth* (St. Louis: CBP Press, 1988), 30. Ronald Allen describes vital preaching in this way: "The turning to God to embrace the offer of salvation is at the same time a turning away from the false gods, false values and evil practices of the world. The preaching of salvation thus becomes a dynamic context by which to call the congregation away from such things as idolatry, participation in injustice and environmental abuse. Why continue to live in Babylon, the city of the great whore, the smoke of whose funeral pyre is already rising, when one can live in the new Jerusalem, drink from the water of life, and behold the unfading glory of God?"

13. Søren Kierkegaard has one of his characters say, "Boredom is the root of all evil!" As quoted in Fred Craddock's *Overhearing the Gospel* (Nashville: Abingdon, 1978), 12.

Chapter 9 The Sermon Journey

1. Thor Hall, *The Future Shape of Preaching* (Philadelphia: Fortress, 1971), 34. Thor Hall years ago spoke of preaching in an exodus culture. This ought to be easy for us, for the Jewish faith was born out of an exodus culture, and the Christian faith out of a "go ye" culture. Everybody in either testament is on a pilgrimage of sorts, from Egypt to Canaan, from Jerusalem to the world. Since this is true we ought to be able to see that movement is more interesting than being stolid. We want the world to move, and our words are the pry bar that sets it in motion.

2. Allen, *Preaching for Growth*, 15. Whatever else the sermon may be about, it should be about God. We have talked a lot in this book about keeping the text central in the sermon. But even more important than that is keeping God at the center of the sermon. It is neither the preacher nor the sermon that is sovereign. It is God. Ronald J. Allen puts it this way: "Things like sociology, psychology, economic and political analysis, community affairs, and institutional promotion can become the functional center of the sermon. One occasionally hears a sermon so void of religious sentiment that it could be comfortably given to an atheist.

"Two factors coincide to point to the necessity of God being the center of the sermon. One is the nature of the gospel itself; it is good news from God for the sake of the redemption of the world. The other is the reason people come to church: they come to be touched by God."

3. Emory A. Griffin, *The Mind Changers* (Wheaton: Tyndale, 1976), 125. One way persuasion is to be done is to focus entirely on the message and how to communicate it. Emory Griffin has this to say: "What all this means is that when we talk about Jesus Christ, we've got to make sure that people focus on the message and not the messenger. . . . And there's nothing quite so affirming as speaking to a group in which every face is gazing up in rapt attention, waiting to agree with whatever we say. But we need to be careful not to play up our own importance. If we fall into this trap people will concentrate on us rather than on the truth we proclaim."

4. Bill Bennett, *Thirty Minutes to Raise the Dead* (Nashville: Nelson, 1991), 146–47. Yet how can we be sure that we are taking the audience with us? A part of the key is surely urgency. Bill Bennett tells about a preacher who was invited to preach at the chapel in a prison. When he arrived there he noticed that two of the many Samsonite chairs were draped. "Who gets the draped chairs?" he asked. He found out that the

draped chairs were for two prisoners who would be attending the Sunday service in the prison a scant twenty-four hours before they were to be executed on Monday morning. "Your sermon," said one of the prisoners, "will be the last sermon those two men will ever hear." Bennett says that the preacher fell on his face before God and said, "Oh God, give me a message for those two men who will be sitting in those draped chairs." One does not have to be loud to be urgent, says Bennett. He must, however, be moved over the lostness of humankind in order to plead in Christ's stead that all who hear him be reconciled to God. This is clearly a message everyone needs whatever status or maturity level they have reached when they sit in attendance at any sermon.

5. G. K. Chesterton, as quoted in A. J. Conyers, *The Eclipse of Heaven* (Downers Grove, IL: InterVarsity, 1982), 87.

6. Clyde Fant, *Preaching for Today* (New York: Harper & Row, 1975), 153.

7. Ibid. Clyde Fant called this kind of preaching "upper garble." This is how he describes the overdone affectation: "Large of gesture, expansive in warmth (sometimes also in girth), he resembles a ministerial Falstaff. Arms akimbo, arms crossed: fingers stabbing the heavens; head cocked; face in a scowl; now beaming like the sun; lips drawn back in the passable imitation of a smile; posturing and posing, gesticulating and declaiming. His vocabulary is even more archaic, dating back to Beowulf or the Venerable Bede."

8. Craddock, *Overhearing the Gospel*, 12, 15, 16. Craddock reminds us yet again that boredom is the root of all evil. But he also reminds us that the not important truths are rarely nimble of foot. Great truths are often pedestrian and will not run and leap unless they are made exciting by an exciting expositor.

9. Miller, *The Empowered Communicator*, 51. "Audience tension and the preacher's self-centeredness keep the same company. Most of the time when we become unmanageably tense in front of a crowd, it is because we have too many of our self-interests at stake." I believe it is this tension that causes us to overreact to the unexpected happenstances that come our way. Thus we appear unfeeling, or inhuman, simply because we will not relax into a conversational style when we preach.

10. Richard Wilbur, *Advice to a Prophet* (New York: Harcourt, Brace and World, 1961), as quoted in Franklin Littell, ed., *Sermons to Intellectuals* (New York: Macmillan, 1963), 19.

> When you come, as soon you must, to the streets of our city,
> Mad-eyed from stating the obvious,
> Not proclaiming our fall, but begging us
> In God's name to have self-pity,

Spare us all the word of the weapons, their force and range,
The long numbers that rocket the mind;
Our slow, unreckoning hearts will be left behind,
Unable to fear what is too strange.

People are bewildered when we throw too much urgency. It is like standing before a crowd for an hour and screaming fire. This is especially confusing when they see no smoke and sit asking themselves for the dull minutes, "Is there a fire or not? Is this urgent or boring?"

11. Miller, *Marketplace Preaching*, 173. To really speak to our community—indeed to create it—we "must have faith in our community. Our community will from time to time affirm our talent by compliment. Let us trust our community's appraisal at such moments. Let us use their compliments as a springboard to take that leap of faith into a strong self-image."

12. Palmer, *The Courage to Teach*, 95. "The hallmark of the community of truth is in its claim that reality is a web of communal relationships and we can know reality only by being in community with it."

Afterword

1. Flannery O'Connor, as quoted in Leland Ryken, *Culture in Christian Perspective* (Portland, OR: Multnomah, 1986), 44.

2. Ibid.

3. C. S. Lewis quoted in Bruce Lockerbie, *The Liberating Word* (Grand Rapids: Eerdmans, 1974), 44.

4. Madeleine L'Engle, *The Irrational Season* (New York: Seabury, 1977), 27.

5. Madeleine L'Engle, *Walking on Water* (Wheaton: Harold Shaw, 1980), 43–48.

6. Aristotle quoted in Lockerbie, *The Liberating Word*, 73, emphasis added.

7. Ibid.

Appendix

1. Haddon W. Robinson, *Biblical Preaching*, 2nd ed. (Grand Rapids: Baker, 1980; Grand Rapids: Baker, 2005), 21. Citation is to the 2005 edition.

2. Pitt-Watson, *A Primer for Preachers*, 14.

3. Ibid., 21.

4. Ibid., 23.

5. Ibid., 21.

6. Ibid., 22.

7. Chapell, *Christ-Centered Preaching*, 2nd ed., 56.

8. Ibid., 178.

9. Taylor, *When God Is Silent*, 115.

10. Ibid., 86–88.

11. Jelaluddin Rumi, "Craftmanship and Emptiness," as quoted in Taylor, *When God Is Silent*, 89.

12. Ibid., 25.

13. Ibid., 29.

14. Ibid., 39.

15. Long, *The Witness of Preaching*, 31.

16. Ibid., 33.

17. Stott, *Between Two Worlds*, 141.

18. Ibid., 145.

19. Ibid., 147.

20. Ibid., 148.

21. Ibid., 149.

22. Ibid.

23. Ibid.

24. Ibid., 151.

25. Eugene L. Lowry, *Doing Time in the Pulpit* (Nashville: Abingdon, 1985), 52.

26. Thomas Mann as quoted in ibid., 29.

27. Ibid., 16.

28. Ibid., 88.

29. Buttrick, *Homiletic*, 24.

30. Ibid., 25.

31. Ibid., 78.

32. Ibid., 140.

33. Ibid., 136.

34. Ibid., 258–62.

35. Coggan, *Preaching: The Sacrament of the Word*, 84.

36. Ibid., 75.

37. Ibid., 79.

38. Ibid., 26.

39. Ibid., 71.

Sources Consulted
in This Book

Achtemeier, Elizabeth. *Preaching as Theology and Art*. Nashville: Abingdon, 1984.

Allen, Ronald J. *Interpreting the Gospel*. St. Louis: Chalice, 1998.

———. *Preaching for Growth*. St. Louis: CBP Press, 1988.

Anderson, Kenton C. *Preaching with Conviction*. Grand Rapids: Kregel, 2001.

Bailey, E. K. and Warren Wiersbe. *Preaching in Black and White*. Grand Rapids: Zondervan, 2003.

Bartow, Charles L. *The Preaching Moment*. Nashville: Abingdon, 1980.

Bennett, Bill. *Thirty Minutes to Raise the Dead*. Nashville: Nelson, 1991.

Bernanos, George. *The Diary of a Country Priest*. New York: Macmillan, 1937.

Broadus, John A. *On the Preparation and Delivery of Sermons*. New York: Harper and Brothers, 1876.

Buerlein, Homer K. *How to Preach More Powerful Sermons*. Philadelphia: Westminster, 1984.

Buttrick, David. *A Captive Voice*. Louisville: Westminster John Knox, 1994.

———. *Homiletic*. Philadelphia: Fortress, 1987.

Chapell, Bryan. *Christ-Centered Preaching*. Grand Rapids: Baker, 2005.

Cionca, John R. *Before You Move*. Grand Rapids: Kregel, 2004.

Claypool, John R. *The Preaching Event*. Waco: Word, 1980.

Coggan, Donald. *Preaching: The Sacrament of the Word.* New York: Crossroad, 1988.

Conyers, A. J. *The Eclipse of Heaven.* Downers Grove, IL: InterVarsity, 1982.

Craddock, Fred. *Overhearing the Gospel.* Nashville: Abingdon, 1978.

———. *Preaching.* Nashville: Abingdon, 1985.

Crenshaw, James. *Trembling at the Threshold of a Biblical Text.* Grand Rapids: Eerdmans, 1994.

Daane, James. *Preaching with Confidence.* Grand Rapids: Eerdmans, 1980.

Dawn, Marva and Eugene Peterson. *The Unnecessary Pastor.* Grand Rapids: Eerdmans, 2000.

Duduit, Michael. *Communicate with Power: Insights from America's Top Ten Communicators.* Grand Rapids: Baker, 1996.

Elliott, Mark Barger. *Creative Styles of Preaching.* Louisville: Westminster John Knox, 2000.

Eslinger, Richard L. *Pitfalls in Preaching.* Grand Rapids: Eerdmans, 1996.

Ezell, Rick. *Hitting a Moving Target.* Grand Rapids: Kregel, 1999.

Fant, Clyde. *Preaching for Today.* New York: Harper & Row, 1975.

Forbes, James. *The Holy Spirit and Preaching.* Nashville: Abingdon, 1989.

Galli, Mark and Craig Brian Larson. *Preaching That Connects.* Grand Rapids: Zondervan, 1994.

Grant, Reg and John Reed. *Telling Stories to Touch the Heart.* Wheaton: Victor, 1990.

Griffin, Emoly. *The Mind Changers.* Wheaton: Tyndale, 1976.

Guinness, Os. *The Call.* Nashville: Word, 1998.

Hall, Thor. *The Future Shape of Preaching.* Philadelphia: Fortress, 1971.

Hauerwas, Stanley and William H. Willimon. *Resident Aliens.* Nashville: Abingdon, 1989.

Honeycutt, Frank G. *Preaching to Skeptics and Seekers.* Nashville: Abingdon, 2001.

Issler, Klaus. *Wasting Time with God.* Downers Grove, IL: InterVarsity, 2001.

Jackson, Gordon S. *Journey Wisdom for the Way.* Colorado Springs: NavPress, 2000.

Jenkins, Philip. *The Next Christendom.* Oxford: Oxford University Press, 2001.

Keck, Leander E. *The Bible in the Pulpit*. Nashville: Abingdon, 1980.

Killinger, John. *Fundamentals of Preaching*. Philadelphia: Fortress, 1957.

———. *Preaching the New Millennium*. Nashville: Abingdon, 1999.

Larsen, David L. *Telling the Old, Old Story*. Wheaton: Crossway, 1995.

L'Engle, Madeleine. *The Irrational Season*. New York: Seabury, 1977.

———. *Walking on Water*. Wheaton: Harold Shaw, 1980.

Lewis, Ralph with Gregg Lewis. *Inductive Preaching: Helping People Listen*. Westchester, IL: Crossway, 1983.

Litchfield, Hugh. *Visualizing the Sermon*. Sioux Falls, SD: Self-published, 1996.

Littell, Franklin. *Sermons to Intellectuals*. New York: Macmillan, 1963.

Lockerbie, Bruce. *The Liberating Word*. Grand Rapids: Eerdmans, 1974.

Long, Thomas G. *Whispering the Lyrics*. Lima, OH: CSS Publishing, 1995.

———. *The Witness of Preaching*. Louisville: Westminster John Knox, 1989.

Loscalzo, Craig A. *Apologetic Preaching*. Downers Grove, IL: InterVarsity, 2000.

———. *Evangelistic Preaching That Connects*. Downers Grove, IL: InterVarsity, 1995.

Lowry, Eugene L. *Doing Time in the Pulpit*. Nashville: Abingdon, 1985.

———. *The Homiletical Plot*. Louisville: Westminster, John Knox, 2001.

———. *The Sermon: Dancing the Edges of Mystery*. Nashville: Abingdon, 1997.

Lueking, F. Dean. *Preaching: The Art of Connecting God and People*. Waco: Word, 1984.

Markquart, Edward. *The Quest for Better Preaching*. Minneapolis: Augsburg, 1988.

McClendon, James. *Biography as Theology*. Nashville: Abingdon, 1974.

McGrath, Alister. *A Passion for the Truth*. Downers Grove, IL: InterVarsity, 1996.

Miller, Calvin. *The Empowered Communicator*. Nashville: Broadman & Holman, 1994.

———. *Marketplace Preaching*. Grand Rapids: Baker, 1995.

———. *The Sermon Maker*. Grand Rapids: Zondervan, 2002.

———. *Spirit, Word, and Story*. Dallas: Word, 1989.

Muggeridge, Malcolm. *Christ in the Media*. Grand Rapids: Eerdmans, 1977.

———. *The Third Testament*. New York: Ballantine, 1976.

Mulder, David P. *Narrative Preaching*. St. Louis: Concordia, 1996.

Nickle, Keith F. *Preaching the Gospel of Luke*. Louisville: Westminster John Knox, 2000.

Oden, Thomas L. *After Modernity . . . What?* Grand Rapids: Zondervan, 1989.

Palmer, Parker. *The Courage to Teach*. San Francisco: Jossey-Bass, 1998.

Pitt-Watson, Ian. *A Primer for Preachers*. Grand Rapids: Baker, 1986.

Reid, John and Reg Grant. *The Power Sermon*. Grand Rapids: Baker, 1993.

Robinson, Haddon W. *Biblical Preaching*. Grand Rapids: Baker, 2005.

Ryken, Leland. *Culture in Christian Perspective*. Portland: Multnomah, 1986.

Seaborn, Joseph Jr. *Celebration of Ministry*. Grand Rapids: Baker, 1990.

Shaddix, James. *The Passion-Driven Sermon*. Nashville: Broadman & Holman, 2003.

Stott, John R.W. *Between Two Worlds*. Grand Rapids: Eerdmans, 1982.

Taylor, Barbara Brown. *The Luminous Web*. Cambridge, MA: Cowley, 2000.

———. *The Preaching Life*. Boston: Cowley, 1993.

———. *When God Is Silent*. Cambridge, MA: Cowley, 1998.

Thompson, James W. *Preaching Like Paul*. Louisville: Westminster John Knox, 2001.

Troeger, Thomas H. *Imaging a Sermon*. Nashville: Abingdon, 1990.

Tucker, Austin B. *A Primer for Pastors*. Grand Rapids: Kregel, 2004.

Wiersbe, Warren. *The Dynamics of Preaching*. Grand Rapids: Baker, 1999.

———. *Preaching and Teaching with Imagination*. Wheaton: Victor, 1994.

Willhite, Keith. *Preaching with Relevance*. Grand Rapids: Kregel, 2001.

Willimon, William H. and Stanley Howerwas. *Preaching to Strangers*. Louisville: Westminster John Knox, 1992.

Wingren, Gustav. *Luther on Vocation*. Philadelphia: Fortress, 1957.

Wogaman, J. Philip. *Speaking the Truth in Love*. Louisville: Westminster John Knox, 1998.

Index

Calvin Miller (D. Min., Midwestern Baptist Theological Seminary), poet, preacher, author, and teacher, has served as a senior pastor in Omaha and as a writer-in-residence and professor of communications and homiletics at Southwestern Baptist Theological Seminary. He is currently a professor of divinity in preaching and pastoral ministry at Samford University's Beeson Divinity School in Birmingham, Alabama. When not teaching or writing, Dr. Miller speaks at a variety of conferences. He has written over forty books, including *The Singer* trilogy.